Advance praise for *Bullseye Marketing*

For years, small- and mid-sized businesses have been the jobs-growth engine of the U.S. economy. In *Bullseye Marketing*, Louis Gudema lays out both a strategic framework as well as detailed specific steps that small- and mid-sized businesses can use to accelerate growth, improve their competitive position and fuel job creation.

> **– Ron Bloom**
> Former "Car Czar" and Assistant to President Obama for Manufacturing Policy

Love it! *Bullseye Marketing* strips the madness away from the traditional paralysis-by-analysis of marketing plans and guides the modern marketer towards an impact target. In a world where low hanging fruit is often overlooked—*Bullseye Marketing* paints a winning equation of making the biggest impact today while setting the foundation for (r) evolutionary marketing success.

> **– David Maffei**
> President of Akumina

Bullseye Marketing is a business book with no BS. Why boil the ocean in trying to understand how to market your product or service and get sales into the pipeline? Three phases: Leverage your existing assets. Focus on the Buy Now prospect. Build awareness and your brand. Simple steps. Data driven. Comprehensive. This marketing How-To must be on your bookshelf or Kindle today.

> **– Jeanne Hopkins**
> Executive Vice President and CMO at Ipswitch

Leading companies are gaining a tremendous competitive advantage by taking advantage of all of the bells and whistles of modern marketing. In *Bullseye Marketing*, Louis Gudema provides a path for people in companies that aren't yet exploiting these tools and techniques to successfully ramp up these programs and gain a similar advantage for themselves.

    – **Jill Rowley**
      Chief Growth Officer at Marketo

Bullseye Marketing hits the mark. It strips away jargon and consultant-speak to help you, a small or medium business leader, caught in the crosshairs of change, turn things around. Reading a few chapters can help you solve today's problems. Reading more of them will help you connect meaningfully and profitably with current and new customers. Louis lays out the steps that work. Your job is to follow them.

    – **Mike Wittenstein**
      Founder of StoryMiners and former IBM Global Services eVisionary

Companies that want to achieve real growth need to focus their marketing efforts on the resources they have, the customers who want to hear from them, and optimizing results based on increases in real business and sales. In *Bullseye Marketing*, Louis Gudema outlines exactly how to grow your business faster using the latest strategic and practical marketing techniques that any business can use today to ignite their growth.

    – **Michael Brenner**
      CEO of Marketing Insider Group and co-author of
      The Content Formula

Bullseye Marketing is not only useful, it is very good! It contains both strategy and tactics for effective marketing. It is a book that I will keep handy to refer to when initiating new marketing initiatives.

    – **Mari Ryan**
      CEO of Advancing Wellness
      Author of *The Thriving Hive*

Bullseye Marketing is written in a non-jargon, readable way that should make it appealing and accessible to the folks who should be reading it—whom Louis describes in the Introduction. This should be an indispensable handbook for them. Bravo for pointing out that all of these ideas won't work for everybody, encouraging people to try it and see what works for them.

> – **Peter Cohen**
> Managing Partner
> SaaS Marketing Strategy Advisors

In *Bullseye Marketing*, Louis Gudema combines marketing insight with thoughtful analysis, and new perspectives with practice experience. Most of all, he provides an accessible, actionable and articulate approach to marketing that is useful—and valuable—to everyone. Highly recommended!

> – **Steve Lishansky**
> CEO, OPTIMIZE International
> Author of *The Ultimate Sales Revolution*

Bullseye Marketing provides a proven, pragmatic method to increase sales. It puts the focus first on how to cost-effectively leverage what Louis calls existing 'marketing assets'. Check this out before you pour more marketing dollars down the customer acquisition rat hole. *Bullseye Marketing* shows you how to do it much faster with a significantly higher ROI.

> – **Kim Wallace**
> Co-author of *Why People Don't Buy Things*

BULLSEYE
MARKETING

How to Grow Your Business Faster

With 100s of best practices & actionable
tips to increase your revenue

LOUIS GUDEMA

To Eleana, Liz and Oma

TABLE OF CONTENTS

TABLE OF FIGURES

Introduction

WHY WE NEED BULLSEYE MARKETING, AND WHO THIS BOOK IS FOR

I HAD BEEN LIVING IN a bubble.

Working in the Boston area, and with some great clients all over the country, I had had the opportunity to work with some of the best marketers in the world. And many were using the latest marketing strategies, software, and data as integral parts of their programs. I assumed everyone did.

But then over time, from my own consulting experience and research[1], I came to realize that I had been living in a bubble. Most businesses—easily over 80%—are seriously under-investing in marketing, to their detriment.

All sorts of great marketing options, and the software to optimize them, exist, yet most of the business world is unaware of them. Or is vaguely aware, and just not using them.

The vast majority of companies don't have anything approaching a robust, always-on marketing program. That lack is especially apparent in small- and mid-sized businesses, those with up to 1,000 employees. But even some enterprises have slowly grown over decades while under-investing in the marketing that could have propelled them to even faster growth.

Companies that market more grow faster

This is a shame because the companies that market the most and the best grow faster.

My study of 85 software companies found that those with the broadest marketing programs grew four to five times faster than those without them.

A study of over 1,000 insurance agencies[2] similarly found significantly faster growth for agencies that had spent the most on marketing. All agencies got business from referrals, but those that invested in marketing got qualified leads and business from many other sources, too.

Consider this quote from the CEO of AFA Protective Systems, which provides fire and security alarm systems, in their annual report:

> Last year I reported that we began to embrace the modern age of marketing. During 2013, the company decided to experiment on a limited basis with various forms of marketing to increase our visibility to potential customers and in turn sales. The year-end results in this regard were very encouraging. In fact, we traced new booked sales attributable to these efforts and learned that they were produced at a rate of ten to one in comparison to amount spent.[3]

Ten dollars of revenue for every dollar spent on marketing: what company wouldn't want that?

Software, insurance, security systems: very different industries with one thing in common. Marketing significantly accelerated growth.

Why don't companies market more?

And yet, the vast majority of companies don't undertake robust marketing programs.

You could say that innovators and early adopters mainly are practicing modern marketing, but that the mainstream of the business world has yet to embrace it.

There are two major reasons for this.

First, marketing is simply not in the DNA of many company founders and CEOs. Most of these leaders are expert in their industry, and they had to become at least competent in sales or their company would have never gotten off the ground. But they're not experienced in marketing, don't understand it, and may think that it's an expense rather than an investment in growth.

Second, marketing has become so complex. Twenty-five or 30 years ago there were only six to eight major marketing channels, such as TV, radio, print, direct mail, billboards, and events. Today, for many marketers and business people, there are simply *too many* options. Gini Dietrich, who is interviewed in chapter 18, has created what she calls the PESO model[4] (Paid, Earned, Shared and Owned) to categorize the dozens of marketing channels today.

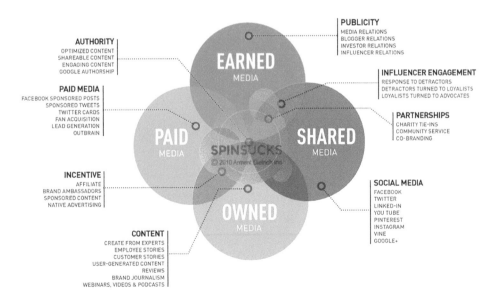

Figure 1. Spin Sucks PESO Model

Compared to those six to eight channels of a few decades ago, Gini today includes close to three dozen channels. Others have put the number of marketing channels today at over 100.[5]

And every year since 2011 Scott Brinker (who is interviewed in chapter 24), puts out an infographic of marketing software vendors. In 2018 it surpassed 6,800 companies in dozens of categories.[6]

Figure 2. 2018 Marketing Technology Landscape

Few marketers would be able to describe what each type of marketing technology is, let alone how to get the maximum benefits from it for their company.

Just to confuse things even more, many consultants and marketing software vendors make incredible claims for programs like social media and "inbound" marketing. With all of those new channels (it seems like there's at least one new one every year), software options, and all the noise, it's hard for businesspeople who are not already deeply steeped in marketing to know what will work best—if at all. And so, not surprisingly, they do nothing.

As a result, most companies under-invest in marketing, if they do it at all. Marketers who are starting, improving or scaling a marketing program often have to overcome internal disinterest if not outright resistance. After all, if your senior executives thought that marketing was such a great idea, the company would probably have been doing it long before now or would be doing a lot more of it.

Who is this book for?

The Bullseye approach described in chapter 1 provides a way to cut through all of this clutter and distraction and grow a successful marketing program that produces real business results. Companies using this approach can expect to grow significantly faster than those in their industry that don't. The book then builds on that strategy with hundreds of actionable tactics and tips for improving your lead generation and brand building programs.

But the Bullseye approach isn't for everyone.

Do you have years of experience managing marketing programs for large, consumer packaged goods companies?

Have you headed up marketing for a software company?

Have you been the CRO for a venture-backed startup?

Then move along. There's little new in this book for you.

If, on the other hand, you work at, or consult to, those 80% or more of companies that have been under-investing in marketing for years, then you will find a lot of useful information here.

Is this a strategy or a bunch of tactics?

Is Bullseye Marketing a strategy, or just a bunch of random tactics?

Fifty years ago marketing and advertising were all about the big idea: big brand campaigns with the Marlboro Man and the Jolly Green Giant. Today marketing is about creating and testing many small ideas, seeing which work, and then scaling those.

Of course you need a marketing strategy. You need to:

- study your competition and the market
- define what differentiates you from your competition (if you don't have any differentiators, you better get some—fast)

- understand your customer, where they're hanging out online and offline, and what motivates them to buy
- have a sales model (direct, online, through distributors and dealers, or all of the above)

You don't need to spend months, though, detailing an in-depth marketing strategy before doing anything.

Over 30 years ago Amar Bhide, now at the Tufts Fletcher School, wrote in his prescient Harvard Business Review article, "Hustle as Strategy"[7], "A surprisingly large number of very successful companies... don't have long-term strategic plans with an obsessive preoccupation on rivalry. They concentrate on operating details and doing things well. Hustle is their style and their strategy. They move fast, and they get it right."

Management consultant and author Tom Peters has similarly tweeted[8]:

Figure 3. Tom Peters tweet about strategy

In describing the startup guerilla marketing program that they successfully carried out against the industry leader, Salesforce founder and CEO Marc Benioff wrote, "One idea alone is a tactic, but if it can be executed a number of different ways, it becomes a great strategy."[9] Today Salesforce is worth over $85 billion.

Bullseye Marketing can be executed in many ways. It is a strategy for turning around marketing and inspiring, or accelerating, revenue growth at a company.

Beyond the book's strategic insights, you can think of it as a kind of checklist. Much of marketing success today is based on tactical execution.

But paradoxically it's not a to-do list. You will find hundreds of actionable ideas in the book. But some will contradict one another because what works for one company or situation won't work for another.

I've included overviews of close to two dozen major marketing tactics, case studies, interviews, and other types of material. Some of the people that I interview disagree with me. That's good! As much as I want to educate, I even more want to encourage an attitude of experimentation.

At the end of each chapter I've listed some of the leading tools for that program. There is no one best tool for everyone.

I developed the Bullseye approach in my work with companies and non-profits in many industries over many years. In working with these companies, I came to realize that I was recommending a particular playbook to successfully grow a marketing program that quickly provided measurable results, such as increases in leads and sales. They not only got a rapid payback from our work but built up confidence within their organization to move into longer-term programs.

I came to call it Bullseye Marketing.

If you do even half of what I propose in this book you'll be way ahead of the vast majority of companies out there.

Avoid analysis paralysis; get to work.

June, 2018

Chapter 1

BULLSEYE MARKETING

LET ME INTRODUCE YOU TO Bullseye Marketing which prioritizes the fastest, least expensive tactics for generating new leads and sales. I'll also share hundreds of actionable insights and tips that you can start using right away.

With Bullseye Marketing you work from the center out because in the center are the fastest and least expensive ways to produce new leads, opportunities and sales.

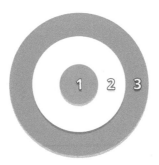

Figure 4. Bullseye Marketing framework

In Phase 1 we take full advantage of the marketing assets that the company already has—such as customers, website traffic, email lists, and our ability to listen—to quickly produce measurable results.

In Phase 2 we generate leads and sales from people who don't yet know about us but who are looking to buy *right now*.

And in Phase 3 we build awareness of our company and offerings with people who are interested in our industry and solutions, could someday be customers, but (as far as we know) are not buying right now. We want to make sure that these people know about us, and think highly of us, so that they will put us high on their short list when they are ready to buy.

Many marketers, and non-marketing executives, are so focused on spreading the word about their great offerings that without realizing it *they do this in reverse order*. They start with programs in the outer ring like social media, content marketing (blogging, videos, speeches, etc.), and display advertising—which usually are among the slowest and most expensive ways to generate new business—and they miss the great opportunities that are right under their noses. And because they do this backward they all too often have poor initial results and soon give up, saying, "We knew it: marketing doesn't work for us."

But it could work if they used Bullseye Marketing.

So let's look more deeply at each phase.

Phase 1—Fully Exploit Your Existing Marketing Assets

Whether you're starting marketing from zero or proposing a major strategic expansion of existing marketing programs, you'll usually need to start out with a small budget and produce some quick, inexpensive results to build confidence among the executives in your company. You may only have six months, if that, to produce some quick wins.

That's where the Phase 1 activities described in chapters 2 through 9 come in. You're going to start with the marketing assets that your company already has and exploit them to quickly produce impressive results.

These are some of the under-utilized marketing assets that you can quickly work magic with:

Customers

Gain a better understanding of customers so that all of your marketing activities can be as effective as possible (I cover this in chapter 3). Market and sell more to your existing customers. It's estimated that it's five to 25 times more expensive to win a new account than to retain and grow an existing one, yet many companies place a much greater emphasis on acquiring new accounts.[10] (Chapter 4)

Website

Your website probably already has a fair amount of traffic, but on most websites 99%—or more—of visitors come and go without anyone knowing who they are or what they want. With the Bullseye approach, you're going to sharpen your message and improve the experience of visitors. (Chapter 5)

Conversion rate optimization

Conversion rate optimization is the process for getting more people, like those who come to your website, to do what you want them to do. You may want people to make a purchase, sign up for a webinar, download an infographic, contact your salespeople, or something else—these are all called "conversions". At a minimum you want their email address and permission to continue to update (market to) them. Improving your conversion rate is perhaps the fastest, least expensive way to increase your leads and reduce your cost per lead. (Chapter 6)

Email lists

Consulting firm McKinsey & Company estimates that email marketing is 40 times more effective for customer acquisition than Facebook and Twitter.[11] And marketers routinely describe email as the digital channel with the highest ROI.[12] Bullseye marketers don't buy lists or spam people; we grow and use a house list to provide useful information that contacts, prospects, and customers value. (Chapter 7)

Remarketing

Remarketing ads are those ads that follow you around the Internet after you've looked at a website. Love it or hate it, remarketing is inexpensive and effective—a combination that we Bullseye marketers always like, especially in Phase 1. (Chapter 8)

The sales team

You're going to work more closely with sales than ever before to better understand your customers, grow your current accounts, and close new accounts. (Chapter 9)

Most companies have low hanging marketing fruit all over the place. You're going to learn how to harvest it.

You can implement some of these Phase 1 activities very quickly and inexpensively; at some companies that I've worked with we doubled or tripled web leads in just a few weeks. That should get the attention of the CEO and others in your company and start to build your credibility.

With your Phase 1 success, you'll be ready to move on to Phase 2.

Phase 2—Sell to People Who Want to Buy Now

Phase 2 is when you focus on getting the attention of new people who intend to buy what you're selling very soon—a perfect audience.

To do this, we focus on "intent data"—information that helps us identify these active shoppers, whether consumers or B2B companies. Here are three ways to identify and take advantage of intent.

Search advertising

People who are searching on certain phrases are very probably researching a purchase. You can connect with people searching for your offerings by running paid search ads, and can get an initial campaign up and running in minutes. (Chapter 11)

How people engage with your content

Track the most frequent visitors to your website, and the people who are especially interested in your content. If a person, or several people from the same company, repeatedly visit your site and engage with your content, that's a good sign that they may be in buying mode. (Chapter 12)

Third-party intent data

Large retailers like Kroger sell their store and website data to non-competitors. And B2B intent data vendors gather information from many websites about the search and reading activities of people from companies; they identify in-market companies by a surge in their searches and reading and sell that information to B2B companies. (Also chapter 12)

By using these expressions of intent in search ads, interaction with your content, and third-party data, you can run an efficient program that identifies the customers who are most likely to buy now.

Phase 3—Cast a Wider Net

With the success of Phases 1 and 2 you should have enough credibility within your company to undertake some longer-range marketing programs. Phase 3 consists of activities that may not produce an immediate return but, when well done, will have an impact over 6, 12, 24 months and beyond.

Some of the programs that you may do in Phase 3 include:

- content marketing (Chapter 14)
- search engine optimization (Chapter 15)
- video, TV and podcasts (Chapter 16)
- social media (Chapter 17)
- PR and influencer marketing (Chapter 18)
- events and trade shows (Chapter 19)
- online and offline display ads (Chapters 20 and 22)
- direct mail (Chapter 21)

In companies that are doing Phase 3 activities well, when sales reps ask a new lead how they heard about the company they'll often get a response like, "I saw you everywhere. I figured I had to talk with you."

The fastest and least expensive leads and sales are, initially anyway, in the center of the Bullseye. As you move out from the center toward the edge the cost for each new lead and sale is likely to increase and your ROI decrease, at least in the short term. Why do it then? Because you can't generate enough new business by only doing the Phase 1 and 2 activities and your company wants more. And even if it's more expensive in the outer ring to acquire new customers, it's still low enough to justify the marketing.

Every company is different, and which channels will work best for you will vary for reasons that we'll discuss later. Every campaign is an experiment.

The Bullseye looks like it has hard edges between each phase. In fact, there is some overlap—leakage even—between phases. For example, improvements that you make to your landing pages as part of conversion rate optimization in Phase 1 will help the performance of your paid search ads in Phase 2. You could host events for current customers in Phase 1, but expand them to a far broader audience in Phase 3.

And, no, you don't necessarily have to do these in this exact sequence. You could ramp up all three phases simultaneously if you have the people, executive buy-in, and resources. But usually you'll be far more successful if you create a solid foundation with the Phase 1 activities before moving on to the other programs.

With the Bullseye approach you're not just throwing out a bunch of random campaigns and hoping that they will have an effect: you're carefully building out an omni-channel marketing program that gets the right message to the right person at the right time.

Now let's drill down into the three Bullseye phases in more detail.

Chapter 2

PHASE 1: FULLY EXPLOIT YOUR EXISTING MARKETING ASSETS

BETTER, FASTER, CHEAPER. USUALLY YOU can't have all three. But you can if you know how to deploy Bullseye Marketing.

At the heart of Bullseye Marketing we take full advantage of the marketing assets that we already have before spending the greater time and money needed for other, less efficient marketing programs.

And since these assets are ours, and ours alone, our competition can't take them away from us. No one can stop us from listening to our customers and producing better offerings for them (which is perhaps the most profound role of marketing). No one can take away our email list, or website, or the opportunity to exploit them better to drive revenue. No one but we can remarket to our website visitors. And no competitor can stop our marketing and sales teams from working together better.

Phase 1 programs are golden opportunities just waiting for you to exploit them.

Some of these programs only take a few weeks to implement. You should be able to complete all of Phase 1 in six months or so. By showing measurable results, you will build the confidence of the executive team in the program and gain their support for expanding into Phases 2 and 3.

But before we drill down into quick-win opportunities like an improved website experience, email marketing, and sales and marketing collaboration, I want to focus on the customer. If we don't understand our customer, it doesn't matter how well we execute those Bullseye Marketing tactics.

Chapter 3

KNOW YOUR CUSTOMER

BUILDING YOUR BUSINESS BEGINS WITH understanding your customer. While many people think of marketing as just being about advertising and promotion, the central role of marketing is actually understanding the customer—the market—and working with the rest of the company to create those products and services that will have a chance for success. And *then* promoting them and generating demand. This is the most strategic role of marketing. Bullseye marketers can start contributing to this in weeks, and it should be a constant activity going forward.

It's not enough to build a better mousetrap if the world is happy with the mousetraps that it already has. Companies introduce tens of thousands of new food products annually and most sink without a trace—and that's just food products. Millions of apps have been developed for Apple, Android, and other platforms, but most get very little usage and even fewer make a meaningful amount of money. It's estimated that less than 10% of new products are still being sold two years later.[13] Many great products have failed because the company was too early to market or too late, or delivered something that—good as it was from a technical or aesthetic point of view—simply wasn't what customers were willing to pay for.

Products and services can have many purposes. Some are necessary for survival, to do things faster and easier, or for knowledge, entertainment, joy, even status. But in business, if the customer isn't willing to pay for it, it doesn't have a value.

Ways to do customer research

As a Bullseye marketer, you need to base your product development and promotions on a genuine understanding of your customers. Don't guess. The first step in gaining customer knowledge is to do research. Here are a few ways to learn about your customers.

Talk to your customers!

The number one way to do customer research is to talk to them! This may seem obvious, but when working with companies, especially startups and small companies, I am amazed at how many executives are resistant to simply sitting down and talking with even a few dozen of their potential customers. But these conversations are by far the fastest, least expensive, and most valuable input that they could get when launching a new company or product.

Don't just *think* about who you want to serve, what you *think* they would find valuable, and whether you can reach them with your offering: talk to them! You'll find people can be remarkably helpful if you say (1) you don't want to sell them anything, and (2) you do want to know what they think and feel.

Here are some questions that I use when interviewing the customers of a service company:

- What services are you using the company for?
- Do you remember how you first heard of them?
- What other companies were you considering?
- Why did you decide to use them?
- How do you feel about the service that they provide? ("feel" rather than "think" to try to elicit emotional responses)

- How could they make your business more successful over the next one-to-two years?
- When choosing a company for this service, which are the three most important considerations? Please rank 1, 2 and 3
  - Industry reputation
  - Quality of work
  - Timeliness of work
  - Responsiveness
  - Price
  - Expertise
  - Other? (What?)

- If their prices had been 10% higher, would you have chosen them anyway? 25%?
- What are your major sources of industry information?
- What else would you like to tell me that I haven't asked?

Depending on the company and the service, the questions can be much more detailed.

And those are just a few initial questions. Key to successful interviewing is making it into a conversation. Listen to how the person responds and ask follow-up questions.

Ideally, you want to talk in person or via a web conference so you can see their expressions when you ask them how they use a product or service, and what they would like and not like.

If you're talking about a new, physical product, you should show them an inexpensive prototype or let them try a sample. But keep the costs down in your first round of research. You could initially use artist renderings or sketches and save on developing production samples until you get favorable feedback. Or print an inexpensive 3D prototype. For a new app or software program, your sample could be as simple as a set of screens—perhaps just "wireframes" that show functionality but have no real colors or design, and have no (expensive) programming behind them. (See fig. 5 on page 20)

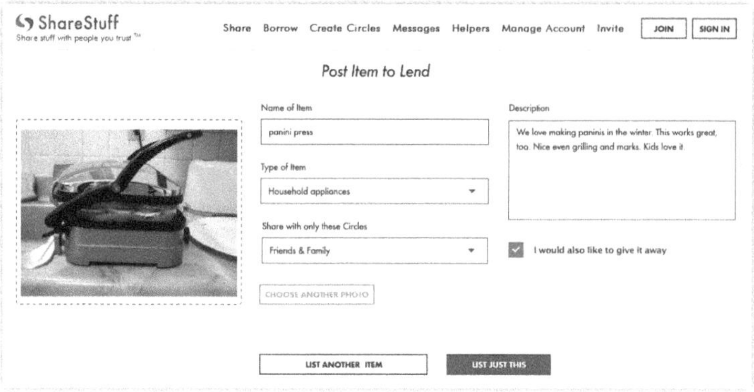

Figure 5. Desktop wireframe

It's important that the people that you're talking with feel comfortable sharing their true feelings with you. You don't want them to be "nice" and just tell you that they think that your service, or your idea for a new product, is great when in fact they don't. You can straight out tell them that you want their honest reactions and feedback, and that they should not be nice, and maybe that will work. Or maybe you will need to have people in your company whom they don't know talk to them, or even hire an outside researcher to do the interviews.

Here's a little secret: often this is not just great research. If you have a good idea for a new product, probably 20% or more of the people you talk with will say, "If you really go ahead with this let me know; I would love to buy it." (If they don't say this, that could be a red light.) But don't try to sell it to them; let them make that kind of remark on their own.

Now, I know, Steve Jobs didn't do customer research. He would dismiss it with an apocryphal quote from Henry Ford who supposedly said, but never actually did, "If I had asked customers what they wanted they would have told me 'a faster horse.'" So Steve Jobs was able to develop great products without talking to customers, great: he was a one-in-a-billion genius. He also had many notable failures such as the Apple III and Lisa. For the rest of us, it's way better if we talk to customers.

Regular, 30-60 minute conversations with customers should be a part of your ongoing marketing and customer retention/growth programs, not just when launching a new company or product. They can be invaluable. I was doing interviews for one client who swore that his customers only cared about price. The very first customer of his that I asked to rank the top three most important buying considerations immediately said, "Well, price isn't in the top three."

And be ready for some of your customers to be unhappy. I was doing interviews for one company and the CEO said, "I don't know why we're talking with our unhappy customers. We know they're unhappy. It just reminds them of that."

Wrong attitude! Heed the words of Bill Gates, "Your most unhappy customers are your greatest source of learning."

Online forums, social media and review sites

As Bullseye marketers, in Phase 1 we're especially interested in that which is fast, inexpensive and effective. You don't necessarily need to hire a market research firm to understand what's important to prospective customers. You can often gather *free* customer insights from masses of people through public sites and industry forums on which people review products and services. Go online and read what your customers are saying about the good, bad and ugly of your existing products, and those of your competitors.

Look at sites such as Facebook, LinkedIn, Twitter, Amazon and Yelp, and technology review sites like Capterra and G2 Crowd. What's going on in conversations about the industry, and the conversations around particular companies and products? What do the customers like? What are their gripes? Are there patterns that can help you identify an unfilled need?

You can use special software tools to help you monitor the social media universe to see what people are saying about you, your industry and competitors outside of your usual social media channels. These range from very deep, expensive programs to free ones with more limited capabilities.[14]

Internet research

The Internet is a great market research tool. Online you can, for example, find out:

- the demographic breakdown of the United States, or of a particular city or state[15]
- the number of people serving in the military, and the states with the highest numbers
- the wealthiest towns
- trends for commercial bakeries[16]
- the size of the market for learning management system software
- the size and growth of cloud hosting[17]
- how many Mexican restaurants there are in San Antonio

Or this nugget from the St. Louis Federal Reserve on the decline in greeting cards sales over the past 15 years:[18]

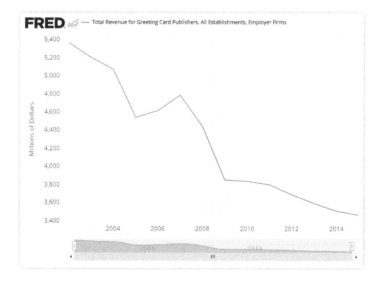

Figure 6. Greeting card sales data from Federal Reserve

With a little online research, you can find out almost anything.

Google Trends and AdWords

Google is your friend. Aside from searching on Google, two useful research tools are Google Trends and Google AdWords.

In Google Trends (www.google.com/trends) you can see how the search interest in terms changes over time, and how strong it is relative to related items. For example, this Trends chart for cookies (blue), cakes (red) and pies (yellow) shows a very big annual spike in interest in cookies every year around Christmas, with a corresponding decline in interest in cakes; a much smaller bump for pies happens around Thanksgiving. And interest in all three continues to rise steadily.

If you're thinking of starting a bakery, this could be very valuable information.

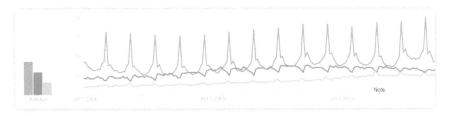

Figure 7. Google Trends on cakes, pies and cookies

Google AdWords isn't just an advertising platform; it also provides very valuable market and customer insights.

In the AdWords Keyword Planner, you can put in a few keywords and it will show you many related terms, how many searches are done nationally and globally each month for those terms, how competitive the market is for those keywords, and estimated cost per click if you decide to advertise for that keyword.

Look at the Keyword Planner data on the next page. If I were starting a bakery that would be making cookies, some type of chocolate chip would definitely be on the menu!

Launch a search campaign on AdWords or Bing, and very quickly you'll find out what keywords people are using to search for your products and services, which ad messages compel them to click and what offers get them to take an action.

Search terms		Avg. monthly searches ?	Competition ?	Suggested bid ?
chocolate chip cookies	⌁	246,000	Low	$1.58
oatmeal raisin cookies	⌁	49,500	Low	$2.56
snickerdoodles	⌁	74,000	Low	$1.00

Figure 8. Google AdWords Keyword Planner data about cookies

Market research resources

Market research and analyst firms regularly conduct market research for companies on virtually any topic. These can give you valuable feedback from hundreds of people—a statistically significant sample—but may cost tens of thousands of dollars. Some online market research tools exist for those with a smaller budget and do-it-yourselfers. These let you survey hundreds of consumers for only a few thousand dollars; I've listed a few in the tools section at the end of this chapter.

You don't have to do all of this research alone, either. There is someone who is often happy to donate her time to help you with your research: your local librarian. Your librarian may have access to many business databases with valuable information.

First establish product/market fit

In the startup world, product/market fit is everything. And although that term may not be used as much in more mature companies, it's just as critical for them.

You achieve product/market fit when you have both a market, and a product that addresses the needs and pains of that market.

There is nothing more classic than an engineer inventing a very elegant new something that is technically the best in its class, and yet it fails as a business. What the engineer thought was important to people was not what the customers actually cared about.

The best way to establish product/market fit is by talking to customers. Talk to dozens of potential customers before developing a new product; the National Science Foundation I-Corps program[19] requires teams to interview at least 100 potential customers. I've seen companies who didn't do their customer research spend millions of dollars on a new product only to find out when it's ready that the market simply doesn't care.

And no amount of advertising and promotion can save a product that doesn't have product/market fit.

Understanding your customer's emotional triggers

> "The difference between the almost right word and the right word is really a large matter—it is the difference between the lightning bug and the lightning."
>
> **Mark Twain**

People buy with emotion and justify with logic, whether they're buying for themselves or for the company that they work for.

Consumers may have many emotional triggers. They buy because something makes them feel fashionable, smart, frugal, modern, or traditional. They buy food because it seems tasty, healthy, or indulgent. One person will want to buy a car that is powerful and loud, and another person will want a car that is self-effacing and green.

In corporations people often buy for emotional reasons, too, even putting the personal career impact of the purchase above the company's interest. For many people at work, the single most important emotion is risk avoidance: they don't want to do anything that could jeopardize their job. That's why, as they *used* to say, "No one ever got fired for buying IBM."

One prominent venture capitalist goes so far as to say that startups aren't selling software, they're selling job promotions.[20]

I've done a lot of marketing work with small colleges and private schools. One year the director of admission at a prominent school tracked whether accepted students revisited on sunny or cloudy/rainy days. He found that those who revisited on sunny days were 10 percentage points more likely to enroll than those who visited on days with bad weather. The school wasn't any different—that's a decision based on emotion.

A classic book about high tech marketing is Geoffrey Moore's *Crossing the Chasm.*[21] In it he describes how difficult it is for early-stage tech companies to move from selling to geeks and early adopters to selling to customers in the mainstream of the market because the *attitudes* of the people in the mainstream are so different from those of the early buyers. Here are some examples of the emotional differences that Moore describes:

Early Adopters	Early Majority
Technologically competent	Not technologically comfortable
Looking for a change agent	Looking for incremental improvements in existing ways of doing business
Will cobble together new technologies to create a significant advantage	Want a whole product
Want innovative, state of the art technology	Want accepted, industry standard technology
Read futurist, tech blogs and publications and attend tech conferences	Read niche industry publications and attend industry conferences
Expect to change jobs and companies often	Want to stay with the same company for many years
Will accept other Early Adopters as references	Will not accept Early Adopters as references

Figure 9. Summary of Crossing the Chasm emotional differentiators

Demographically those people may be very similar, but their attitudes, career goals and emotions are entirely different. To an early adopter you can successfully make the pitch "Be the first in your industry to use our innovative product!" To a member of the mainstream market that may be the worst possible message.

Companies research the specific words that will spark customer emotions and inspire them to act. Messages with those words can produce 50% to 100% more responses than those without them.[22]

For both consumers and people working in companies, attitudes are more important than demographics. Learn about your customer's attitudes and emotional triggers.

Developing customer personas

Once you've done your research, including talking with actual customers, develop buyer personas that will help keep your marketing team—and your entire company—focused on who your customer is and what they want from your company, its products, and content.

Personas are actionable profiles of customers, based on research, that describe their attitudes, demographics, reasons for buying, and goals. These are not real people, but composite profiles that represent a significant portion of your customers. Developing personas is central to refining your customer understanding. If you haven't done this before, it's best to start with just three to five personas.

Your senior executives, product development, and sales teams should be part of your persona development because they all need to buy into and use the personas. It will make a big difference throughout a B2B company, for example, if you decide that your target market and personas are with small office/home office (SOHO) customers or large enterprises. For a B2C company, just consider the differences if you're selling to a discount shopper or a luxury customer. Ultimately these personas are driven by, or drive, your entire corporate and product strategy.

For B2C companies your buyers will typically be individuals, or possibly a couple. For B2B companies your buyer is often a team. You may need to develop personas for each of those buying team members so you can create more effective marketing, and materials for your sales team.

Here are a couple of sample personas.

For an apparel company:

Name: Angela

Age: 24

Income: $45,000

Occupation: real estate

Relationship status: dating, but not a top priority

Housing: urban apartment with one roommate

Watches: Romcoms, Stranger Things, Gilmore Girls re-runs, ESPN 30 for 30. Digests most media on MacBook

Shops: Gap, American Apparel, Urban Outfitters, Kroger

News outlets: Twitter, Facebook, Buzzfeed, Reddit

Favorite social apps: Snapchat and Instagram

"I'm very career focused and like having my own money that I can spend however I wish. I'll start saving when I settle down. Right now the best use of my money includes getting together with friends."

Angela has been interested in real estate since high school. She did well in school but has always enjoyed work more than reading and writing papers, and was happy to finish school and get into the real world. She is very conscientious, which has made her successful in landing and keeping jobs.

For work she likes clothing that is professional and not so tied to current trends that she'll need to replace it in six months; her work clothes tend to project her more conservative, reliable nature. Outside of work she dresses more stylishly and is happy to spend money for clothes, eating out with friends and going to concerts.

Figure 10. Consumer Persona Board

For an industrial equipment company:

Name: David

Age: 51

Income: $325,000

Occupation: COO at a mid-sized manufacturing company

Information he trusts: Business Week, WSJ, Economist, his network of peers, industry associations, industry conferences. Doesn't use social media.

"I'm not interested in projected ROI; I want to know what you'll replace that makes buying from you free."

David has been at the same company for 17 years and is well respected in his industry. He has people coming to him with new ideas all the time, but he is more concerned with operational excellence and reliability than innovation. He'll leave innovation to others in the company who are working on products.

David has deep technical expertise in his field, so he can evaluate new technologies himself. And when he can't, he relies on a team of others at his company whom he consults on major operational changes.

He's evaluated on:

- delivery of products on time and within defined quality standards
- maintaining better than industry-average operating margins
- high employee satisfaction and engagement
- high customer satisfaction based on Net Promoter Score®

Figure 11. Industrial Persona Board

Different marketers put different content into their personas, and it can vary considerably by industry. For example, to better understand their customer some marketers include a "day in the life" section. Some people use categorical names like "Designer Danielle" or "Retiree Ron". We'll go over other matters that you may want to put into your personas shortly.

Personas are useful for taking that huge number of potential, face-less customers and putting a face on them. They clarify who you are speaking and selling to. They should be helpful for your marketing team when they are creating campaigns and content.

Remember: base your personas on actual research, not just what you imagine. If you Google "questions when creating personas" you'll find links to articles with five, eight, 20, 55, 100, even 150 questions to consider, although some of the 100+ suggested questions include such unknowable or low-value ones as Where does he fall in the birth order; Did his parents have a permissive parenting style; and Did he enjoy his college experience? There is no one way to do anything that I discuss in this book, but the following should help you find your way when creating personas.

Here are some demographic factors to consider when creating the personas of consumers:

- age
- gender
- sexual orientation
- level of education
- where they live (cities and states; urban, suburban and rural)
- home ownership status
- employment status, income and net worth
- relationship status
- do they have children
- where they get their information and what they do for entertainment (favorite websites, TV shows, movies, artists, etc.)

For a particular product or service you may want to focus on other considerations that could be important such as race, whether they're religious, their political orientation, are they concerned with being fashionable or casual in their style, what kind of food do they eat, what do they do for fun, are they tech savvy, are they looking for bargains or status purchases, and so on.

Matters of attitude are more important than demographics. You can have two working, suburban, college educated, married 45-year-old white women with two children each who nonetheless have very different attitudes about work, child raising, nutrition, clothes, how to best spend their family's entertainment and vacation dollars, the best cars, and much more. This is especially important because, on average, moms spend the most money in day-to-day family purchases while dads will have a much larger role in the purchase and maintenance of big-ticket items.[23] Just the attitude of the mother toward the most important attribute of a car—environmentally friendly versus safe versus sporty—could have a huge impact on which cars they'd consider.

Some of the attitudinal factors to consider when you create your personas include:

- Why do they buy your product (necessity, status, entertainment)?
- What are the most important considerations in the purchase?
- How often do they buy it?
- Is this a new or replacement purchase?
- An impulse or considered purchase?
- What is their attitude toward your brand?

For B2B purchases the buying team might include five to 10 people, including:

- CEO, COO, and CFO
- line of business manager
- IT manager
- IT specialist
- procurement
- internal end user

B2B personas include such factors as:

- What's their title and responsibility?
- What is their role in this purchase?
- What are their personal and professional goals?
- Are they a risk taker or risk avoider?
- RACI: Are they Responsible, Accountable, Consulted, and/or Informed on this purchase?

Interview with Jeanne Hopkins: Personalization versus personas

Jeanne Hopkins is the Executive Vice President and Chief Marketing Officer at Ipswitch.

Louis: When you start at a company do you look at developing personas and journey maps and doing those sorts of exercises as part of developing your marketing programs?

Jeanne: That's the Holy Grail. Everybody wants to be able to do that. Who are you selling to? Are you selling to Debby, or are you selling to Dan? What do they look like? What is their pain? Every company has different personas. So you're constantly trying to figure out who you're selling to.

Louis: In terms of personas, you're an advisor to BrightInfo. And there are other companies, like Evergage and others that have website personalization also. And we've been talking about one-to-one marketing for twenty years, and now we're talking personalization a lot. And I'm wondering if personalization eliminates or overrides the need for personas.

Jeanne: Oh, that's a good question. So, personalization based on the IP address of who's coming and what they actually choose?

Louis: Personalization based on all sorts of factors: based on their keywords, based on their actions, based on the previous interaction that you have recorded in your CRM and your marketing automation system. Within one persona you might have many, many journeys. Amazon doesn't have 15 personas. Amazon has millions of personalized experiences. Does personalization ultimately eliminate or override personas?

Jeanne: Wow. Oh boy—is this heresy? But when we talk about personas, I still think that for many marketers it's good to have a good picture in your head of what that person looks like. "The targeted marketing software customer is a marketing vice president, 46 years old, drives a Volvo station wagon or SUV, and has 2.2 children, lives in the suburbs and works 65 hours a week and tries really hard to take a vacation." So you can really understand what that person looks like; you're visualizing that person. It helps a lot to have a picture in your head about who you're talking to.

Sometimes you need a visual of who you're actually speaking to, and that's where I think the persona development comes in. You need the shorthand to say, "Well, this persona: this is something that would resonate with them."

A value proposition for The Walt Disney Company

A value proposition is a useful way for a company to explain to itself and the world what it does and why it does it. As an internal instrument, the value proposition can serve as the North Star for people at the company, always guiding their actions. For the world the value proposition is central to the company's brand: the promise that it is making to them.

The Walt Disney Company is one of the most valuable brands in the world but, surprisingly, it does not express a true, customer-focused value proposition. Repeatedly the company describes itself in terms such as:

> The Walt Disney Company, together with its subsidiaries and affiliates, is a leading diversified international entertainment and media enterprise with five business segments: media

networks, parks and resorts, studio entertainment, consumer products and interactive.

There's only one thing missing from those: the customer. The Disney descriptions are company- and shareholder-centric. While maximizing shareholder value is an important component of any public company, it only happens in the long run by providing a true value to customers.

A value proposition is a customer-centric statement that includes:

- What product or services does the company provide the customer?
- Who is the customer and how is that valuable to them?
- What is unique about the way this company provides that value?

This is a potential value proposition for Disney:

> The Walt Disney Company provides magical, many-in-a-lifetime experiences for children of all ages.
>
> These unique experiences are created through the ingenuity and storytelling ability of Disney employees and delivered in a consistent yet surprising manner. For decades people at Disney have delighted people by bringing to life such characters as Mickey Mouse, The Lion King, Belle, The Pirates of the Caribbean, Jessie, the students in High School Musical, and Anna and Elsa through media networks, parks and resorts, studio entertainment, consumer products and interactive. Not only do people interact with Disney creative across many media, but throughout their lifetime: people who grew up with Disney then in turn trust Disney to entertain and educate their children, too.
>
> The Disney operational excellence, which is studied by companies in many industries, allows us to provide these experiences in a way that maximizes profitability and shareholder value.

This is a far more balanced value proposition that puts the customer — "children of all ages"—first. It provides some detail on what Disney provides and its goal: to delight the customer. And it also describes some of the company's unique creative and operational components on which Disney builds to meet the needs of the customers and shareholders.

Taking a strategic role

Now that you've done a lot of research into your customers and market, you may be ready not just to develop and manage successful advertising and promotion campaigns but to take a more strategic role at your company. You should, ultimately, be able to help your product people and executives understand what your customers want, how much they may be willing to pay for it, how providing that would differentiate you from your competition, the size of your potential market, and other critical matters.

Many people have a fundamental misunderstanding of marketing. They equate marketing with advertising and promotion, and they think its sole purpose is to help increase the awareness of the company and close new accounts.

Marketing should have a much deeper and more profound role in a company, and as a Bullseye marketer you know that advertising and promotion to new accounts are among the last things you should be doing.

That is the ultimate role of marketing, but it isn't the primary focus of this book. So we're not going to spend a lot of time on product and corporate strategy. But do keep in mind the bigger, strategic role that you should also play.

Tools for customer research

Ask Your Target Market provides inexpensive consumer research.

GutCheck is a qualitative market research tool.

Precision Sample helps companies create panels for research.

You can use SurveyMonkey and SurveyGizmo to conduct online surveys.

Qualtrics provides a range of tools for online surveys, customer product feedback, and customer experience insights.

Chapter 4

SELL MORE TO YOUR CURRENT CUSTOMERS

YOUR BEST BULLSEYE OPPORTUNITY IS to sell more to your current customers.

Many companies focus too much on closing new accounts. But it is far less expensive to sell more to existing customers than to land a new customer, whether you're selling to consumers or other companies. Depending on the company and industry, landing new customers costs five to 25 times more than retaining and growing an existing one. Since these new sales are so much easier and less expensive to close, they have a much higher profit, too. Increasing customer retention rates by 5% increases profits by 25% to 95%.[24]

In higher education they understand that retaining students is as important as landing new ones: after all, what's the point if every time the admission office lets a new student in the front door two are walking out the back? So they stay close to their customers (students and parents) and are constantly looking at programs to improve their retention rates. They call this "enrollment management."

In some companies, such as SaaS (Software as a Service) companies, retaining customers is a KPI (key performance indicator). The loss of customers is called churn. The best SaaS companies lose less than five percent of customers annually.

For some B2B companies just a few, large customers account for a disproportionate share of their sales and profits. Perhaps just 20% of customers provide 80% of profits (an example of the "80-20 Rule", also called the Pareto Rule[25]). In higher ed fundraising, which definitely requires marketing support, the proportions can be even more extreme: sometimes 95% of money raised comes from just five percent of donors. Those few, vital accounts demand special attention and programs.

If you're retaining and growing current accounts at a high rate, you then want to turn those customers into advocates, because people today believe recommendations from friends and professional colleagues—and even strangers on social media—more than they believe your marketing. And recommendations are free; you'll never do marketing cheaper than free.

For all of these reasons, increasing customer satisfaction and retention and selling more to existing customers are key parts of your Phase 1 Bullseye activities. Let's get to it!

The one question to ask

In 2003, Bain business strategist Fred Reichheld wrote an article for The Harvard Business Review entitled "The One Number You Need to Grow"[26]. Reichheld had researched customer loyalty and, expanding on some original insights from Enterprise Rent-A-Car, he outlined what would become known as the Net Promoter Score® (NPS ®).[27]

With NPS you ask customers one question: "How likely is it that you would recommend [company X] to a friend or colleague?" They are asked to respond on a 0-10 scale. A rating of 9 or 10 is considered a promoter, 7-8 is neutral, and 6 or below is a detractor. To find the Net Promoter Score, you subtract the percentage of detractors from the percentage of promoters. According to Reichheld, companies with a high NPS grow the fastest and those with a low NPS have slow or no growth, or may even be in decline. You want to have a positive NPS, and the best companies have an NPS of 60-80, or better.

This question is often followed up with a second, open-ended question: What is the reason for your answer?

The NPS can provide a valuable baseline for companies and a way to measure improvement. And that second, open-ended question can be invaluable research, too, because you find out what are the most important issues affecting your customers. The NPS answers can provide important information to salespeople for follow-ups since the respondent should not be anonymous, but asked to identify themselves.

Reichfeld developed the NPS when social media was still pretty young. Companies such as Facebook, Twitter, Yelp, and Pinterest didn't even exist; LinkedIn was only a year old. While it has its critics (or detractors ;-) the Net Promoter Score is more important today than ever with the ability of a positive recommendation or negative comment on social media to be seen by so many people almost instantly, and for the insights it gives into your customers.

Create a great customer experience

To sell more to current customers, they have to like what you're providing—and maybe even be delighted by it. You're selling an experience that starts with the very first marketing or sales interaction that they have with you and hopefully will continue for years.

A common framework for understanding the customer experience is the 5Es:

Entice: How do customers first hear of us? How are they lured into possibly doing business with us?

Enter: What's their initial experience with us?

Engage: How do we interact with them as they do business with us?

Exit: What is the end of their experience like?

Extend: How do we encourage repeat business?

Consider the 5Es as they apply to the in-restaurant customer experience for a pizza shop.

Entice

- Their storefront, signage, website, listing on Yelp, Facebook page

Enter

- How the store looks (Its design: Is it clean? Pleasant? Comfortable?)
- Are customers acknowledged or greeted when they first arrive?

Engage

- Offerings:
  - The types of pizzas and toppings they offer
  - The drinks, salads, desserts, and other foods offered besides the pizza
  - Their prices
- How customers order:
  - How the staff interacts with customers. Are they friendly? Curt?
  - How long do customers have to wait?
  - Which methods can customers pay with?
- How they serve the food:
  - Are the pizzas properly prepared? How quickly are they ready?
  - Are they served on a flat sheet? On some nice stand? What kind of plates and utensils do they use?
  - What is the quality of the pizzas?
  - How are complaints handled?

Exit
- What do customers do with their refuse when they're done at the restaurant?
- Any "thanks" or other message as customers leave?

Extend
- A loyalty program. Email or text communication with program members.
- Et cetera.

For a take-out customer, there would be additional/different elements to the experience.

And that's all just for buying a pizza!

Imagine how complex the customer experience is for a hospital, or an airport, an online retailer, or a B2B company selling and servicing multi-million dollar equipment, or providing a complex service (like managing marketing campaigns) over a period of years.

All of these categories of interactions are called touchpoints, and you use them to analyze and design an ideal customer experience (CX).

Note a few key things to keep in mind about CX touchpoints:

- Each touchpoint includes a customer expectation, experience, and emotion.
- Touchpoints should be viewed from the customer point of view, not from the company orientation of "sales," "marketing," "operations," and "customer service."

You have two groups of people who need to be involved in creating a great customer experience: customers and employees.

Designing a great CX begins with customer research. (By now you should expect that, right? We're not flying by the seat of our pants here, people.) In the previous chapter, I presented ideas about how to research your customers.

Here are a few that are important for CX research:

- Talk to customers.
- Conduct usability and customer satisfaction studies of your products and services.
- Look at the usability of your website.
  - Can people achieve what they want to?
  - Where are they leaving when you would expect them to stay? (Ecommerce companies have learned that they need to offer "free shipping" because otherwise many people abandon the purchase when faced with that additional cost near the end of checkout.)
- What are customers saying online about you and your competitors?
- What insights do you get when you simulate the customer experience by using "secret shoppers"?

Employees are the front-line representatives of your organization. Not only do they have the most direct experience with customers but, unless your operation is completely automated, they can also have the greatest impact on the customer experience. Companies need to engage employees from the start in understanding the customer experience and empower them to improve it. The best companies create groups of employees to study and improve the customer experience.

You need to remember that you have more than one CX; even the pizza shop has people who eat in the store and do take-out. For larger companies, there are far more interactions and touchpoints. And in many B2B situations, the users of your products and services may not be the people who authorize the purchase or pay for it. Your CX studies and improvements need to account for all of your stakeholders.

This customer experience work is not something that should be left to a few senior executives to try to do on their own in one or two meetings. An initial customer experience program can take months to show results in the form of greater customer success, reduced complaints, and improved customer satisfaction and Net Promoter Scores. In the best organizations, it is a never-ending mission.

Creating customer journey maps

To create an effective presence in the mind of your customers, you first need to understand where they are—online and offline—and what they want to do at each point of their journey. Obviously, the buyer of an industrial pump has a very different customer journey than the buyer of a pizza. And even within a company, you will have potentially many different journey maps for different personas and products. Customer journey maps can be a central tool for understanding and improving the customer experience and creating a successful marketing program.

Below is a customer journey map which shows the good, neutral and bad of the current touchpoints that a customer has when interacting with a company.[28] Note how the customer's emotions are shown at each touchpoint. Those touchpoints with negative or neutral emotions, as well as especially important touchpoints, are ideal to target for improvement.

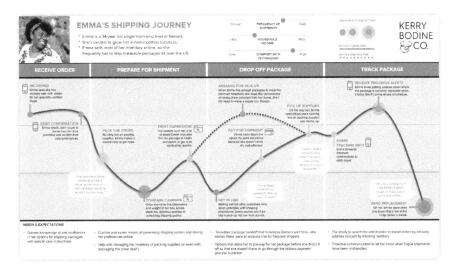

Figure 12. Customer journey map

The needs and expectations of the customer at each touchpoint are described in the bottom section of this journey map.

The map will vary depending on how you sell and service your products. The customer experience is very different depending on whether you sell directly; online; through retailers, dealers, or distributors; and how you handle returns and service in each of those channels.

Multiple stakeholders may exist behind a single customer or persona. The person who experiences the tech product failure may not be the person who calls support (in the company or a family). Both companies and consumers may have buying teams.

Organizations use customer journey maps to understand their many customer touchpoints which can include store visits, visits to the website, use of an app, interaction with a social media account, viewing of ads, interactions with salespeople, experience with the product return process and so on. (Note that your touchpoints aren't places, they are experiences that the customer has.) There is no single way to create a journey map—if you search Google for them you'll find a tremendous variety of customer journey maps—and they can be quite complex. They can also be a very important tool in understanding and improving the customer experience and creating an omni-channel marketing program.

Customer journey maps describe the customer experience from their points of view, not the point of view of your internal processes. For example, if a customer needs to return a product their experience starts with the decision to return it and finding out how to do that, which is before their first interaction with your team. Later you may connect your internal marketing and sales processes with the touchpoints.

Journey maps can contain descriptive and prescriptive information. In fact, you could have an entire journey map—or "experience map"—that only describes the current state of the customer experience, and a separate one describing an ideal future state, including the content that you'll provide at each touchpoint. Or you could combine that descriptive and prescriptive information into the same journey map.

Your maps should also note places in the journey where the customer is anonymous and when they're known. For example, your website may deliver different content—or an entirely different experience—to a known prospect than to an anonymous website visitor.

Customer journey maps can require months of time and lots of research. The best are based on customer input, such as interviews, surveys, and analytics. And you can also look at the data that you have about how you're interacting with customers before and after the sale. There is no one way to do journey maps. Do them so that they're useful for you.

And if a competitor provides some part of an experience that's better than yours, don't be afraid to copy them until you can improve on it. I'm always amazed, for example, when I go to a retail website that is clearly inferior to Amazon; the experience delivered by the market leader is out there for everyone to see—and copy.

Improving the customer's experience is an effort that involves all parts of the company. With attention to this over time employees should become more and more customer focused and empathetic.

A Bullseye approach to customer journey maps

In Forrester Research's 2015 report, "Mapping the Customer Journey"[29] Tony Costa and Joana van den Brink-Quintanilha describe four approaches companies use to successfully create journey maps:

- Hypothesis-first: a one-to-two day workshop potentially followed by validation research
- Research-first: several weeks of customer research and analysis, followed by journey map development
- Co-creation: a one-day workshop with customers as participants
- Quick-fire: a 60 to 90 minute small internal group workshop to work on deepening customer empathy and improving one key touchpoint

While the first three approaches require more time and resources, the Quick-fire approach achieves significant results in a single day. For example, an airline might use a Quick-fire workshop to improve their customer experience when rebooking flights, or a retailer might use one to improve its product return experience.

The Quick-fire approach can create quick wins, customer empathy, buy-in and momentum behind the idea of using customer journey maps. That sounds like a perfect place to start with journey maps when implementing the Bullseye approach. You could create some in Phase 1, have successes, and build the internal support for deeper customer research and involvement in later journey map creation using the other three approaches that require more time and resources.

Examples of great customer experience

Many industries have produced examples of great customer experience enabled by digital and mobile.

- Uber transformed the experience of taxi riders at virtually every touchpoint, and gained a valuation of tens of billions of dollars in just a few years as a result:
  - You can hail a cab with a mobile app.
  - In advance, you can see who the driver will be, their rating from other passengers, and their type of vehicle.
  - While you wait, you can see where the car is and when it will arrive.
  - The cars are typically well cared for, and the drivers pleasant and polite, because they know that they will be rated.
  - Payment is pre-authorized to your credit card, so you always have the money to pay, and the tip is included.
- Customers can deposit checks and perform many other banking functions via mobile apps.
- For builders who order concrete, it's just as bad if it arrives early as if it arrives late. Industrial concrete provider Cemex

developed a mobile app to let customers see the status and delivery date of their order.[30]

- Many companies, like UPS and FedEx, let consumers track the status of their orders.
- On the Zappos Twitter feed, they describe themselves as "a service company that happens to sell shoes, clothes, & more!" A founding principle of Zappos was that customers could return a purchase for any reason, no questions asked. Early on Zappos learned that people who returned their *first* purchase became their most loyal and valuable customers because they had tested the Zappos customer promise and found it was true.
- Twenty years ago I did a video for IBM about how Shell Chemicals changed its relationship with customers from order-to-order to something more like a utility. Shell began to monitor the customers' chemical inventories for them and assured them that they would never run out. (Today it might be part of a Chemicals as a Service offering.[31]) It's much harder for a competitor to dislodge a vendor who has established a subscription relationship.

Those examples demonstrate that you don't need to have a digital product to take advantage of digital and mobile touchpoints.

People love positive interactions with other people and improving those interactions, rather than automating or eliminating them, may produce your greatest leaps in customer experience.

- Online pharmacy PillPack learned that while getting their prescriptions reliably pre-packaged was important, what its elderly customers most value is being able to talk to a person when they have a question. So PillPack provides 24/7 customer service by phone.
- HubSpot provides a three-month onboarding service for new customers. It's mandatory, and customers pay for it, but HubSpot—like many other software companies—has learned

that providing enhanced training, support, and tips in the first few weeks is critical to customer success.

- McKinsey tells the story of a little girl visiting a Disney theme park who threw her doll into a construction site.[32] The Disney employees could have ignored it, but instead staff retrieved the doll, cleaned and restyled her hair, made her a new dress in the wardrobe department, and even had the doll's picture taken at a party with other Disney princesses. That's what empowered employees can do.

- In his 1990 book *Customers for Life*, Texas car dealer Carl Sewell describes how he develops long-term relationships with customers. One of his tenets is to never charge a customer for something that you would do for a friend for free. Today they are still selling services.

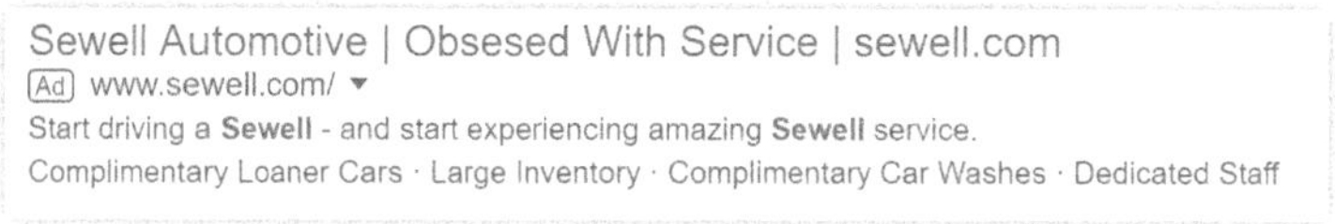

Sewell Automotive | Obsesed With Service | sewell.com
[Ad] www.sewell.com/ ▾
Start driving a **Sewell** - and start experiencing amazing **Sewell** service.
Complimentary Loaner Cars · Large Inventory · Complimentary Car Washes · Dedicated Staff

---

Figure 13. Car dealer AdWords ad emphasizing service

- In the documentary "Springsteen & I," a couple describes how they arrived at a Bruce Springsteen concert where they had the cheapest balcony seats farthest from the stage. A representative of Springsteen then approached them and exchanged their tickets for seats in the front row—where they had an experience that they'll remember for the rest of their lives.

If digital offers the fastest and best customer experience, use it. But when in-person is required, provide that.

The economic value of a great customer experience

Every year Forrester surveys tens of thousands of consumers and publishes its Customer Experience Index. USAA is often at the top, with companies such as Southwest Airlines, Amazon, Zappos, Kaiser Permanente and others moving in and out of the top tier, too.

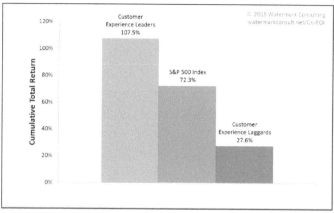

Figure 14. Watermark Consulting customer experience leader analysis

Jon Picoult at Watermark Consulting has taken the results of Forrester's survey and correlated them with shareholder value.[33] He has found that the stock of public companies that rank high for customer experience significantly outperform both companies with poor CX and the market in general, and typically the companies that provide poor customer experience underperform the market.

Give customers what they want, and they'll give you what you want.

Ways to sell more to current customers

Here are some ways you can market to, improve the experience of, and sell more to your customers.

Salespeople

Many companies split sales responsibilities between "hunters," whose job is to close new accounts, and "farmers," who are responsible for growing existing accounts.

The two roles typically represent two different sales personalities.

Hunters are your stereotypical sales people who are solely focused on finding and closing new accounts, collecting their commissions, and then moving on to the next opportunity.

Farmers are concerned with long-term relationships. Farmers build on the initial customer relationship to learn more about what the customer needs, and how the vendor can provide it. Farmers know that the relationships that they're building may take months or years to produce results. Many hunters would not accept sales timeframes of that length.

Farmers want to take care of "their" customers, and they want the internal resources to provide solutions to do that.

Of course, people are not so easily split into two types. Hunters often need a bit of farmer in them to truly understand prospects. And farmers need a bit of hunter in them to build on the initial engagement and expand into other parts of the company.

Outside of these sales roles, companies are increasingly embracing customer success as a philosophy and role. Customer success teams work with accounts as soon as they're won to onboard them, understand their opportunities and challenges, and help them get the most from the vendor's products and services.

Call them what you will, the important thing is that you have people in your organization who have an explicit responsibility to grow current accounts, and that they have the tools to do so.

Website

Your website is a great way not just to gather insight into what customers want but also to engage with them, support and upsell them.

Using a marketing automation program, you can track what customers are looking at down to the individual. Analyzing these interactions across all of your contacts in an account may give the "farmers" in your company insight into what an organization is looking for now (see more on the role of sales in account based marketing below).

If you have a customers-only section to your website, requiring registration and login, you can provide custom content there. You could have private, branded portals for your most important customers. Many companies crowdsource their support function to an online community of customers answering questions for one another in a knowledgebase; the company may give an annual award to the customer who provides the most frequent/best advice.

And once people have visited customer-only pages, you could target them with remarketing ads about customer-only events and offers.

Email

Just as email is a powerful channel for customer acquisition, it can also be central to customer satisfaction, retention, and growth.

The first step in using email to sell more to your customers is to create segments of them. You can create segments based on what or how much they're bought in the past, geography, industry, or whatever other factors are important in your company.

Ecommerce companies with large lists create RFM cells based on Recency (how recently a person bought), Frequency (how often they buy) and Monetization (their average purchase). Using a 1-5 scale for each of the three factors, with 5 being the best, they can create 125 or more cells of current customers and test frequency of emails and different offers with each cell to maximize profits.

Create unique content for your customers. Customers need a different webinar than your prospects. If I'm a long-time customer, I don't want to get the email offering 25% off the first year to new customers. Why, I might wonder, are your newest customers getting this, but not your most loyal ones?

So you need to segment and understand what messages and content will be most meaningful for existing customers.

Newsletters are just a special type of email, and they can be valuable for increasing sales to current customers. The mistake that many companies make is using the newsletter to talk about themselves (We have a new logo! We have a new customer!). Fill your newsletter with information that adds value for your customer; sometimes that's as easy as refocusing an article from "this is what we did for a customer" to "this is what a company achieved (with our help)". Make the customer the hero of your stories.

Social media

As I'll discuss in chapter 17, social media is not a great customer acquisition channel for most companies—at least not as good as email and many other programs.

Social media can play a significant role in growing customer satisfaction within existing accounts, though.

First, even without a significant following, you can listen to the conversation about your company and your competitors on social media to understand what customers like and dislike about you and them, and then react to those insights and individual comments.

Social media properties, especially on Facebook and Twitter, can be central to a company's customer support. Some companies have social media "support" accounts separate from their main accounts. Two keys to successful social media customer support are (1) quickly respond to customers who post there, and (2) immediately take the issue offline. You don't want a long, potentially embarrassing exchange to live forever on social media.

Create a customer-only group on Facebook or LinkedIn and facilitate conversation between customers, and between them and you.

And you can use YouTube for customer support by posting videos demonstrating how to use and fix your products.

Events

In-person events are one of the strongest brand building activities, and B2C companies may even sell a significant amount of products at one. In our increasingly digital world, the personal touch means even more.

Whether B2C or B2B, companies have held successful customer events such as:

- special, customer-only receptions, classes, tastings, lunches, and parties

- annual users conferences, especially for B2B and tech companies
- hosting local events for affiliate groups, such as:
  - a bike shop hosting weekly rides and free repair clinics
  - bookstores hosting authors' readings
  - tech companies hosting meetings for startups

Every element of an event is part of the customer experience including the invitations, venue, decorations, music, food, activities, Wi-Fi and follow-up. Make it memorable, and on brand.

You can also provide online and virtual events, of course, such as webinars. And combine the physical and digital with augmented reality.

Loyalty marketing

You don't need to be an airline (miles) or credit card company (points) to reward your customers with a loyalty program.

- Dry cleaners provide discount coupon books to their best customers.
- Bookstores and pizza shops provide loyalty cards so that after eight or 10 purchases the next one is free.
- CVS uses data to personalize the discount offered to each customer on the checkout receipt. If a customer's average purchase is, for example, $20, CVS may offer a discount if they spend $30 or $40. If their average purchase is $40, though, the starting point for the discount may be higher.
- Bertucci's offered diners contest cards that could only be redeemed on a future visit.

Text messages

Text messaging lets you take advantage of the platform in your customer's pocket and purse: their smartphone. Over 95% of texts are read. Can you claim that for your other marketing channels? (Text messaging is also called SMS, which means "Short Message Service".)

It makes the most sense to use texts to reach existing customers who already trust you and are willing to give you their mobile phone information. Of course, the very first thing you need is permission from people to text them. Legally and ethically you need to get people to opt-in to text messages before sending them.

Text messages may be especially effective for retailers and other B2C companies. They may boost sales with timely texts such as "Show this message to get 20% off today on...

snow shovels before the storm hits

or

fall fashions that have just arrived

or

food on your way home from work

You also can use texts to improve your customers' experience and bind them closer to you. For example, you can use text messages to let customers know the status of their order, and to confirm an appointment.

Use common sense, of course. Don't send texts in the middle of the night (be especially careful about this if the people you're texting aren't all local). Too many of us sleep with our phone near our bed and don't want to get woken at 3 am with a commercial message.

If you're new to text messaging, it may seem uncomfortable or intrusive when you first do it. But if your customers have given you permission, go for it.

Account based marketing

Account based marketing (ABM) is basically a new name for a B2B strategy that has been around forever under such names as key, strategic, or target account marketing. Rather than casting a wide net for new customers, as is done with much marketing, ABM is sometimes referred to as "spear fishing"—focusing personalized marketing on perhaps just a few dozen especially large, important accounts. While it can be used to land new accounts, ABM is especially effective for growing your most important existing accounts.

ABM requires deep cooperation between sales and marketing in terms of:

- identifying the most important accounts and most important people on their buying teams
- understanding the personas
- developing personalized content that speaks to that particular company's issues
- getting it to people at the right time

Helpful content created by marketing is valuable in educating the people at the target company and creating at least interest in, if not preference for, the vendor. And with ABM you direct the content toward those individuals rather than waiting for them to find it.

A major role of marketing in ABM is the development of personalized content, which may take considerable effort for each company. If it's possible in the vendor's business, an effective tactic can be to send the prospect a one or two-page benchmark summary of their company's performance, or some other highly personalized content, and suggest a competitive analysis as a foot-in-the-door next step. It's hard for companies to ignore competitive information. Some vendors use expensive and creative dimensional mailers to gain the attention of people in target accounts, or one-to-one personalized events. Companies may need a drip program of several pieces of personalized content to get the desired meetings.

You also can customize your messages with personalized landing pages, remarketing ads, display ads, emails, LinkedIn ads, and so forth. Some tools let you target ads to particular individuals or companies. These are perfect for ABM.

ABM speaks the language of sales, which is usually more interested in closing and growing *accounts* than with *individual* leads. In some companies the ABM team pairs with an account based sales counterpart. As ABM matures in a company, it may involve other areas beyond sales and marketing, too, such as customer service, support, and even product development—in short, the entire customer experience.

ABM is not a short-term marketing program; it is an approach that will reap rewards over months and years. Farmers welcome.

Since the accounts are already known before the ABM program begins, and the contacts are known or identified early on, ABM has different metrics than other marketing programs. You may measure:

- how many of the buying team members you are interacting with
- how much time they are spending with your company online and offline, in any form
- acceleration and growth of deals and improving close rates

ITSMA claims that ABM "has the highest Return on Investment of any B2B marketing strategy or tactic. Period."[35] Perhaps that is achieved because it isn't just a marketing campaign; ABM is a program that involves the entire company up to the highest executives. And it helps close and grow the accounts that have the highest lifetime value.

Tools to sell more to your customers

If you are going to have more than a couple dozen customers, a foundational tool for marketing and sales success is the customer relationship management (CRM) system or database. Leading small company CRMs include HubSpot, Freshsales, Pipeline Deals, ProsperWorks, InfusionSoft and Act-On; larger company CRMs include Salesforce, SAP, and Oracle. There are many others.

Account based marketing tools include:

The DiscoverOrg platform helps ABM teams put together information on the key contacts, organizational structure and trigger events of targeted accounts.

Demandbase and El Toro target ads by IP address. Vendor ads only show to the companies targeted.

With LinkedIn, you can target ads to people by title in specific companies, and with uploaded customer email lists.

Terminus provides cookie-based targeting that supports showing a vendor's online ads only to the specific individuals targeted by the ABM program.

Engagio supplements traditional contact-based marketing automation programs with account-based and outbound marketing capabilities and analytics.

Chapter 5

WEBSITE

THERE ARE COUNTLESS TYPES OF websites, such as:

- corporate (IBM, GM)
- social media (Facebook, Pinterest, TripAdvisor)
- ecommerce (Amazon, Walmart, Wayfair)
- SaaS software (Slack, Trello, Optimizely)
- non-profit (Red Cross, Partners in Health, Human Rights Watch)
- schools and colleges
- entertainment
- games
- blogs, personal expression

So there's no way that in just a few pages I could successfully describe how to create every type of website. That said, here are 10 tips that should help.

1. Establish goals

What do you want to achieve with your website? Generate leads? Sell products? Build your personal brand? Attract donations? Volunteers? Provide a platform for social connections? For personal expression?

You need to define your goals before you put much effort into the messaging, information architecture, technology, and so forth.

2. Speak to the customer

The home page is the most-visited page on most websites, and most website visitors are first-time visitors, so make sure that you have a single, compelling, customer-centric message on your home page that quickly communicates who you are and why visitors should care.

Having a single, compelling message means that you should not use a carousel—those slide shows of several images and messages that change every few seconds. Instead of conveying several messages—the hope of people using carousels—carousels dilute all of your messages and frustrate your visitors. In 2013 the shouldiuseacarousel.com website was created, and it well communicates the case against carousels.

Here is the before and after of a website home page for a client of mine that prints custom labels for food companies. Their customers include major brands like Whole Foods, Williams-Sonoma, Wegmans, and Dunkin' Donuts, but you wouldn't know it by looking at their original website, which was very cluttered.

Figure 15. QSX Labels legacy website

After the redesign, they presented a strong message around their core service, and their website was full of conversion opportunities that made it easy for companies to order from them. Their new website is also mobile-ready, unlike their old one.

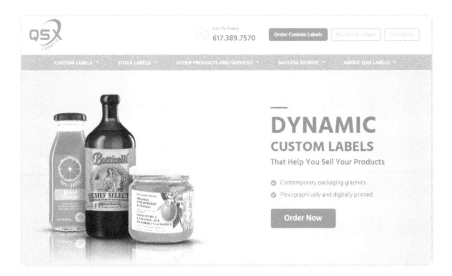

Figure 16. QSX Labels new website

3. Information architecture and navigation

The *information architecture* (IA) of a site is how it is organized. The *navigation* is the on-screen menus and similar devices that people use to move through the content.

When developing your IA keep in mind what your visitor is coming to the site to do, and make it easy for them to do it. Also remember that many of your visitors—maybe a majority—are looking at your site on a phone, and you need an experience that will work for them. Because of its small screen, developing for mobile is more challenging and less forgiving. Start with the mobile experience and work out from there to small tablets and then desktops. Website designers call this approach "mobile first."

My philosophy of navigation is to keep it simple and to use Web-standard conventions like having the main desktop navigation across the top of the page. Maybe a game site could create a different navigation experience, but for 99.9% of sites you'll want to make it as fast and easy as possible for people to do what they want to do and get to your content. Cars can be as different as a Hummer, a Ferrari and a Smart Car, but they all have the steering wheel in the front seat. Save your creativity for your content.

In your navigation, avoid drop-down and fly-out menus: they clutter up the screen and get in the way of other content. And they aren't easy for search engines to analyze.

4. Chunk your content

You should break up your content between pages, and within pages.

One contemporary website design trend is long, multi-topic scrolling pages. The only problem is people don't like to scroll down long, multi-topic pages. Heat maps show that on almost any web page the farther down content is, the less it is read. That's why when Google is indexing a page it weights the content at the top of the page more heavily than that farther down.

For one client I re-engineered their website from long, scrolling pages into many shorter, single-topic pages with a traditional navigation at the top. The average time-on-site for a visit immediately jumped up 50%.

So if you have content that you don't care if people read, feel free to put it at the bottom of a long, multi-topic page. But if you think that all of your content is important, break it up into shorter pages and make it easy for people to navigate to them.

There's nothing wrong with having long, *single*-topic pages of content; some studies have shown that blog posts with 2,500-3,000 words get higher readership and sharing than shorter pieces. But make it easy for people to scan and take in what you are saying by chunking your content.

- Break your content up into short sections with headlines and subheads to guide the reader and enable them to scan a page to see if they're interested.
- Use numbered and bulleted lists.
- Use images to emphasize important points.

5. Segment and personalize content

In 1998 Jeff Bezos said, "If we have 4.5 million customers, we shouldn't have one store. We should have 4.5 million stores."[36]

That vision was way ahead of its time, but it has come to pass. Today Amazon has hundreds of millions of customers and hundreds of millions of home pages. They personalize based on previous purchases, browsing, and other factors.

You don't need to have an ecommerce site to create a personalized website. Leading marketing automation and experience management platforms, and even lighter solutions aimed at smaller sites, let you personalize content based on such factors as which pages the person has previously visited, their geolocation, how often they visit, their relationship to you (customer, partner, etc.), what other site they were referred from, and their corporate domain. You could personalize the home page message for each known visitor.

Figure 17. Personalized home page

Optimizely customized their home page experience for 16 market segments, including key accounts that they were targeting with an account based marketing program.[37] With targeted home page messages they caught the attention of visitors and achieved significantly greater engagement.

6. Provide calls to action

Your website should have many calls to action (CTAs) throughout it encouraging site visitors to do what you want them to (those goals you started with). You can offer visitors the opportunity to sign up for upcoming physical and digital events, register for a free trial, access content, make a purchase, make a donation, join, volunteer, and much more.

Pay special attention to the next chapter on conversion rate optimization for all sorts of tips on using CTAs and increasing conversions.

7. Include social media buttons

You want social media and email buttons on your website. But what do you want them to do?

Figure 18. Social media buttons

On many corporate sites the social media buttons are low on the page—maybe even in the footer—and take you to that company's Facebook, Twitter and other social media accounts with the hope that you'll then follow them.

On news and ecommerce sites the social media and email buttons are often high on the page—sometimes at the very top—to encourage people to share that page's content with their social media followers.

Which purpose is more important for your company?

8. Make your site accessible

Companies need to make their websites accessible to the visually impaired. Over three million Americans are blind and many use screen reading software to access the Internet. Other people are color blind: think of reading a subway map with color-coded lines when you can't distinguish between colors. Companies may need to provide text explanations for critical color-based information.

Some of the things you need to do to create an accessible website include:

- Structure menus and pages so screen readers can navigate and read them
- Use descriptive alt tags on all images (alt tags are read by the screen readers to explain what the image is/says)
- Provide transcripts for your videos and podcasts

If you don't want to make your website accessible to help the two-to-three percent of people who are visually impaired do business with you, or to be nice, you need to do it because the Americans with Disabilities Act (ADA) requires it.

Enter the attorneys.

Hundreds of class action lawsuits have been filed to require organizations to make their websites accessible. For now, these usually target larger companies with deep pockets: retailers have faced the most suits, as have restaurant chains, universities, banks, and other industries.

These suits charge that not only do the inaccessible websites stop the plaintiffs from doing business with the organization, they also make it impossible for them to apply for jobs. Most defendants settle.

Better get on it.

9. Optimize for search engines

Of course, you want your website content to be read by as many people as possible, and so you need to optimize your site and content for high rankings on Google and Bing. Be sure to read the search engine optimization chapter in Phase 3 and apply its recommendations to your site.

10. Use the right technology

You should plan to update your site regularly, if for no other reason than that Google likes sites with fresh content. And you don't want your IT department to be a bottleneck. So you will need a content management system (CMS) to empower many people to make website changes. Some vendors these days call their CMS an "experience manager."

There are hundreds of content management systems available. Some are tailored for particular uses such as community sites or ecommerce sites or educational institutions.

If many of the people in your organization who will be posting content to the site don't have deep tech experience, then you need a CMS that's easy to use. When considering a new CMS don't just watch demos, but have the end users in your organization try the contenders out for themselves.

The CMS should also have a permissions structure that enables you to say which parts of the website each person can edit, and what their level of privileges are. For example, some people may be able to create and edit, but not publish without someone else first approving it.

Tools for website management

WordPress, Drupal, Sitecore, and Adobe Experience Manager are leading website content management systems/experience managers. You can also find many industry-specific programs, such as ecommerce or community platforms.

Evergage, BrightInfo, and Optimizely support website personalization and can be integrated with marketing automation programs.

Chapter 6

CONVERSION RATE OPTIMIZATION

CONVERSION RATE OPTIMIZATION IS ONE of the most important elements of a Bullseye marketing program. Starting serious marketing efforts without first optimizing your website for conversions is like turning on a spigot and trying to fill a bucket that's full of holes.

You should always have an objective for people coming to your website. At a minimum, you want to get their contact information and permission to send them updates (aka market to them). Conversion rate optimization (CRO) is the practice of constantly improving the rate of people completing your desired actions, whether it's making a purchase, downloading an ebook, signing up for a webinar, or something else.

The logic of CRO is simple: it's much easier, faster, and cheaper to get twice as many of the people who are already coming to a website to do something than it is to double the number of people coming to the site.

As you'll see, doubling your conversion rate is not as hard as you might think. And when you do double it, you've also cut in half the cost of those web leads or sales.

Ecommerce companies know that the vast majority of people who come to their site won't actually buy something on their first visit, but their lifetime value as a customer will be several times higher if the company can get that site visitor's email address and market to them. So right on their home page many ecommerce sites will interrupt the first time visitor's buying experience and give them an incentive to provide their email address or text information.

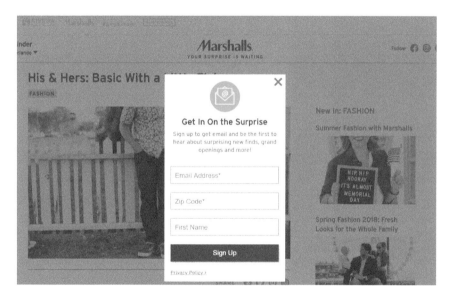

Figure 19. Home page pop-up offers

Of course, it's even better if the site visitors also buy. So ecommerce sites run countless tests regarding pricing, images, colors, layout, and so forth, to encourage that, too. Those all are part of conversion rate optimization.

Direct marketing success factors

Many digital marketing programs are forms of direct marketing. And, in order, the three most important components contributing to the success of direct marketing campaigns are:

1. List or audience
2. Offer
3. Creative

Before going deeper into CRO and other marketing tactics, let's consider each for a moment because they will impact much of what we do.

List: A direct marketing list is traditionally just that: a list of thousands or millions of people and their addresses and other information. In large-scale consumer direct marketing programs, marketers enrich those lists with such additional information as the consumer's approximate income, credit rating, type of car that they drive, and magazines that they subscribe to. In a B2B campaign, additional data may include the size and location of the prospect's company, company's industry, previous business relationship with the company, title of the person, and much, much more. Some direct marketers add *thousands* of data points to each profile and use advanced analytics to target their messages.

I'm using the term "list" broadly. I consider a list to be that traditional kind, such as for email marketing and direct mail, but also more broadly your audience. You need to get in front of the right people and get them to your website to have Bullseye marketing success.

Offer: Once you've found your audience, you need to get them to act. To get people to give up something you value (their money, or their contact information), you need to give them something that they value. That may simply be your product or service, but often it is a discount, information, entertainment—value comes in many forms. You need to understand your customers to know what will move them to act. You then use calls to action—such as "Click here to do X" or "Take advantage of our 10% discount; offer good today only"—to get them act on your offer

Creative: Direct marketers have always tested different creative: messages, colors, photos, layouts, and so on.

Just changing the color of a button, changing the button text from "Submit" to "Download your free ebook", adding the word "free" to a headline, or redesigning a landing page can make a significant difference. Superior creative can more than double your conversion rates.

Your landing page copy can make a big difference. Some tried and true techniques are:

- bandwagon effect ("Being used by 150,000 people!")
- halo effect ("Brought to you by the people who made [last year's great product, movie, etc.]")
- scarcity ("Only X left!", "Offer good today only!")
- social proof, such as reviews and testimonials
- use the word "you" in your copy
- describe benefits not features
- use the word "because"—studies have shown that providing even the feeblest reason increases cooperation
- include emotional trigger words

Doubling your conversion rates with better creative is huge, of course. But getting in front of the right audience with a superior offer can produce conversion rate improvements of *several hundred* percent.

And that translates into dropping the cost per lead by 75% or more.

Website conversion rate optimization

You need to get the most from the people who are visiting your website.

Most people will start on your home page or a page that's especially well optimized for search. In my experience, the three most popular pages for a corporate site are

- home page
- top product/service pages
- careers page

Since we're concerned with marketing and revenue, we're not going to worry about the careers page. But if someone has enough interest in you to come to your site and go to one of your product/ service pages, it's a good idea to do what you can to get them to start interacting with you.

To do that, you need to spread offers and calls to action all over your site.

Here are a few companies that demonstrate how.

Jeff Bezos knows more about Internet business than anyone. When he bought The Washington Post it was losing money, partly because it was giving its great writing away for free. So he put up a paywall. This is what the home page looks like now if you're not a paying subscriber. (See fig. 20 on next page)

Conversion optimization is not subtle, although it is not always as in-your-face as this.

But it worked: within a couple of years The Post was once again profitable.

Figure 20. Home page with calls to action

For a company like Slack that delivers its software via the Internet, it's a no-brainer: let people buy your software, or at least sign up for the free version of your software, right on your home page.

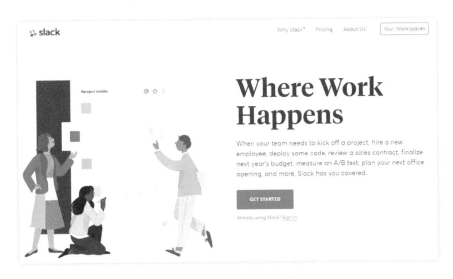

Figure 21. Home page account sign-up

SaaS software companies are one of the few types of firms that can use their home page as a prime CRO landing page.

Dell EMC sells high-end computer memory and other systems; a single deal can be worth tens of millions of dollars. They think that getting people to their conference is so significant that they will sometimes devote their entire home page to promoting it.

Figure 22. Home page with conference promotion

A primary marketing goal for many medical institutions is to get more appointments scheduled with new patients. So Cleveland Clinic, a premier institution, provides multiple ways for people to move the conversation forward on most website pages (See fig. 23 on next page):

- A phone number
- That orange appointments button
- Live chat
- Email

Even subtle changes to a regular web page—like an orange button versus a gray one—can make a big difference. Or the location of the Contact Us button: make sure that there's one at the top of your page, it will produce far better results than one in the footer.

Figure 23. Prominent website contact options

The key point is to make it as easy as possible for people to connect with you in whatever way they prefer.

Chat pop-ups are proving to be a very effective way for companies to start to engage one-to-one with people visiting their websites, especially with those people on pages that suggest stronger buying intent, like a pricing page.

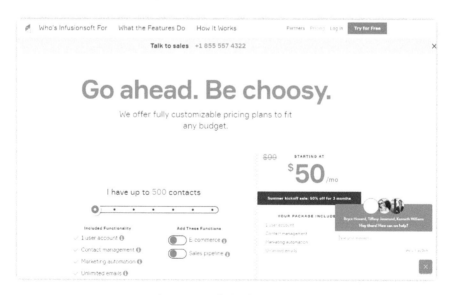

Figure 24. Website chat pop-up

And some companies are automating at least part of these conversations with chatbots. The chatbots can be programmed with branching conversations to qualify a visitor and move the appropriate ones on to a live salesperson, or save the salesperson's time and get the visitor the information that they need instead. Or direct them to support if that's what they need. These chatbots only cost a few hundred dollars a month, making them far less expensive than a person, can be trained quickly and don't mind working 24/7.

Often pop-ups are launched when a person is about to leave your site. These can be triggered by the cursor moving toward the URL address box (presumably to type in a different site) or, if they just arrived, to the Back button. These "exit intent pop-ups" display a "Wait! Don't go yet!" offer such as this one:

Figure 25. Exit intent pop-up

While you may not use these devices on every page of your site—you might exempt your career pages, for example—they can significantly increase business from people who are showing real interest in the products and services that you're offering.

Landing pages

Landing pages are a special kind of website page. They are the pages with forms that you direct people to from your website buttons, ads, social media posts, direct mail, and other calls to action.

When people come to your landing pages, often at considerable expense to you, you want them to fill in the form with accurate information, immediately do business with you, or give you permission to market to them. That is why you brought them to the landing page.

Several guidelines for the creation of effective landing pages are:

- The landing page should make it easy for the person to take advantage of the offer that brought them to the page.
- Usually, the landing page will have a prominent headline with explanatory text on one side and the form on the other side; pages with the text on the top and the form below tend not to perform as well.
- Only one subject and offer per landing page. Don't try to do too much. You can experiment with secondary offers far down at the bottom of the page, but don't make them so prominent that they're competing with your primary offer and goal.
- You should not have the website navigation on the landing page. Various studies have shown that you'll get a higher conversion rate without navigation giving the person an easy way to move on to other parts of the site. Only the company logo should be on the top and clickable to get to the full website.[38]
- You can test such creative options as:
  - including a phone number
  - different wording, images, and colors
  - different call-to-action button colors, designs, and text (for example, "Get your free ebook" instead of "Download")

This landing page checks all the boxes:

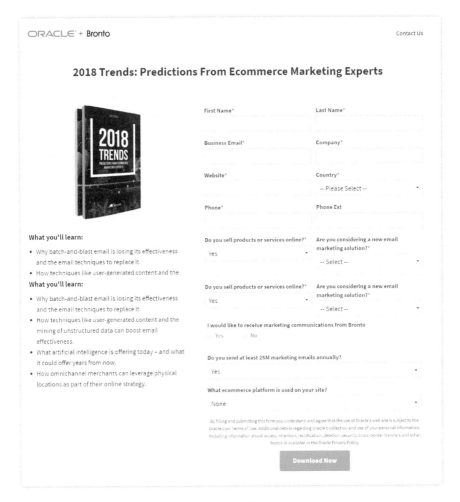

Figure 26. Landing page

Make sure that your landing pages look good and work well on smartphones. Since the mobile screen is so much smaller, you have far fewer options. The first absolute rule is that you need a mobile-ready website, typically a responsive site. The mobile landing page text and form fields should be large enough that they're easily read and completed.

On the left is what an Oracle form looked like on its site before it was responsive, and on the right is the mobile-friendly version of the same form. The latter is far easier to deal with on a small, smartphone screen.

Figure 27. Mobile non-responsive (left) and responsive (right) forms

And one part of the tips I gave above may be changing: increasingly sites use an initial page with the information, offer and a big yes button (of some sort) which then takes the person to the page with just the form. Shouldn't that cut responses in half? Maybe not: it's often intended to create a superior mobile experience and eliminate the need for the person to scroll down to a form on their phone. The extra click is easier.

When offering a report or infographic, I recommend that you ask people to provide an email address and then send them a download link or other information, rather than giving them all the information online after they fill out the form. First, for you that guarantees that they'll put in a valid email address, not something like a@a.com; and for them they'll have a link that they can use to download the materials to their desktop and mobile devices—wherever they want to read them—and even do so more than once.

Test, test, test. You may be surprised at what can make a difference—digital marketers usually are!

A rough rule of thumb is that landing pages usually have a conversion rate of only about three percent, but if the creative is optimized you can double that to perhaps six percent. Right there you've doubled your leads while cutting your cost per lead in half.

However, a superior offer can dramatically improve on that with some companies reporting 50% or higher landing page form completions with great offers.

How much information should you ask for?

If you're asking people to fill out a form, how much information can you ask for? At what point will you drive them away?

It depends on the value of your offer. If people think of it as a very valuable offer, they may be willing to provide quite a lot of information. This form by tech analyst firm Gartner requires a dozen pieces of information to get their report. (See fig. 28 on the next page)

I once worked with a company that needed a lot of information for the first sales call. I wondered if we couldn't pre-qualify prospects and speed up the work of the salespeople by asking prospects those questions in advance of a call. So I created a form with over 20 fields to it. These were detailed questions about what they wanted to do, how soon they needed it, and so on. It would take a person at least five to 10 minutes to fill out the whole thing.

And many people did. Just in case someone didn't want to bother, we gave them an out at the very top: we told them that they could call us (phone number provided) or use a link to go to a much shorter form and fill that out—but few people did. We got *four times* more qualified leads from that very long form than from the short one.

Why?

I think a major reason was that we called it a "fee request form." Many people probably thought that if they filled it out, they would get a proposal or information on our fees; that was our offer. And they may have thought that they would not need to talk with a salesperson; lots of people don't want to talk with a salesperson.

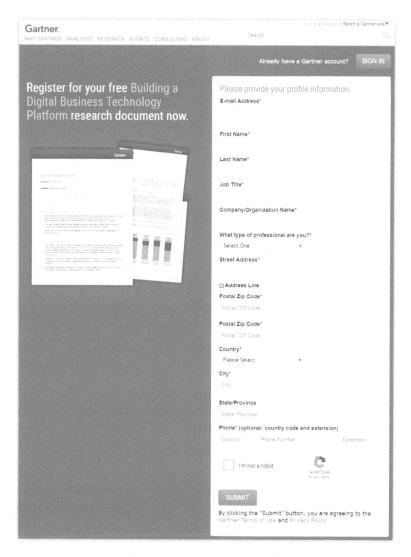

Figure 28. Form with many fields

From a sales point of view, we knew that if someone was going to take the time to fill out our very long form they were probably fairly serious.

So my recommendation, based on industry data and my experience, is to go to the extremes. Either use a very short form—possibly only initially asking for just their email address—to get lots of signups to build your database, or use a very long form that by its very nature will put you in touch with only the most serious prospects.

A third option is to use progressive profiling. With progressive profiling, you start with one or a few questions and each time the person requests something else from your site you ask just a few more questions. Over time you build up a rich profile of the person. Many marketing automation programs provide progressive profiling.

Marketing apps

Interactive marketing apps are an advanced form of conversion optimization. They are based on the idea that people may value an experience with your company that is more enjoyable than filling out a form. You only have to look at how many people take and share Buzzfeed quizzes to realize how much people like interactive content.

Marketing apps bring a kind of gamified experience to marketing and can include quizzes, assessments, configurators, ROI calculators, games, interactive infographics, graders, and more.

When WordStream was sold, founder Larry Kim wrote on LinkedIn, "My most spectacular growth hack is the AdWords Grader. We showcase the product by grading AdWords account performance."[39] People have used the HubSpot Website Grader over four million times,[40] making it one of their strongest lead generation tools.

Thank You pages

Once the person has filled out a form and submitted it, you're done with them for now, right? Wrong! You've got a very interested person in front of you. Offer them even more.

The Thank You page is a great opportunity to say more than, "Thank you, the webinar registration information has been emailed to you."

You now can give them more information, show a couple more offers, even provide a "Would you like to talk to a rep right now?" button.

Figure 29. Thank You page with multiple options

Or you may send a Thank You email with more offers.

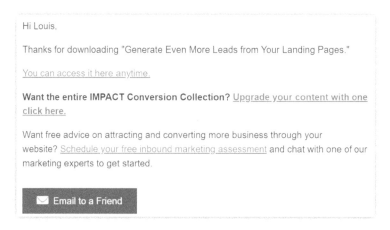

Figure 30. Thank You email with offers

You can also include social sharing buttons: make it easy for people to tell their friends about the valuable offer that they were smart enough to take advantage of.

Call tracking

So far I've focused primarily on the digital conversion experience, but of course there are other options such as business reply mail envelopes, postcards, and a telephone number.

When a prospect calls your company, they are likely to be more highly motivated than if they filled out a form. Call tracking is a way for you to improve the call experience over time and to understand which of your campaigns are generating leads.

With call tracking your company gets a pool of unique phone numbers. You then use different ones throughout your campaigns: one for mail, one for billboards, one on your website, and so on. You can even dynamically include unique numbers on different AdWords ads and track responses at the keyword and ad level. The numbers all forward to your regular sales or customer support lines, but you have reports on which channel they came from.

That's the campaign analytics part. The conversion optimization part is that you can record the calls ("this call may be monitored or recorded for quality assurance purposes"). You then can use the recordings to review how your business development reps—the people who answered the calls—did, and to train them to improve in the future.

Now that you know some of the most effective ways to improve your conversion rates, you're probably going to be looking at websites, offers, landing pages and even business phone calls differently than before. Great! There's a lot to gain by being critical and running many tests to see what actually works for your company.

Tools for conversion optimization

WordStream has a free Landing Page Grader.

With Optimizely, VWO and Unbounce you can run A/B tests on landing pages and other website elements, and they provide other optimization tools.

ion interactive and SnapApp provide tools for creating interactive marketing experiences.

HotJar and Crazy Egg are tools for analyzing the behavior of people on individual pages of your website, including how far down the page visitors go.

CallRail is a call tracking vendor.

Chapter 7

EMAIL MARKETING

EMAIL IS THE 500-POUND GORILLA of Bullseye Marketing.

- If you build your list from customers and prospects, you should have an excellent list. You are sending messages primarily to people who have already done business with you or are interested enough in you that they have asked to receive your emails.
- You can segment and personalize so that people are getting the most tailored, valuable messages.
- Over 99% of the people that you send an email to will receive it.
- You have the tools and metrics to constantly improve your email campaigns to make them increasingly more effective.
- Good emails get high response rates: not just opens, but clicks, forwards and—most importantly—conversions.
- It is inexpensive. You pay for staff time and creative, of course, but compared to the high cost of physical direct mail and some other channels, an email program is a bargain.

Even Millennials, who are rumored to prefer tools like Snapchat and Instagram, like brands to use emails—and engage with them.[41]

So let's talk about what goes into making email marketing work for you.

Build your own list

The first rule of 21st century email marketing is to build your own list. As described in the previous chapter, give people who come to your website many opportunities to opt-in to receiving your emails. Offer them 10% off their first purchase, or a free ebook, or a webinar—whatever works for your customers. Have your salespeople collect business cards and systematically enter them into your CRM.

When visitors are leaving your site, you can give them one more opportunity to sign up to receive your content with an exit-intent pop-up.

But don't buy lists. If you do buy a list, you are likely to find:

- Major email platforms won't even import it because they have algorithms to detect lists with a high percentage of bad email addresses (after all, you aren't the first person the list has been sold to).
- If you use one of the email service providers who will work with a bought list, you'll find that many of the names are bad and get rejected even by them.
- You'll want to set up a different web domain for those bought list mailings because you don't want your real domain getting blacklisted as a source of spam.
- You'll get a historically low response rate to what you send.
- The email list broker will be last seen riding off into the distance, waving your check and laughing maniacally.

If, nonetheless, you decide to go ahead with buying a list, then make sure you do use a different email service provider who will permit its use. And use the email you send to promote a really attractive offer that will entice people to come to your site and use your awesome landing page to opt-in to becoming part of your house list and receiving emails in the future.

Later we'll talk about a special case in which you didn't build the list: pre-event lists provided by trade shows and conferences where you're exhibiting.

The CAN-SPAM Act

The name of the CAN-SPAM Act was meant to suggest that the law, which took effect in 2003, would "can" (stop) spam. But its regulations are so loose that people immediately started to joke that with it you can spam. Under the law, commercial emails must do the following to avoid being considered spam:

- have accurate header information, such as the From and Reply-To information
- use non-deceptive Subject lines
- identify that the message is an ad
- include the physical address (in the footer, usually)
- provide a way for people to unsubscribe, and honor those requests promptly
- make sure that any company that you hire to do email marketing for you complies with these requirements.

That's a pretty low bar.

The potential penalties for violating the CAN-SPAM Act are high; *each* individual email sent is subject to penalties of over $40,000, so you could be facing millions of dollars in penalties for even a single email blast with just a few dozen addresses that are in violation.[42] And the CAN-SPAM act doesn't just apply to large/bulk email blasts, it applies to one-to-one "commercial" emails, too, although it seems to be ignored by virtually all companies at that level.

Individuals who receive emails that don't comply with the requirements cannot sue, and there is a limited right of action by corporations. Most actions are taken by prosecutors or the Federal Trade Commission (FTC) against large, bulk spammers.

Segment your lists

As a Bullseye marketer, you know that the most important factor in direct response campaigns is the quality of your list. Email programs, when integrated with data from your marketing automation program, CRM, and other sources, provide very advanced tools to target the right list.

People in different stages of the buying/customer funnel are just some of the segments that you'll want to create and develop different content for. These include:

- contacts
- qualified prospects
- active leads
- customers

You may also have separate segments for partners, the press, analysts, and others.

Beyond these high-level segments, you can segment far more based on the nature of what you're selling, the size of your lists, and what you find to be effective. Important segments could include:

- demographics (gender, age, location)
- business demographics (size of company, industry, title in company)
- amount and type of interactions with your website, emails and other marketing
- recency, size or type of previous purchases
- self-identified interests: ask people on your email sign-up form which subjects they are interested in getting information about, and let them manage those preference in the future

Three types of marketing data

You can use three types of data to enhance your customer and prospect targeting.

First party data

First party data is your data. It includes previous customer buying history, how a person interacts with your website, emails and other content (what marketing automation vendor Eloqua calls a person's "digital body language"), their attendance on webinars and at physical events, and so on. First party data rules, and it's inexpensive for you to gather and use. In Phase 1, you can mostly rely on first party data.

Third party data

You buy third party data from vendors, and it can include more information about the person or account:

- what they've bought from others in the past
- their behavior on other websites (have they recently started researching and reading articles about your type of products?)
- what kind of car they drive
- have they filed any patents

And so on. There are thousands of third party data types you could enrich your data with. Tens of thousands of retailers and publishers are pooling their anonymized data in data co-ops.[43]

Second party data

Second party data is essentially private third party data. Second party data is created and collected in partnership with another company but not distributed broadly by data merchants.

> For example, if you do a campaign jointly with another company, or if you swap data with another company. You're getting data directly from the source, not through a data merchant, and it may be deeper and tied to particular individuals.
>
> Some companies gather and buy thousands of data points for each contact. By using first-, second- and third-party data, you can significantly improve the segmentation, targeting, personalization and effectiveness of your email and other marketing.

Personalize

Personalization can dramatically enhance the effectiveness of your emails.

Personalization once meant a personal greeting, like "Hi Louis", or using the person's name in the Subject line. How 2007.

Your emails will be many times more effective the more that they speak to the current status, pains and interests of the customer. An email in response to an abandoned ecommerce shopping cart is perhaps the ultimate in timely, personalized communication.

Just as an ecommerce site can send emails promoting the types of products that the person has bought in the past or—based on lessons learned from predictive analytics—is likely to buy in the future, B2B companies should personalize their messages.

Based on a person's website behavior, companies can remind people of their interest in a product when it goes on sale.

The ultimate in personalization is when you base your entire email strategy on it. Amazon may have a few high-level segments, such as by country. But after that their emails are almost entirely personalized for each of their several hundred million customers based on the massive amount of data Amazon has collected from their browsing and shopping habits, as well as what they can learn about them from other web activity and third-party data.

Use calls to action

If you're a consultant or otherwise need to promote your industry knowledge and thought leadership, you may be sending regular emails with just your insights and no strong calls to action, sort of like emailed blog posts.

Most companies, though, will be looking for direct, traceable results from their email campaigns such as downloads, event sign-ups, and sales.

Generally you should only have one call to action per email. This email from DigitalMarketer has a big reply button to register at the top, and also right within the email is a cool clock ticking down to the event that's adding a sense of urgency. At the end of the email is a link to reply, too. So there's only one call to action.

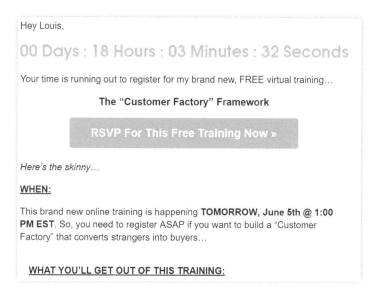

Figure 31. Email with one calls to action buttons

Usually you'll find that the links/offers at the top of the email get the most clicks. I've seen it over and over again. We spend all that time crafting our email masterpieces, but most people don't read to the end. The lower you go in an email (or on a web page), the fewer clicks your links and buttons will usually get.

So if you do have a single call to action, put the link or button for it at the beginning and end of your email.

How often should you send emails?

A few years ago I saw the CMO of Vistaprint talk, and he said that they had done tests and found that their emails produced the most business if they emailed their customers every day. "I know we shouldn't do it, but that's what the data show," he said. Vistaprint sells to very small business; organizations as different as 1-800-Flowers and WGBH also send out emails daily, or almost daily, to people on their lists. Around holidays like Mother's Day, some send more than once a day.

Edible Arrangements	Inbox	🌼 Think Spring! 🌼 - Plus, FREE delivery is happening NOW! edibleÂ® handcraftible - order you	May 16
Edible Arrangements	Inbox	FREE delivery?! Yes, please! - Surprise someone today & SAVE! edibleÂ® Surprise someone too	May 15
Edible Arrangements	Inbox	You're going to love this. - (HINT: It's a SWEET deal for you!) edibleÂ® (HINT: It's a SWEET deal	May 14
Edible Arrangements	Inbox	Forgot Mother's Day? It's Not Too Late - Last Chance to WOW Mom! edibleÂ® Mother's Day Ch	May 13
Edible Arrangements	Inbox	Today is Mother's Day. Still open and delivering! - Order now for pickup or delivery and WOW M	May 13
Edible Arrangements	Inbox	You're not too late! - Order now. Get it for Mother's Day! edibleÂ® Mother's Day Chocolate Dipped	May 12
Edible Arrangements	Inbox	Mother's Day is TOMORROW! - Order right now & SAVE! - No rush fees! edibleÂ® Mother's Day	May 12
Edible Arrangements	Inbox	Quit Procrastinating This Mother's Day! - Find a Gift for Mom Today! edibleÂ® Mother's Day Cho	May 11
Edible Arrangements	Inbox	🕐 Tick, Tock... don't forget about Mom! - Shop our Mother's Day Collection Now! - NO Rush Fe	May 11
Edible Arrangements	Inbox	▢ NEW MESSAGE - Trust us. You want to read this. edibleÂ® Mother's Day Chocolate Dipped Fr	May 11
Edible Arrangements	Inbox	Our NEW Deal of the Day is HERE! - Shop Now. Save BIG. WOW Mom. edibleÂ® deal of the day	May 11
Edible Arrangements	Inbox	Our NEW Deal of the Day is HERE! - Shop Now. Save BIG. WOW Mom. edibleÂ® deal of the day	May 11
Edible Arrangements	Inbox	⏱ HOURS LEFT! - Get today's deal before it's gone! edibleÂ® Get today's deal before it's gone! n	May 10
Edible Arrangements	Inbox	▢ NEW MESSAGE - Don't leave this unread! edibleÂ® Mother's Day Chocolate Dipped Fruit? An	May 10
Edible Arrangements	Inbox	3 Days Until Mother's Day! - Order Now & Save BIG! edibleÂ® deal of the day - click to reveal the	May 10
Edible Arrangements	Inbox	Last Chance for FREE Delivery! - Hurry! This deal ends tonight! edibleÂ® Hurry! This deal ends to	May 9
Edible Arrangements	Inbox	IT'S HERE! - Shop our Mother's Day Collection NOW! edibleÂ® Shop our Mother's Day Collection	May 9
Edible Arrangements	Inbox	NEW Deal of the Day! - Reveal today's offer NOW! edibleÂ® Reveal today's offer NOW! mother's	May 9
Edible Arrangements	Inbox	🎁 MYSTERY OFFER INSIDE! 🎁 - What could it be? edibleÂ® What could it be? edibleÂ® is love	May 8

Figure 32. Inbox showing cadence of email promotions

The rate of optimal email frequency is going to be different for every company. The only way you'll know what cadence is best for you is to test. Most important, though, is that once you have established a cadence, stick to it.

Generally, you have to expect that .25% or more of your list will unsubscribe each time you send an email. So over time, your email list will become more focused on people who really do want to hear from you. And you should be making enough valuable offers on your website and elsewhere that you can constantly grow your list even with those unsubscribes.

So how often should you email? Most likely it's far more often than you think.

When should you send?

Like the question *how often* should you send, *when* you should send can vary significantly depending on who you are marketing to. Generally, email service providers report that open rates are significantly higher on weekdays. Some categories, like emails related to hobbies and ecommerce, perform a bit better on weekends than other categories, but may still not be as good as they are during the week.[44]

For example:

- If you're marketing to business people, you may find that early morning and late afternoon emails get the best response.
- If you're marketing to doctors who do not read their email during the day, then evening emails may work best.
- If you're marketing to bartenders and others who work at night, then you want to send during the day.
- If you're marketing to senior executives, many people have found that messages early on Saturday morning are particularly effective because the weekend is when they catch up with their less urgent reading.

There is no magic day/time for all people.

Email programs also give you the option to customize sends by each recipient's time zone. After all, 8 am in New York is 5 am in San Francisco and 8 pm in Hong Kong. Staggering sends by time zone is a helpful feature if you're sending to a national or international list.

Use UTM tracking codes

UTM tracking codes are a way to measure the effectiveness of almost any online marketing program, including your emails.

Even if you're not familiar with UTMs (Urchin Tracking Module; Urchin was the company that developed the software that eventually became Google Analytics), you may have noticed them in URLs. They show up after the specific page URL and look something like this:

> http://revenueassociates.biz/bullseye-marketing-framework/?utm_source=newsletter&utm_medium=email&utm_campaign=june_newsletter

By creating and using custom UTMs, you can track in Google Analytics which website traffic was generated by your emails, social media posts, ads, and so on.

However, they're not absolutely reliable because people often copy an entire URL, including the UTM code, and send, re-post or re-use it and it will appear in your reports that the traffic came from the original source, not the new source that the URL with UTM was pasted into.

You can easily create URLs with UTMs using Google's URL Builder.[45] (Fig. 33)

Some other tools like Hootsuite also provide UTM builders.

And keep in mind that UTMs are case sensitive, so be consistent and always use lower case.

Email data: Open rates aren't absolutely reliable

Email programs give you many metrics such as delivery rates, open rates, clicks, forwards, bounces, and unsubscribes. That open rate data is not reliable.

Campaign URL Builder

This tool allows you to easily add campaign parameters to URLs so you can track Custom Campaigns in Google Analytics.

Enter the website URL and campaign information

Fill out the required fields (marked with *) in the form below, and once complete the full campaign URL will be generated for you. *Note: the generated URL is automatically updated as you make changes.*

* Website URL

The full website URL (e.g. `https://www.example.com`)

* Campaign Source

The referrer: (e.g. `google` , `newsletter`)

Figure 33. Google URL builder for UTMs

There are too many different email clients, and ways to even define what an open is, for open rates to be absolutely meaningful. If your email program says, for example, that 16.8% of recipients opened an email, that's probably not accurate. It could be more or less.

However, the data are relatively reliable. By that I mean that if you see that certain topics have higher open rates over time, then since it's all in one system with a relatively consistent set of recipients you can probably trust that people are especially interested in those topics.

Subject lines

The most important factor in email opens is the reputation of the sender. If people know that you're sending them valuable information that they requested, they'll continue to open your emails. If you send them garbage, they won't.

Figure 34. Mobile email inbox

That said, different email Subject lines definitely can have a significant impact. Political campaigns raise hundreds of millions of dollars by optimizing their emails and Subject lines. Two Subject lines that were especially effective for the 2012 Obama campaign[46] were, "I will be outspent" and "Hey".

Personalization is good, especially if you're going past the first name in Subject line bit. "Louis, your test results are ready."

Urgency, fear of missing out, status and other appeals may be effective, such as "Last chance" or "Only a few left."

How-tos and numbers are usually effective in blog post headlines and tweets and may work for emails, too, such as, "7 ways to improve your email open rates."

One study[47] found that adding a special offer to the Subject line—like free shipping or buy one, get one free—actually produced lower open and conversion rates. Too salesy, I guess.

Like all marketing, message fatigue will eventually set in. Whatever is working now will eventually need to be replaced.

And beyond the Subject line, be attentive to what you say with the first 6 or 7 words of your message because many email programs will display them in the preview of an email client. Use those first few words to give the recipient another reason to open your emails.

Mobile

Half or more of your emails are being read on smartphones, or will be soon, so make sure they look good and work well on mobile.

Next.

Just some of the ways to use email

Here are just a few of the ways that Bullseye marketers can use emails to promote and grow your business.

Updates/newsletters

Periodic updates on what you're doing, including links to recent blog posts and product update information, can be greatly beneficial. Just make sure that you're writing it from the point of view of the customer. Use "How the Patel family lowered their utility bills with new solar panels" rather than "We installed new solar panels for the Patel family."

Retail promos
Many online retailers send daily, or near daily, emails with that day's deals.

Test drive sign-ups, and getting started tips
Of course you'll be sending emails to people who sign up for free product trials. Then also follow up over the next few days with daily tips on how they can get the most out of their trial, as well as a reminder just a few days before the trial will end. You can personalize these with messages, such as, "I see that you're using X feature a lot. That's one of my favorites. Here are some tips on how to get the most from it."

Pre-conference promos
If you're an exhibitor at a conference or trade show, a few weeks before the event you may be given a list of people who have registered. You can send them information about why they should stop by your booth, including your special trade show offer. This is one of those rare cases where you'll send emails to people who have not yet opted-in to receive yours.

Promote webinars and events
You'll want to send at least three emails inviting people to your webinars and other events, as well as a reminder email a day or so before the event. You can send an email with a link to a video of the webinar shortly afterward, too.

Automate these multi-email "drip" or "nurture" campaigns with a marketing automation program. You tee up all of the emails in advance with decision tree-like logic: If they responded to message A, then skip messages B and C; if they did not respond to message A, send message B. If they responded affirmatively to messages A, B or C, then send message D, and so on.

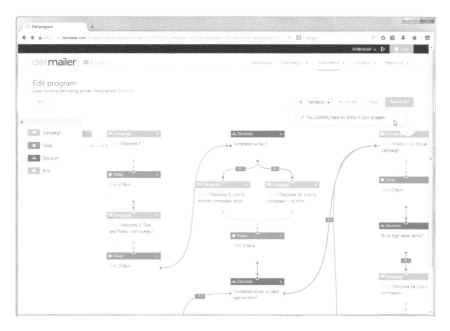

Figure 35. dotmailer branching lead nurturing campaign builder

And you can use your email lists to create custom lists to target ads to on social media platforms like Facebook and LinkedIn. Marketing tends to be more effective when customers see your messages in more than one channel, and combining email and targeted ads in this way (with remarketing, which I describe in the next chapter) can be especially inexpensive and effective.

Thank yous, rewards to loyal customers

You wouldn't be there without your customers. Let your most valuable customers know how much you appreciate them with an occasional thank you and reward.

Case Study: MailChimp product launch email

This is one of my favorite business blog posts of all time.[48] MailChimp CEO Ben Chestnut wrote it in 2013, and I still remember it: how many blog posts can you say that about? Even though the product that MailChimp is promoting ultimately didn't make it—that happens—it's such a well-written post that I didn't know whether to put it here or in the chapter on content.

The post:

- uses storytelling and a humble, on-brand tone
- is full of useful information about how to create, target and measure an email campaign
- promotes their new product without giving it a hard sell

It's like a triple bank shot in pool.

This has been reprinted in full except for links.

"Behind the Scenes: How We Do Our <u>Own</u> Email Marketing at MailChimp"[49]

Last month, we sent an email announcement to customers about our new SMS app Gather. I guess you could call it "email marketing," though we rarely think of it that way (we just call it "talking to customers"). But the marketing team put it together, with some help from our mobile team, and a *bajillion* annoying edits from me. I thought I'd share all the edits I made, and why I made them, in case you find this sort of thing interesting.

First, here's the final version of the email that we eventually sent:

Now, let's go over the process we went through to get there.

Targeting

The goal was simple enough: Tell our customers about Gather. Gather is an SMS app that's designed specifically for people who host events. It's not exactly for *everyone*, so we certainly shouldn't send it to everyone. Our list of users has more than 2.8 million subscribers. Not gonna lie—I was sort of tempted to send this email to that entire list. But that would've resulted in a ton of backlash, unsubscribes, account cancellations, angry tweets, and—worst of all—loss of trust in our brand.

So we started looking for *segments* of the list that we thought would most likely find this useful (and least likely find it irrelevant).

Our first thought was to segment by industry. There are quite a few people in our system who've indicated they're in the "Entertainment and Events" industry:

That whittles the list down significantly, but it's still a pretty big group.

Then we remembered that Gather was only available on the iPhone. And like many mobile app developers, we've learned the hard way that you really don't want to irk the Android users out there. So we did this:

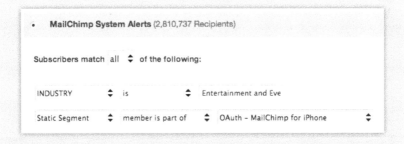

That static segment is a feature in MailChimp where we can use our API to sync data from our user database. Among many other things, our user database stores information about which external apps each account has linked to.

In the example above, you see MailChimp customers who are in the events industry, *and* who've logged in to our MailChimp mobile app for iPhone. But I felt a little uneasy about this segment of the list. The industry "Entertainment and Events" just seemed too broad (What, exactly, is "entertainment"?). At the same time, it was too narrow—there are plenty of people out there who host events, but wouldn't consider themselves in the "Events" industry.

I really wanted us to focus on "tech-savvy people who host events." So this is the segment of our list that we ultimately chose:

These are MailChimp customers who have used our integration with Eventbrite. Integrating two SaaS products like MailChimp and Eventbrite is a decent indicator that these people are tech-savvy, and wouldn't be scared to try Gather.

We make the act of segmenting your list super easy. But the discussion of *how we should segment the list* took place over 2-3 days. That seems awfully long, but this is important stuff. Nine times out of 10, I also include the criteria, "is very engaged." That little added element removes all the disengaged subscribers, who are more likely to complain or unsubscribe, or to tweet mean things about your brand. I believe your main goal of segmenting your list is not to *increase* relevancy (that's your content's job) but to reduce irrelevancy.

Content and design

After the segment of our list was settled, we tackled design and content. This was our very first stab at the email announcement:

It was such a pretty email. It took a lot to get that done. Back in July of last year, we built an online service that generates quick images of app screenshots inside of various mobile devices. That led us to creating a Tumblr of random hands holding smartphones, mostly for laughs (it's pretty challenging to get a good shot of a hand holding a phone). So you *could* say the photo at the top of the email was months in the making. The marketing team certainly was proud of it.

But I had a problem with it.

This was my basic feedback:

By the way, my actual feedback was mostly face-to-face. I didn't mark up the email in red like these diagrams. I'm not a jerk, really! The red marks are just an easy way to recount my edits to you.

First, the subject line was a little too salesy, and was missing context:

"A Few Ways to Use Gather, MailChimp's SMS App for Events"

We didn't even introduce Gather yet—let alone say, "Hi, we're MailChimp!"— to the recipient. So why are we already talking about all the ways you can use it? It's a well written subject, but we were getting ahead of ourselves. Remember, this is an introductory email.

So we changed it to:

"Announcing Gather, a MailChimp App for Events"

It's still a little slick and salesy, but hey—we're selling something. It's honest, and it's a more polite way to introduce ourselves.

"Who the [bleep] is Gather?"

Next, I was concerned that our recipients would open the email, see the Gather logo, and think, "Who the [bleep] is Gather?!? This is spam!!!!" These customers signed up for MailChimp, and therefore are only expecting emails from MailChimp. So I asked for the MailChimp logo at the top of the email. Wouldn't want to get shut down by my own Compliance Team.

Proper introductions

Finally, I wasn't happy about placing that large photograph of the iPhone so high on the email. I wanted to get some text above that photo, where people can skim or scan really fast and decide if the email is useful to them. Plopping a giant image at the top is disrespectful, in my opinion. You're asking the recipient to basically wait (or click) for an image to download? That's kinda like the old "skip intro" days of web design (seriously, don't be a Flashole).

So we moved the intro paragraph above the big pretty picture.

And here's the second draft:

That's better placement of the intro copy, but this didn't feel like the way we'd write. It's nice that we provide some context about why they're receiving the email in the first place ("Since you use MailChimp and Eventbrite..."), but I still didn't think it felt quite right. Our style has refined a little over the years, but we're still trying to keep it a little weird. This copy was missing something MailChimpy.

My advice to all new email marketers is to figure out your brand's natural Voice and Tone as soon as you can (we're lucky enough to have ours documented by some brilliant people). If you're not quite there yet, blogging can help you write more confidently, and the feedback in your customers' comments will help you calibrate your style over time. Once you've got that figured out, writing email newsletters gets soooo much easier, and you'll be able to spot when you're a little "off brand."

My feedback:

Here's the revision:

Okay, my writers are making fun of me. Clearly, they're getting tired of my edits. But this is actually kind of funny, and does a really good job of explaining how the app works. Most importantly, it's a true story! (I get lost a lot.) I loved it because it was humble, and it was human. That's perfectly "on brand" for MailChimp.

With this new intro, it didn't make sense to list all the ways you can use Gather. So the team chopped the rest of the email down to a very simple "go try it if you're interested:"

By now, about 4 days had passed from when we started working on this email. And wouldn't you know it, our dang mobile team went and *launched the Android version of Gather*. Sigh. People are always changing things around here. That means more last-minute edits (#agilemarketing). So we changed the image of the phone to Android (What the heck, we've got an app for that!), and we mentioned Android in the copy.

too late to send them an email. His frustration led to the idea for Gather, a simple app that lets event organizers send SMS notifications from a private number, and allows attendees to contact organizers, too.

gather by MailChimp

Android

If you're interested in giving Gather a try, check it out at gather.mailchimpapp.com. It's available for both iOS and Android in the United States, Canada, and United Kingdom.

Cheers,
The MailChimp Team

Always give
something useful.

PS. If you're interested in event-based email marketing, you can read our blog post about Rockhouse Partners, who have some great strategies to encourage engagement, like using small events to promote bigger events and offering special deals for out-of-town attendees.

Always be useful

We try to include something useful in every email. If the announcement was totally useless, let's at least give the recipient a case study, or something educational (even if it points to some other resource). So at the bottom of the email, we added a postscript that linked to one of our blog posts about Rockhouse Partners, an entertainment agency that uses our geo targeting feature to help them with their events. That was a blog post from November 2012. How lucky are we to have that content to point to?

Lesson: always be blogging.

The results

The campaign got an open rate of 32.6% (the list average for general announcements is 24.7%) and a click rate of 6.3% (average is 1.8%). Meanwhile, 0.22% of recipients unsubscribed. And it only received one complaint.

Most importantly, sales went up. You can see clearly how sales picked up on the day the email was sent:

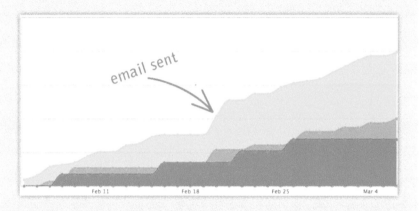

Word got out on Twitter, and sales are picking up speed. The different colors you see are the different price tiers. Cyan is the cheapest price plan, which has grown the most.

Being human is hard.

My point of all this is that sooner or later, you're going to want to send an email campaign that sells something. When that time comes, it'll be easy to just put on the Sales Guy Hat and run through the motions, doing the same stuff you've seen other companies do. You write a salesy subject line, throw in some aggressive copy, add a slick product photo, and "blast" it out to the masses. Because that's what you see polluting *your* inbox, right? Please don't do that. Email marketing is your chance to connect with your customers in a *human* way. Be human!

Tools for email marketing

Constant Contact and MailChimp are two leading email platforms for small and mid-sized companies.

All of the marketing automation programs and marketing clouds have integrated email programs.

Bronto, dotmailer and Klaviyo are email programs that support larger B2C and ecommerce campaigns.

Epsilon, Experian, Bombora, Harte-Hanks, Aberdeen, and Tech-Target gather and sell third-party data.

Chapter 8

REMARKETING

REMARKETING IS THE MARKETING TACTIC that people love to hate.

Remarketing ads are the ones that you see after you've visited a site. For example, you look at the page for a particular book on Amazon and immediately you start to see ads for that book on other sites. That's remarketing (sometimes called "retargeting").

Do you think that it's kind of creepy? Annoying? Maybe. But it's very effective.

As a Bullseye marketer, you know that the most important factor in direct response marketing is targeting the right audience. Remarketing is so effective because you're only advertising to people who have already spent some time on your website. That's a great audience! You're way more likely to close a sale with them than someone who has never heard of you before.

And you can be very specific with your ads. If someone visited a page about a particular product or service, you show them ads just for that.

You only pay for remarketing ads when people click on them, so you can get thousands of impressions without paying anything for them.

The CPM—cost per thousand impressions, a common pricing method for display ads—can be very low. And your remarketing ads may show on some high-quality sites that you might not be able to afford to advertise on if you had to buy one of their minimum packages.

You can manage remarketing programs through Google, Facebook, LinkedIn, Twitter and some third party ad management software.

Here are a few tips:

- Run your remarketing on appropriate websites and social media channels—wherever your customer is.
- Put the remarketing tags from the services you plan to use on your website asap. You can be building your remarketing cookie pool while you're developing the strategy and creative and getting the campaigns set up.
- Create different ads for each product, so the ads that people see are personalized to what they were looking at.
- Use remarketing to supplement your paid search ad campaigns on AdWords and Bing. Search ads (in Phase 2) are a great way of building your website traffic with qualified visitors, and build a larger, highly-targeted remarketing pool in the process.
- Use custom combination lists. With a custom combination list, you can exclude people who converted from your remarketing pool so that you don't waste your money and annoy people who already did convert.
- You could, however, use remarketing to promote supplemental items to people who did make a purchase. Would you like a tie with that shirt?
- Consider the buying cycle for your products and show remarketing ads for that period of time. If people typically complete a purchase of your product within one to two weeks, there's no reason to show them ads for 90 days or more.
- If you have customer-only pages on your website which require a login, you can create a special remarketing list of people who visit those pages and show customer-only messages to them.

- Experiment with bidding higher for ads for your higher margin products.
- Accelerate the delivery of ads, so people see them as soon as they leave your site. I've seen remarketing ads within 30-60 seconds of visiting a site.
- Experiment with Google's "similar audiences" feature to show your ads to people with interests similar to those in your remarketing list. (That's not a Bullseye list, though, so I'd recommend you do that as part of your Phase 2 or 3 marketing efforts.)
- Combine remarketing with other ad targeting techniques such as geographic and dayparting to make your remarketing ads even more effective.
- To cut down on the creep factor, limit how often people will see your campaign to perhaps just three times a day. Or maybe not: experiment with how much you show your ads and see which converts best.

You may—or may not—like them, but remarketing ads work.

Be careful with medical remarketing

Generally with remarketing you want to shows ads for what the person specifically was looking at on your website. One exception is medical services.

Let's say that a person came to a hospital or medical center website and looked at the pages on diabetes or cancer. It would be inappropriate to then target them with remarketing ads that contain copy about the specific condition that they were reading about.

This is one of the few cases in which, instead, you could show them more general remarketing ads for the institution but not for the particular service.

Use all of your powers

Just using remarketing can significantly improve the results that you're getting from website visitors, AdWords, and other marketing programs. And you can target even more precisely within the people in your remarketing pool.

Watchfinder is a British company that sells high-end, pre-owned watches; their average sale is several thousand dollars. At those prices most people who visit their website don't make a purchase on their first visit, so Watchfinder chose remarketing as a way to stay in front of customers during the several weeks that they might be considering a decision.[50]

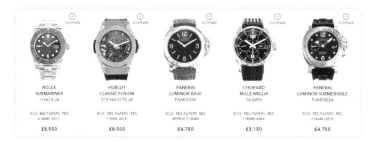

Figure 36. Website retail offers

They and their agency decided to remarket differently to different segments. They created 20 highly focused audiences in Google Analytics with separate messages and ads for each. Lists included such factors as which brands visitors viewed, how many pages they looked at, time on site, and even select ISPs (Internet service providers) in the London financial district. They geo-targeted ads to people in London encouraging them to visit the local store.

After six months their average order had increased 13%, cost per acquisition had dropped 34%, and the campaign ROI was 1,300%.

PS: The list that performed the best was people who had browsed for 10 minutes or more on their initial visit without making a purchase.

Mobile app remarketing

You don't have to be a player of smartphone games to use mobile apps. You probably have many on your phone for news, weather, banking, social media, entertainment and other purposes. In fact, a large majority of the time that the average adult spends on their phone is in apps.

But that usage is highly concentrated, and most people use a new app only a few times.

You can use remarketing to re-engage with people who have downloaded your app. Depending on the platform, these campaigns can be targeted by how they have used your app.

You also can remarket specifically to people who visited your website on their phones. And since that's where people spend a majority of their screen time these days, for many campaigns that could be critical.

 ## Tools for remarketing

Google AdWords, Facebook, LinkedIn, and Twitter.
Perfect Audience supports more sophisticated cross-device
remarketing.

.

Chapter 9

MARKETING AND SALES COLLABORATION

BULLSEYE MARKETERS WILL WANT TO embrace sales and marketing collaboration because companies that get this right grow much faster.

I once had a meeting with the CEO, VP of Sales, and VP of Marketing of a client, with the CEO sitting in the middle between the other two. That physical arrangement also reflected their relationships: the two VPs simply could not agree on anything. That company was having problems.

With sales and marketing working together, though, all pulling in the same direction, wonders can happen.

Sales and marketing collaboration is often discussed in the context of B2B companies. (And it is usually called "sales and marketing alignment", but I prefer "collaboration" as introduced by Tom Barrieau.[51]) But many B2C companies have sales people, too: clothing stores, bakeries, auto repair shops all have front-line sales reps; attorneys and financial service advisors are selling every day. So with a little tweaking, everything in this chapter should be usable in almost any company.

Sales sells to people, marketing to personas

Sales and marketing have many reasons why they might not work together well, but one is that they start with a fundamentally different view of the business universe.

Salespeople sell to individuals and small buying teams. They are always trying to understand their customer, their particular needs, and how that person can be motivated to buy from them.

Marketers, on the other hand, typically start with personas: a fictional composite of the customer based on research. Sometimes these have names like Marketing Mary and Homeowner Henry. These personas and market segments drive marketing messaging and targeting.

As more sophisticated companies add more and more data to their customer records, they will create deeper profiles of individual customers. Like the recommendations on Amazon, they will become increasingly personalized. But no matter how much data they use, the customer record will never have the nuanced personal knowledge that a salesperson can.

On the other hand, the salesperson will never command the breadth of knowledge that is in the customer record. They certainly won't remember every piece of content that the customer looked at, and every interaction that they've had with the company.

Both sales and marketing have great, but incomplete, knowledge. The magic happens when they respect one another and begin true collaboration.

Involve sales in developing personas

The first step in sales and marketing collaboration is a joint agreement on who the customer is. In chapter 3 I talked about developing personas so everyone on the marketing team understands their customers better. Sales should be actively involved in the development of those personas.

No one in your company has more day-to-day contact with customers than sales. They know better than anyone the messages that move customers to buy, their objections, and how to successfully address them.

Take advantage of that knowledge when creating your personas and work with your sales team so they are fully invested in them.

Jointly define a lead

A major role of marketing is to generate qualified leads for sales, so you first need to agree on what that even means. If you don't you'll end up with snarky comments like "The leads from marketing are junk" and "sales never follows up on the great leads that marketing gets them."

The stages that a prospect goes through can include (each company may define these a little differently):

- contact: anyone who interacts with the company
- prospect: a contact who fits the profile of a possible customer
- marketing qualified lead (MQL): a prospect who has been reviewed by marketing and found to meet the definition of a lead agreed upon by sales and marketing
- sales qualified lead (SQL): an MQL who has been contacted by sales, and they agree that the lead is at a point where they should try to close a sale with them. Leads generated by sales, such as by teleprospecting, may never be an MQL and may immediately become an SQL.
- opportunity: A person/company that is ready to buy... from someone. A salesperson has talked with them and knows their needs and requirements. They are ready for, or have received, a proposal.
- customer

Defining who a lead is, and which leads marketing should pass on to sales, are critical early steps in this.

The more data from past sales that you bring to the process of defining a qualified lead, the better. Without data, you're just guessing.

Usually a person in marketing needs to talk with a prospect to qualify them and send them on to sales. You may find out that someone who seems to be from the right kind of company and is very actively

engaged is just researching something that they're personally interested in, but that their company has no plans to buy anytime soon
(much to their regret). Sales wants to close deals; they need leads who
are serious about buying—now.

In many B2B companies, a quarter to a third of MQLs get rejected
by sales and sent back to marketing for further nurturing. Sales and
marketing need to constantly work together to reduce that as much
as possible.

Marketing TLAs (Three Letter Acronyms)

As we go deeper into these marketing tactics you'll see more
of these TLAs. Don't even think about memorizing them; I
don't even use all of these in this book. You'll get comfortable
with the important ones over time.

ABM	Account Based Marketing
ACV	Annual Contract Value
AOV	Average Order Value
API	Application Programming Interface
ARR	Annual Recurring Revenue
B2B	Business to Business
B2C	Business to Consumer
BDR	Business Development Representative (see SDR)
CAC	Customer Acquisition Cost
CEO	Chief Executive Officer
CFO	Chief Financial Officer
CMO	Chief Marketing Officer
CMS	Content Management System
CPA	Cost Per Action, or Cost Per Acquisition
CPC	Cost Per Click
CPG	Consumer Packaged Goods
CPL	Cost Per Lead
CPM	Cost Per Thousand
CRM	Customer Relationship Management (software)
CRO	Conversion Rate Optimization
CRO	Chief Revenue Officer
CTR	Click Through Rate
DAM	Digital Asset Management
DMP	Data Management Platform
DSP	Demand Side Platform

ECM	Enterprise Content Management
EMS	Event Management Software
ICP	Ideal Customer Profile
KPI	Key Performance Indicator
LTV	Lifetime Value
MAP	Marketing Automation Program
MCM	Marketing Campaign Management
MQL	Marketing Qualified Lead
MRR	Monthly Recurring Revenue
OVP	Online Video Platform
PPA	Pay Per Acquisition
PPC	Pay Per Click
ROI	Return on Investment
SDR	Sales Development Representative (see BDR)
SEM	Search Engine Marketing
SEO	Search Engine Optimization
SLA	Service Level Agreement
SMM	Social Media Marketing
SQL	Sales Qualified Lead
UGC	User Generated Content
URL	Uniform Resource Locator
VDP	Variable Data Printing
VOC	Voice of Customer
YOY	Year Over Year

Create goals and responsibilities

Once you've defined a qualified lead, you can jointly decide who is responsible for generating them. Marketing and sales each have specific roles and responsibilities.

Marketing will generate new leads through integrated programs that include email marketing, remarketing, search marketing, content marketing, display ads, and other tactics. Sales will generally generate its leads through outbound calling, which may be done by junior BDRs and SDRs, and by personal networking at events, references, and "social selling." Social selling involves engaging with people who fit the profile of a prospect who are active on social media.

Sales and marketing should create an agreement on how many leads of what type each is responsible for generating each week. And sales should also agree on how it will react to MQLs delivered to them.

Usually this involves prioritizing them with some leads requiring immediate outreach—and I do mean immediate—while others can be called in an hour or a day. Marketing and sales will usually agree that someone who filled out a sales contact form and is from the right kind of company goes directly to sales for immediate action.

Depending on the season, and other factors, the two groups may need to modify these goals from time to time. If it's late in the summer, for example, and neither is generating as many leads as they have committed to, for a few weeks they may need to relax their definition of a qualified lead.

Create a written SLA

Write it down!

Sales and marketing collaboration requires a formal service level agreement between the two. Put it in writing. Make your commitments explicit.

This will likely take several meetings over a number of weeks, but the time investment is well worth it.

Putting it in writing doesn't mean it never changes. As you work together more, you'll learn how to work together better, and you'll update the SLA.

As they say in Hollywood, "Of course we need a contract. Otherwise, what would we re-negotiate?"

Interview with Zorian Rotenberg: How marketing and sales can work together more successfully

Zorian Rotenberg is co-founder and CEO at Atiim. At the time of this interview, he was the VP of Sales and Marketing at InsightSquared.

Zorian: You need a service level agreement, an SLA, with sales. And when I say an SLA, I mean people literally should write it out and draw a line in the sand on what marketing will provide not only in number of leads but in dollar value. This SLA should include the timing or when sales will call the high scoring leads and when they will call all other leads. A lot of disagreements can end when you have that in place. And it's a continuous, iterative process. It can take some time to iterate and improve. But you basically have a service level agreement with sales that says, "We're going to deliver to you X number of these types of leads, Y number of other types of leads. And for the first type which we'll say is the high scoring ones, you have to call them within five minutes. There will be very few of these very high scoring leads, but they're the hot leads. Then there's a second tranche that's not as hot, and sales agrees to call them within 30-60 minutes. And then there may be a third tranche for some companies, and you can call them during the same day but certainly not right away." So you have to show the order of priority and decide that the call is going to be based on that priority. You can't tell sales that you have to call all of them in five minutes, because it's a simple calculation that it's impossible to do that. So you have to have an agreement around what's possible and what's not and have a mutual understanding.

Louis: I've heard from people in marketing even at some big companies that I've worked with who say that sales sometimes doesn't follow up for a week or more, and it just is insanity.

Zorian: Yes. Absolutely. It happens all the time. And I think the reasons are two-fold. One, there's no agreement on what a hot lead is. And there's likely no SLA in the first place because when you put a SLA in place, it forces you to agree with sales on the definition of a "lead." And the second reason is that most people are not able to measure or track leads and follow-ups well enough. You should have exception reports that are produced every night. We have a nightly report, and InsightSquared makes the product that does this report, that shows how many of our hot or marketing qualified leads are not being contacted by the sales team. And, for example, one time it showed a lot of leads weren't being followed up on, and it caused us to bring in another inbound SDR and put him on the team. We doubled the team in a few weeks because we realized that marketing was significantly outgrowing the capacity of the sales team, of the inbound sales team, to handle our leads. It's a good problem—it's a champagne problem, right?

Louis: Yes, that's a good problem to have. So do you have goals around what percent of your leads are inbound leads and what percent are generated by sales teleprospecting?

Zorian: We don't look at percentage of leads generated. We focus more on opportunities generated. In terms of leads, it's not so important at a strategic level but only at a tactical level in marketing. Opportunities are what you attempt to close in any given selling period—it's all the potential deals your sales reps are pursuing to close, but only 10% to 30% of them will end up as won deals for most companies depending on the business, industry, sales process, etc. And, basically, we look at that. And roughly 60% of our opportunities are generated by the sales outbound prospecting team and 40% by marketing, but marketing opportunities convert at about a 20% win rate which is quite a bit higher than the win rate on other sources. So while marketing produces fewer count of opportunities, those end up converting into about 70% of the deals, so fewer opportunities which drive a vast majority of closed deals. And this makes sense because those folks who inbound are ones who already have an interest and we were able to catch them with lead generation or, as we like to call them, dragnet and other fishnet strategies for catching leads.

Hold weekly meetings

Once you have your SLA in place, the leaders of sales and marketing should continue to meet weekly to review how they are doing in terms of their goals and responsibilities.

In these meetings you can review the data for each team and discuss if you need to adjust the goals and responsibilities. As described before, some of these adjustments may be seasonal or short-term in nature.

These are the serious meetings, but sales and marketing should also get together occasionally just for fun. Maybe it's to celebrate a big win, or making a quarterly or yearly goal, or maybe it's just an occasional happy hour after work. Knowing the people that you're working with as more than emails and Slack messages can really help bond your teams and see you through the inevitable challenges.

Take a sales rep to lunch

As Bullseye marketers we should be talking with customers ourselves and bringing research to sales. But whether it's an enterprise sales rep closing $1 million deals or a retail salesperson in the clothes section helping people buy something that looks good on them, salespeople have orders of magnitude more customer contact than we ever will. So be close to your salespeople and learn from them about your customers.

Take one of your most experienced, successful salespeople to lunch and find out from them what customers really think about your offerings. What do they like? What are their objections? And how does the salesperson deal with those objections? Good salespeople listen; this is an opportunity for you to listen to them.

Arrange a ride along and go on some sales calls, or be a "trainee" in the store for a day or two to learn more about how the actual sales process goes and what customers are saying.

This is invaluable research for creating better personas, products, offers and promotions, and also for creating late stage content that can help your salespeople close the next deal.

Create content for sales to use

Content can be a critical tool for reps to use to close deals. Bullseye marketers need to work closely with sales to understand their content needs and develop it for them.

Many marketers focus primarily, or exclusively, on "top of funnel" content designed to attract more prospects and leads. New contacts are important, of course, but only a small number of them will turn into opportunities, and even fewer will become customers. You have a much better chance of closing a deal with an SQL who has already been interacting with your company. Help your sales reps get it done.

Typically the late stage content needed to close a deal is different from the early stage content needed to attract prospects. An infographic may help attract new contacts, but it won't close a deal. Your sales people can help you understand the issues of the different people on the buying committee. A CFO may want an ROI calculator while business unit managers may want case studies and success story videos.

Sales reps may also need the ability to customize content for a particular prospect. This may be as simple as adding the prospect's logo to a piece of content, or as complex as a multi-page benchmark report comparing a company with industry averages. If you're in a heavily regulated industry such as financial services, however, you may want to limit how much reps can edit text so that they don't inadvertently violate industry rules.

Help sales be first responders

We all know about first responders in public safety: the police, firefighter and EMT personnel who are trained to be the first to respond to an emergency.

I first heard of how important it is for sales to respond first when the agency that I then owned was doing work for a company that makes software to serve the hospitality industry. Hotels or other facilities that responded first to an RFP to host an event had a 50+ percent chance of winning the deal. Similarly, according to one study of over 15,000 leads and 100,000 call attempts, responding within five minutes makes you four times more likely to reach the person than if you called just five minutes later, and 10 times more likely to reach them than if you waited an hour.[52]

The swift sales rep has tremendous advantages because they're way more memorable than if they're the fourth or fifth company to respond, hours or days later. In one sales opportunity that I managed a VP of Marketing at a $700 million company filled out a contact us form on the company's website. I called in under five minutes. Her reaction was, "Either you have nothing to do, or you're incredibly responsive." I assured her that it was the latter. And that stuck with her. Whenever she introduced me to others at her company during the sales process, she invariably said, "He's the guy who called me back in less than five minutes." It was a very smooth sales process for a six-figure engagement that closed very swiftly.

They're not going to save lives, but sales first responders can create tremendous value for themselves and their companies. So as a Bullseye marketer, help them do that.

Put in place the right technology

Several thousand companies provide some flavor of technology related to sales and marketing. These include technologies in dozens of categories for managing customer contacts, marketing data, email, website management, proposal generation, electronic signatures and much, much more.

Marketing and sales can significantly improve their collaboration by jointly and actively using two technologies in particular: the customer relationship management system (CRM) and a marketing automation program.

CRM: The customer relationship management software stores and manages information about people and accounts in every stage of the marketing and sales cycle. Advanced CRMs include analytics, tracking of social media engagement, integration of third party data, support tickets, and features for HR and other parts of the company. The CRM software is central to the success of any company that wants to grow beyond a few dozen customers that are being tracked in a spreadsheet.

"Customer relationship management", as distinct from the software, is the strategies and practices for managing all of these interactions. But when implementing CRM software, many companies fail to fully take advantage of the power of these systems. According to some surveys, a majority of CRM implementations fail to achieve their goals due to a combination of unclear goals, poor planning, lack of executive buy-in, insufficient training, and other factors.

Keeping the information in the CRM system up to date is key to managing sales and predicting pipeline. A CRM system that's used to track not just sales opportunities and orders but also customer support interactions, support tickets, and other issues with existing customers can help provide a 360-degree view of the customer and be critical in growing those all-important existing accounts.

Sales management needs to make sure that reps are entering all of their activity information into the CRM and that they are updating the opportunities so that your reports and forecasts are accurate. Keeping the CRM updated is not stupid paperwork: managers need to be able to look at all of the information on each opportunity anytime they want to, as well as individual rep and team data. Up to date information on individual opportunities can be invaluable if an account executive walks out the door.

An advanced CRM will also include automated account news (management changes, new initiatives, patents, etc.) and data (quarterly and annual revenue and profits, total employees, number of locations, etc.) as well as updates from social media and blogs signaling the most important current issues at an account. Using third party services to add this information to the CRM can significantly enhance the targeting of marketing and lead scoring, and cut down the research time needed by sales reps.

For marketing, the CRM contains invaluable data for tracking campaign performance beyond leads to opportunities and wins, as well as identifying the most promising accounts and individuals within accounts, and other data for analyzing programs and planning future efforts.

Marketing automation: When fully implemented, marketing automation programs (MAP) are a combination of email marketing, customer behavior tracking, lead scoring, lead nurturing, website personalization, sales alerts and more.

Some marketing automation systems began as email marketing programs which then added programmatic actions based on the response of the prospect. There is a good illustration of an automated campaign in the earlier chapter on email marketing; some of these can include an automated alert to the sales rep based on the actions of the prospect.

Lead scoring versus predictive analytics

Lead scoring and predictive analytics can both be used for segmenting. Predictive analytics, though, can take you much further.

Lead scoring is a relatively simple process. For example, B2B lead scoring is often done on two axes:

- Firmographics and Demographics: Type of company, size of company, title of person, etc.
- Activity: How often have they recently engaged with your website, messages, events, etc. , and which products are they interested in?

Lead Scoring Matrix				
D E M O	High	C	B	A
	Medium	D	C	B
	Low	E	D	C
		Low	Medium	High
		Actions/Interest		

Figure 37. Lead scoring matrix

The leads in the upper right corner are the best and require immediate attention. Marketing can nurture mid-level leads over time, and ignore the people in the lower left.

Just this level of scoring can be very helpful in identifying your most promising prospects for sending on to sales.

Predictive analytics is way ahead of lead scoring, though, in helping companies retain customers, close new business, and serve their customers better.

You're familiar with predictive analytics, although you may not know it was called that. Let's look at a few examples.

Imagine that you have a friend who's a woman in her thirties. She's married with one child around two years old. And on Pinterest you suddenly see her pinning things like this:

| Maternity red wrap | Pregnant black dress | Pregnant - white towel |
| Elegant | Pretty! | Cute |

Figure 38. Pinterest pins for maternity dresses[53]

You might deduce that she is pregnant again. Given her demographic profile and social media behavior, it's a reasonable guess. And if you did guess that, you'd be engaging in an informal form of predictive analytics.

Now imagine that you're a retailer and a female who's around 16 years old suddenly starts looking at items on your ecommerce site that are typically bought by women who are pregnant. And she buys some of them on your site and in your stores.

So, to encourage her to buy more, you send her a few coupons for similar items. And before you know it, her angry father is in your store accusing you of encouraging his teenage daughter to get pregnant.

This happened to Target.[54] But what the father soon found out was that his daughter actually was pregnant.

Target realized that pregnant women in the second trimester often buy unscented lotions as well as supplements like calcium, magnesium, zinc, and other items. That behavior identified likely customers, but then Target had to be careful about how they marketed to them because a pregnant woman doesn't want to get a flyer with the headline "Congratulations!" if she hasn't registered on a Target baby wish list.

Target knew the girl was pregnant before the father did. That's the power of predictive analytics. Nonetheless, the incident was instructive, and Target changed how they use that knowledge.

Finally, when Netflix presents you with these suggestions?

Figure 39. Netflix recommendations

Or Amazon shows this:

Figure 40. Amazon recommendations

Yes, all predictive analytics.

A spokesperson for Netflix described the breadth of the company's data and signals: "We monitor what you watch, how often you watch things. Does a movie have a happy ending, what's the level of romance, what's the level of violence, is it a cerebral kind of movie or is it light and funny?"[55]

Large B2B companies have been using predictive analytics for years, to better prioritize sales leads, determine which products a prospect would be most likely to buy, nurture contacts who aren't yet ready to buy, and develop more reliable sales forecasting. It used to be that only the largest companies had the data and data scientists to do it, but that's now changing.

SaaS companies are democratizing predictive analytics (PA). These companies are providing cloud-based B2B PA services that eliminate the need to hire increasingly-pricey data scientists internally. The PA firms start with the client's internal CRM and marketing automation data, and then add data about prospects from thousands of public sources such as company revenue and income, number of employees, number and location of offices, executive management changes, credit history, social media activity, press releases, news articles, job openings, patent filings, and so on.

From this, they use data science to identify common characteristics of the accounts that were won by sales and predict the likelihood of closing each prospect. A simple example: a good signal for an office supply company to contact a prospect may be when they sign a lease for a new building or put out a press release about expanding to more cities or hiring many new people.

That one's easy. But often the signals are far more obscure than that. For a company selling CAD-CAM software, a key signal was the number of design engineer job openings that their prospects were posting.

With PA, sales receives prioritized leads and salespeople have important new information about the accounts, which cuts down on their research time. Marketing has segments of lower-priority prospects to nurture. And PA can be equally useful in retaining and growing existing accounts.

This goes way beyond the lead scoring of a marketing automation system, as valuable as that is. Marketing automation typically only uses the information from the CRM and the activities of a prospect interacting with the company's website, emails, and other communications. Predictive analytics companies are adding a huge amount of data to that and then sifting through all of it to find the most useful buying signals.

Figure 41. Lead scoring versus predictive analytics

Predictive analytics is the only way for large companies to act on leads at scale. For example, Adobe gets thousands of leads a day. To be able to score those accurately, and only send the best leads on to sales, they tried a test of PA and AI against traditional rules-based lead scoring for a year. Half of the leads went to PA, and they scored half of the leads in the traditional manner.

The results? Predictive created:

- 46% fewer marketing qualified leads (MQLs)
- 26% higher acceptance of the MQLs by sales
- 26% increase in pipeline

In other words, fewer, better leads were going to sales, and they were creating more sales opportunities from those fewer qualified leads. And with PA, Adobe could process 95% of those thousands of leads a day within *one minute*. After a year they went to 100% predictive analytics.[56]

Predictive analytics is not for small companies; it requires too much data. You typically need at least several hundred existing customers and tens of thousands of prospects in the CRM. But for mid-sized and enterprise companies predictive analytics can create a huge competitive advantage.

Develop an account based marketing program

In chapter 4 on selling more to current customers, I described how to implement an account based marketing program. ABM requires tight cooperation between marketing and sales from Day One. At some companies, ABM is their most productive revenue generation program. As Bullseye marketers, we definitely want to be on top of this.

 Tools for sales and marketing collaboration

InfusionSoft, GetResponse and Act-On are leading marketing automation programs for small companies.

HubSpot may be a good fit for small- and mid-sized companies.

Oracle Eloqua, Marketo, Silverpop, and Pardot provide marketing automation programs for mid-market and enterprises.

Lattice Engines and Infer are SaaS predictive analytics vendors.

OpenTable and Yelp can help you take a sales rep to lunch.

Chapter 10

PHASE 2: SELL TO PEOPLE WHO WANT TO BUY NOW

WHEN EXPANDING YOUR MARKETING BEYOND existing marketing assets and current customers, you can use three methods to target people: demographic, psychographic, and intent. By targeting by customer intent, you'll produce your most effective marketing.

With **demographic** profiling, you're reaching people who are most broadly potential customers. As discussed in chapter 3, consumer demographics could include age, gender, income, where they live, race, education and so on. B2B demographic data can include the industry of the company, location, and size, as well as the departments and titles of people. But people with similar demographics may have very different preferences. Many people in my neighborhood are similar to me demographically, but some have very different tastes when it comes to food, cars, entertainment, vacations, fashion and so on.

Psychographic profiling gets to those personal and organizational personalities and preferences. Does the person like cars that are safe, fast, or green? Do they like to vacation in all-inclusive resorts or urban

Airbnb apartments? Is their fashion taste trendy or conservative? For corporate buyers consider the *Crossing the Chasm* factors in chapter 3.

Psychographic profiling is based on much more data. In the past, large consumer companies added thousands of data points to each customer's profile; today they may be adding tens of thousands. Data science and predictive analytics are then used to select the best customers or accounts to target.

But neither demographic nor psychographic profiling answers the most important question: Who wants to buy what you're selling *now*?

It's a lot faster, easier and cheaper to convert people who are interested in buying into customers than to get people—no matter how well they match your ideal customer profile—to buy if they're just not interested or haven't budgeted for the purchase this year.

That's where **intent data** comes in. Intent data helps you identify and target people who are in active buying mode.

Search marketing is based on intent data. And the keyword phrases people are searching with can help tell you where in the buying process they are: early exploration, comparing solutions, or making final reviews of vendors.

You may collect intent data from your website. If you're using a marketing automation program it will help you track people—and accounts—who are more actively visiting your site now and researching what you sell.

Depending on your business, you may also be able to buy from third parties intent data based on the online behavior of people.

Your best prospects are at the intersection of demographics, psychographics, and intent. (See fig. 42)

Sometimes you'll identify people whose behavior suggests intent, but whose demographics don't fit your potential customer profile. Those people are often called "students", or "tire kickers", or people who are writing books.

Combining demographic, psychographic, and intent data can give you a very high quality set of people and accounts to target with programs from direct mail to account based marketing.

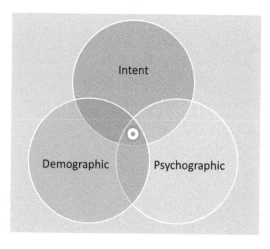

Figure 42. Bullseye intersection of demographics, psychographics, and intent

Chapter 11

SEARCH ADVERTISING

MOST PEOPLE WHO ARE CONSIDERING a purchase these days start their research by searching online. They intend to buy soon. We want them to buy from us.

Unfortunately, a majority of clicks typically happen on just the first three links on the search engine results page (SERP) on Google and Bing. In many industries, your chance of getting in those first three links is very low, or may take a long time as I'll discuss in chapter 15 on search engine optimization.

But anyone can quickly get high on page one with search ads.

And if your organic link *is* high on page one, also having search ads will usually increase your organic click-throughs, too.

Search ad success factors

A successful paid search program involves several moving parts:

- targeting
- offers
- ads

- landing pages/conversion experience
- remarketing
- tailored mobile and desktop approaches
- analytics

When all of these are working in combination, you can fine tune your campaigns to produce a consistent, high ROI.

This is probably the most tactical chapter in the book. We'll be down in the weeds more than usual. You'll get dozens of tips about ways to get profitable AdWords results.

This image of a Space Shuttle cockpit[57] reminds me of the complexity of managing search ad campaigns, and you may feel that way if it's the first time that you're looking at the AdWords management console. But press on.

Figure 43. Space Shuttle cockpit

If the AdWords management console provides too much information, hire an experienced AdWords firm or consultant to manage it for you.

Targeting your ads

Search ads are an ideal Phase 2 Bullseye technique because they are mainly seen by people who are looking for your products and services right now. The ads are the most direct way to grow your leads and opportunities beyond your current customers and others who you are already in touch with through your email lists and other channels.

But only if you target your ads properly.

Earlier I described, in order, the three most important factors in direct marketing success—and search ads are a form of direct marketing:

1. List/audience
2. Offer
3. Creative

Proper targeting of your ads is how you make sure that they're appearing in front of the right audience.

AdWords targeting starts with identifying the best keywords. With paid ads, Bullseye marketers will usually want to tightly target your ads to the best prospects. Later, if the program is proving successful in terms of leads, opportunities, and sales, you can broaden it.

To target your ads, you have to consider the intent of the searcher. Imagine that you're selling email marketing software. People searching on:

- "email marketing" could just be interested in how to do it
- "email marketing software" are much more likely to be looking into buying the software
- "email marketing software pricing" would most likely be seriously considering a purchase

Researching and deciding on the keyword phrases that you're going to focus on is the first step. A great tool for this is the Google AdWords Keyword Planner.[58] Here are some of the results it delivers when looking in the Boston metropolitan area for keywords related to Thai restaurants:

☐	Keyword (by relevance)	Avg. monthly searches	Competition	Top of page bid (low range)	Top of page bid (high range)
☐	thai restaurant	1K – 10K	Low	$2.25	$6.91
☐	thai food	1K – 10K	Low	$2.10	$5.36
☐	thai food near me	10K – 100K	Low	$3.30	$7.47
☐	thai restaurant n...	1K – 10K	Low	$1.51	$7.17

Figure 44. Google AdWords Keyword Planner

Two things:

1. People search for "Thai food" and "Thai restaurant" roughly the same amount. If I was promoting a Thai restaurant, I'd use both. Google treats singular and plural keywords the same, so I don't need to worry about that.
2. There's not a lot of competition for paid ads for either phrase. That's a good place to be in. It's always cheaper to produce results, in any marketing channel, when you're one of the first to be using it.

Google automatically handles those "near me" searches by showing restaurants in my city.

This very rough data, though, is only what you see if you are new to AdWords and have a zero monthly spend. A company that's spending money on active campaigns sees this much more detailed data:

Keyword (by relevance)	Avg. monthly searches	Competition
thai restaurant	4,400	Low
thai food	8,100	Low

Figure 45. Google AdWords Keyword Planner

That's much more helpful.

Let's say that you're marketing a new marketing automation software program. Here are some of the suggested keywords from Google's Keyword Planner.

Keyword ↑	Avg. monthly searches	Competition
best marketing automation software	140	High
email marketing software	2,400	High
marketing automation	6,600	High
marketing automation programs	40	High
marketing automation software	1,600	High
marketing automation software pricing	10	High
marketing automation tools	720	High

Figure 46. AdWords Keyword Planner results for "marketing automation programs"

"Marketing automation" is too broad. Clearly "marketing automation program" would be a perfect, Bullseye keyword, but Google tells us—and they should know—that, surprisingly, there are only 40 searches on that phrase in the typical month. "Marketing automation software," though, is a synonym and it has 1,600 searches per month. Let's add in "best marketing automation software" and a few others, too. Those people are searching for what we're selling.

Cost per click historically ranges from about $12 per click to over $50 depending on the term. The higher cost per click likely indicates that the vendors have found those to be the most effective keyword phrases for actually closing new business and are willing to pay more for them. Those are Bullseye material, if your ROI supports them.

Once you have targeted all of the most focused keywords, if you aren't getting enough clicks and leads you could move out to broader terms. Here the keywords are still relevant, like "email automation software" (email marketing being a part of marketing automation), "lead scoring software" and "website personalization software." These searchers are people that are at least looking for a part of your marketing automation program, and you may be able to convince them that they need the whole thing.

If that still isn't enough, and you have the budget, you could target keywords such as "best marketing software" and "marketing software tools." But that's more of a Phase 3 activity: expanding awareness of your offerings to the broader market. In Phase 2 we're more focused on search ad programs that can produce opportunities and sales now.

So start with those Bullseye keywords and see where they take you first.

You could also include keywords for marketing automation competitors in your program, such as Eloqua, Marketo, and HubSpot. They tend to get a lot of searches, and the clicks are less expensive. Since the vast majority of clicks will be on the organic results, this could be an inexpensive way to build your brand awareness.

Keyword	Avg. monthly searches		Competition
eloqua	9,900		Low
getresponse	14,800		Low
hubspot	135,000		Low
marketo	33,100		Low
pardot	18,100		Low

Figure 47. AdWords Keyword Planner competitive analysis

Only run competitive ads against brands that you often win business over. Most people searching on a specific brand name are either already a customer of that brand or are late in their decision-making process and researching reviews, etc.; they may not be interested anymore in considering other options. In my experience, advertising on competitor keywords usually has a low ROI.

And don't always trust Google to tell you which keywords to advertise on. I did work with a company that provides professional services for Open edX, the elearning platform developed by Harvard and MIT. We were only interested in advertising to companies and institutions searching for those services, but Google would suggest we broaden our keywords to include such phrases as "edX courses" and "mooc courses." People doing those searches, though, were looking for courses, not the software or its service providers. Again, consider the intent of the searcher.

After you've chosen your Bullseye keywords, you can use the several keyword match types Google provides (Exact, Phrase, Broad, and Modified Broad) to tightly or broadly target.

Companies with big budgets might start with broad match, cast a wide net, and narrow down based on the search phrases that people used. From a Bullseye point of view, though, exact match is the way to start out. You can test your most tightly targeted searchers and see if the channel works for you. With success, widen out using phrase and broad matches and see if you can also produce profitable results with them.

AdWords has one more important match type: <u>negative matching</u>. As you run your campaigns and look at the actual search phrases that people are using to find and click on your ads (in AdWords' Keywords-Search Terms section), you'll see an astonishingly wide range of search keyword phrases. Some of those are from people clearly looking for something other than what you're selling, yet they clicked on your ad, and you're paying for that. Let's say that you're marketing a luxury resort, but in your AdWords Search Terms report you find search phrases such as "cheap resorts" popping up; you need to add "cheap" into your campaign negative keywords.

Regularly add negative keywords to your campaigns to knock out those unwanted clicks. This is one of the ways that you can continually improve the performance of your campaigns and lower their cost.

You can use some of the tools described at the end of this chapter to find additional keywords, including ones that your competitors are using.

Google provides you with many other targeting options for your campaigns. Here are three important ones:

- *Locations*: Geo-targeting is a very important factor in campaign success. Even if you're a national business with stores in 100 cities, it's unlikely that people will drive more than a few miles to your stores. So you should run 100 separate, geo-targeted campaigns rather than one national campaign.
- *Scheduling*: You can set the specific days and times of the week that your ads will run using dayparting. You may find, for example, that people searching in the middle of the night don't turn into customers, so you should schedule your ads to run Monday through Friday from 8 am to 6 pm. Or maybe you're a restaurant that only wants to advertise to people making a late dinner plan, so you advertise Friday, Saturday, and Sunday from 5 pm to 8 pm. As you get deeper into your campaign data, you can see which times have the lowest cost per acquisition and target them. Besides when your ads appear, you can also adjust your bids by day and time.
- *Demographics*: You can target your search ads to display only to certain people based on age and gender.

If you're new to AdWords, you likely will want to start with automated bidding and let Google handle that. But as you get more comfortable with all of the levers at your command you can move to manually manage at least some of your bids; this can be very useful for increasing your impression share (what percentage of all searches on your keywords your ads appear for) and the position of your ads.

In all these ways you can focus in on your best prospects and get the most from your search ad program.

BTW, beyond search ads, Google provides intent targeting of people on its Google Display Network whose behavior tells Google that they are in-market now for a particular product or service. These may be more useful for selling to consumers than B2B. For example, Google says that there are several billion impressions weekly for people looking to buy baby and children's products, and several hundred thousand impressions weekly for people looking for desktop computers. When creating a display ad campaign, you can specify a custom intent audience in the Audiences section of the AdWords manager.

Offers

You can think of search advertising as a process of making and carrying through on promises. In your ads, you're making promises: 10% off! Sign up for a webinar. Free consultation! Smooth shave! Early Bird pricing! In your ads, you promote your offers. On your website, you fulfill the promise.

These are ads for cheap airfares.

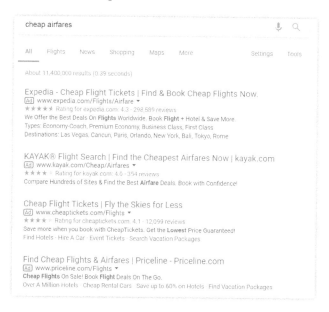

Figure 48. Search ads for "cheap airfares"

The offers are bold: Cheap Flight Tickets. Find the Cheapest Airfares Now. Find Cheap Flights & Airfares.

Some of these mattress ads also have strong offers:

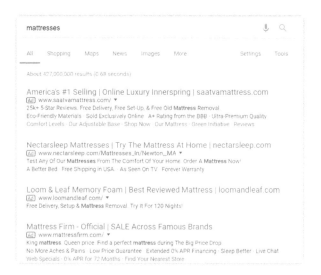

Figure 49. Google search ads for "mattresses"

The first ad uses the bandwagon "America's #1 Selling" appeal with offers in the next line for free delivery, free set-up, and free old mattress removal. The second ad offers you the option to test the mattress at home, with free shipping. The third offers a 120-night trial period. And the fourth is running a sale.

When companies offer a discount they may say something like "$200 off" or "Up to 50% off". If you're offering a discount or sale, test whether an amount or a percentage off is more profitable.

The most important factor in your offer is relevance. If someone is searching for cheap airfares, make sure that's what your ads offer. Search advertising is no place for bait and switch.

The only way to know what offers will move the needle for your company is to do lots of testing.

Ads

Ads are part of the third factor in direct marketing success: creative.

Combined, the two headlines and one description in a Google search ad can have 140 characters. (This is the format in 2018, but it could always change.) How much can you say in an ad that has two 30-character phrases (which usually follow one another separated by a dash) with an 80 character description below the URL? Enough. Especially when you add in extensions.

But keep in mind that the 80-character description field may not appear on the mobile version of the ads. So if mobile is important, get your critical information and offers into your headline fields—preferably the first one.

People aren't entirely, or even primarily, rational in their buying decisions, and even less so in their clicking decisions, so use the psychological motivators such as scarcity and the bandwagon effect, described in chapter 6, in your ads to improve results.

Did you notice anything unusual about those cheap airfare and mattress ads? Look at them again before reading the next paragraph.

Figure 50. Mobile Google search ads

Those ads all use initial caps for all of their words. Many businesses have found that they get the most engagement with ads with initial caps. Test it for yourself.

If the keyword appears in your ad, Google will bold it there, which can lead to a higher click rate. You have the opportunity to automate the copy in your ads to include the person's search phrase. Google calls this Keyword Insertion.

Extensions are those additional pieces of information that Google may show below the description field of your ad. You can use extensions to include your phone number, address, price, reviews, links and other information in your ads. They are a great addition, make your ad physically larger so it stands out more and is more likely to be clicked, and they're free—so what's not to like? Google will decide when to display your extensions based your ad's position and Ad Rank.

Speaking of ad position, how do you get your ad to display on top?

Do you always want your ad to display on top?

The top placement doesn't always go to the highest bidder, so offering Google more money isn't necessarily the best way to optimize your campaigns.

Ad placement is determined by Ad Rank which, Google says, "gives your ad a score based on your bid, the quality of your ads and landing page, and the expected impact of extensions and other ad formats."

This gets back to search ads being a promise fulfilled. Create ads that speak to the intent of the person using a particular search phrase, develop landing pages that speak to that same promise, use the extensions, and offer a competitive (or automated) bid.

Do you always want to be the top placed ad? Not necessarily. The top position usually is considerably more expensive than the second[59], so you'll need to decide if the additional cost is worth it for you. The AdWords management console shows you the average positions for your ads, and you can manage those Ad Rank factors to attempt to move your ads up or down to find the most profitable position for them.

Landing pages

In chapter 6, I discussed conversion rate optimization. If you don't remember it well—and there was a lot there—it's worth a re-read. Great landing pages are central to paid search campaign success.

What's especially important about search ad campaign landing pages is that they should strongly relate to the promise of the ad. This will not only help your conversion rates but will also improve your Google Ad Rank.

Here's an example of how Firestone provides an outstanding conversion experience for their search ads.[60] This is their ad that I saw when I searched:

Figure 51. Firestone search ad

I was searching for "car tires," and that's what the headline and ad are all about; some of their competitors mixed in many other car services in their ads.

When I click on the Firestone ads I go to this landing page:

Figure 52. Firestone landing page

The Firestone landing page prominently offers a $100 off deal. It promises me an easy process for finding tires ("Let us find your tires in three easy steps"). I can fill out a form right on that page to move this process forward—a form with the headline "Get the right tires" and the promise, on the button, to "Get tire pricing"—which was promised twice in its ad.

The excellent Firestone approach is even more apparent when you look at mobile, where their same ad appears.

Firestone displays its $100 off deal right at the top, where you're most likely to see it on a phone. Firestone also has a dealer locator and their "Get the Right Tires" form on the first two screens.

Firestone gets so much right:

- Their ad is solely focused on the search phrase.
- They have a clear offer.
- Their landing page is focused; on mobile, it shows important information on the first one or two screens.
- Their landing page makes it easy to convert; people don't need to go several clicks deep to accomplish anything.

Remember: people get to these landing pages from *paid* ads. In this case, every click costs $2.50-3.00. Companies should be making the most of what they spend for those clicks.

Firestone nails it.

Figure 53. Firestone mobile landing page

How much should you spend for a click?

If you search on "womens razors" you'll find ads from many companies. Google's Keyword Planner shows that each click will cost up to $2.50. Since it may take 25 clicks or more to get a single sale (we'll talk about that below), why would companies pay over $60 to sell a razor that sells for much less than that?

A classic business model is to "lose money on the razor and make money on the blades"; that idea can apply to many industries. For example, the margins on printer toner cartridges (the "blades" of that industry) are very high—that's where most of the profits are, not in selling the printer.

This is all based on the idea of the lifetime value (LTV) of the customer. Whatever business you're in, you want to understand what is an average customer's LTV to you and base your marketing ROI calculations on that. If a razor company knows that on average they will ultimately make $2,500 in profits on a customer, then it's well worth paying $60, or more, to win them.

Here are some examples of the average costs per clicks in 2017 for some of the more expensive search terms:

Keyword	Suggested CPC Bid
Mesothelioma	$600
Network managed services	$161.73
Virtualization cloud computing	$108.91
Auto insurance	$77.39
Best IT consulting firms	$59.60
Business online storage	$45.40
Reverse mortgages	$37.41
Printed circuit board designers	$36.32
Load testing machines	$20.45

Figure 54. AdWords keywords with high costs per click

Look at that first search term. "Mesothelioma" has long been the most expensive keyword. Attorneys know that cases filed for people with this cancer, typically caused by an exposure to asbestos, usually settle before trial and often for million-dollar-plus amounts. The attorney can make hundreds of thousands of dollars on a single case, so they're willing to pay over ten thousand dollars to get a client.

For some companies that provide enterprise technology, a single deal can be worth millions of dollars, and a new customer can be worth many times that. They are happy to pay thousands of dollars for a single, good lead.

Use call tracking

People who call are often higher quality leads than ones who fill out a form. Call tracking is a good way to find out which campaigns are bringing the most calls to your business.

You can supercharge your call tracking in AdWords by having a unique phone number for each ad, although all of the calls redirect to your regular numbers. Then through integration with Google Analytics, you can track not only the ads that are driving calls but even which keywords and offers are working for you.

Remarketing

Even with great offers and well-designed landing pages, most people who come to them won't convert. In many industries only two to three percent of people who come to landing pages after clicking on a search ad convert, although that rate may be three to five times higher for the top 10% of advertisers.[61] Remarketing gives you another chance. It is a perfect complement to search ads and may increase your campaign results by 50% or more.

I've written about remarketing in chapter 8, so it would be worth your time to re-read that now. You will want custom remarketing ads that target the people who came to a particular campaign landing page with information about that product, and in your remarketing ads you can reinforce the offers you made that brought the person to you in the first place.

One type of remarketing that is especially applicable for search ad campaigns is Remarketing Lists for Search Ads (RLSA). You can use this to create ad groups that only show ads to people who are on your remarketing list. You may want to experiment with targeting with RLSA for those less focused, less expensive keywords.

Mobile/Desktop

People behave differently on their smartphones than on desktop. Even though many searches start on mobile and continue on desktop, people on the move often use their phones to find something that they need right now like a restaurant, store or gas station.

There may be times when you want to advertise specifically to people on smartphones. An obvious case is when you're marketing a mobile app or a service that is smartphone or tablet specific. Or maybe you want to target people who are attending a conference or event. Or people stranded at airports: Red Roof Inn tied localized search ads into flight cancellation data and saw their bookings leap.[62]

In the past people didn't buy or fill out forms as much on mobile, but as companies have gotten better at developing good mobile experiences that difference seems to be rapidly disappearing.

Conversion tracking and analytics

As always we have campaign metrics and business metrics. To a Bullseye marketer like you, the business metrics are, of course, the most important. You'll use the campaign metrics to help achieve those business goals.

The most important business metric is ROI. When calculating ROI, you divide your profits (not sales: profits) by costs. And remember that your costs include not just AdWords clicks but also such items as staff time, campaign management software, and fees for creative.

The first two things you want to do, if you haven't already, is setup Google Analytics conversion tracking and connect AdWords with your CRM. Conversion tracking can be set up for completion of a website activity, such as a purchase, registration, or download; installation of an app and in-app activities; phone calls; and other activities.

For an ecommerce site, your conversion is a sale and it can be relatively simple to calculate ROI. For a complex B2B sale that goes on for months, your conversion may be just one early touchpoint on a long path towards closing the deal. You may need to do more complex attribution modeling, taking into consideration all of the interactions with the customer. The connection to the CRM is critical for doing this.

If you've looked at the AdWords administrative interface, what they call the AdWords Experience, you've probably noticed that AdWords provides you with a firehose of data about the performance of campaigns, ads, keywords, quality score, and on and on. Use this to continuously improve your campaign's performance:

- Add negative keywords to focus your targeting
- Drop your poorly performing ads and experiment with new ones
- Improve your quality score to reduce your costs
- Increase your impression share to increase opportunities (but sometimes gaining the last bit of impression share can be prohibitively expensive)
- Experiment with different ad positions to see which are most cost-effective
- Fine tune your dayparting and other campaign settings

Of course, your most expensive clicks may or may not be your most effective. That's where your conversion tracking comes into play. Use conversion tracking to analyze results at the keyword and ad level, and you can focus on what's truly generating business results.

What about Bing?

In this chapter, I've only mentioned Google AdWords. It was easier than always writing "Google and Bing." So now I'm writing "and Bing."

Google dominates the growing mobile search market with about 95% globally[63], and has 90% of the desktop market.[64] Your target audience may be using Bing. Bing users skew older, are Windows users, and tend to be in the U.S.[65] Companies that have a clientele that is not as tech-savvy, and which isn't inclined to download another browser or even go to a different search engine than the Windows default Bing, may find it a valuable search ad channel.

The management of Bing ads is similar to Google, and many search ad management tools support Bing, too. In the Bing interface, you can import your AdWords campaigns and set it up to automatically update with changes that you make to the campaigns on AdWords.

Often the CPC on Bing is lower than on AdWords. Use Bing conversion tracking and Google Analytics to track the effectiveness of your Bing campaigns separately.

I got into a lot of detail there. That's where digital marketing lives or dies. But always keep in mind what we're focused on in Phase 2 with AdWords: who is in market and interested in buying your offering now. Optimizing for that should drive all of your decisions.

Tools for search advertising

AdWords management console is fine for managing smaller campaigns.

WordStream is an ad management program for small and mid-sized companies.

Marin is an ad management program geared more to mid-sized and large companies.

SEMrush and SpyFu can show you the keywords and ads that your competitors are using, and lots of other search ad data.

Most large marketing clouds include ad management tools.

Large companies and agencies may use predictive analytics to help manage their ad programs.

Chapter 12

TARGETING PROSPECTS WITH OTHER KINDS OF INTENT DATA

BEYOND SEARCH, THERE ARE OTHER ways to identify people who are in-market now. These include people and accounts visiting your website and otherwise engaging with your content (tracked as first party data), from companies that sell their own data, and companies that aggregate data from many websites about the search and content consumption of people online (providing you with third party data).

Website and other intent data you own

If a person starts coming to your website frequently and looking at content about a particular product or service, that's a good signal that they are interested in doing business with you. This doesn't just apply to website visits; opening and forwarding emails, attending webinars, clicking on your remarketing ads and even getting information from your reps at trade shows are all signals of potential intent.

A marketing automation program can help you track these inter-actions and, if you set up rules, even send alerts to your salespeople about the most active people. Another way for marketing and sales to collaborate is to link your CRM and marketing automation program and then alert a sales rep if a person they've sent a proposal to has revisited the website.

A key metric for account based marketing success (as discussed in chapter 4), is a surge in traffic to your website, and engaging with your other content, from multiple people at an account. And the more people who are engaging with your content from a particular account, the more likely it is that they are interested in what you're selling.

Third party intent data sources

It's been said that data is the new oil that powers our increasingly digital economy.

And major companies are drilling into their data, refining it, and selling it to others for them to use to power their marketing.

Kroger, the nation's largest supermarket chain, and Amazon use their combination of in-store and online data to identify in-market customers and target them better—for themselves, for advertisers on their sites, and for purchasers of their data. Some other retailers do, too, and for decades credit card companies have sold the purchase history of customers.

Bombora and The Big Willow are two companies that provide B2B intent data by aggregating data from many websites. TechTarget collects and sells data from its 140+ tech information websites.

In all of these cases the companies are looking for a change in behavior—a "surge" of interest to identify people who are in-market now, and sell this data to marketers for better targeting.

Chapter 13

PHASE 3: CAST A WIDER NET

PHASE 3 BULLSEYE PROGRAMS ARE long-term and may not produce measurable results for a year or two—or even longer. They are intended to grow awareness of your brand and offerings among people and accounts who may want to buy them sometime but aren't, so far as we know, in market at this time.

Many people think of Phase 3 programs like social media, content marketing, inbound marketing, and display ads as the definition of marketing. But, as you should recognize by now, many other programs are quicker and more cost-effective.

However, in the long run, having a strong brand can be tremendously valuable. Typically companies with strong brands have more loyal customers who are willing to pay more. And their customer acquisition costs are lower.

So in this section we'll dive down into successfully implementing these long-term programs.

Chapter 14

CONTENT MARKETING

EVERYTHING THAT YOU CREATE IS content. Every web page, email, and tweet, every late stage ROI calculator to help sales close deals, every customer newsletter. In one sense saying that we're doing "content marketing" seems obvious, or redundant: kind of like saying that we're doing "water swimming."

But it's not redundant. Content marketing is a particular strategy using content to build your brand and awareness, and ultimately more leads, opportunities and sales, by providing useful and entertaining content. It is not a direct response program like the almost daily emails from 1-800-Flowers and Vistaprint described in chapter 7, or search ads. Those programs can produce results in the first hour; content marketing takes longer.

But just because it takes a while to have an impact doesn't mean you shouldn't do it. You should.

For almost any purchase these days, people check out content online first. People interested in fashion look at blogs and videos. People buying a new HDTV or car look at a variety of reviews and articles. Business buyers typically look at several pieces of content in the process of making a buying decision; they also use late-stage content to help convince other members of the buying team.[66] And long before the buying process even begins, people are keeping up with topics that interest them personally or professionally. You want them to find your content in all of the stages of their vetting and buying process.

The work that you did in Phase 1 in understanding your customers and defining personas will be critical for your content marketing. You'll need to create content that speaks to those personas in a voice that is not just appropriate but compelling.

Create great content!

This is your chance to tell your company's story in the best, most engaging way possible. And if you're at a small company, developing great creative that people remember and share can help level the field against larger competitors. You may not be able to match their ad budgets, but nothing is stopping you from creating memorable, useful content.

Think of the best content that you ever saw. Quickly: what comes to mind when you think of a great video, or blog post, or infographic? (For me, one that comes quickly to mind is that blog post on creating a great email from the founder of MailChimp that's in chapter 7.) Don't copy it, but be inspired. Do something even better. Dare to be remarkable.

Tell stories: people relate to and remember stories much better than they remember facts.

And use emotions. Storytelling almost invariably provokes emotions because of its arc from challenge to success or failure. Emotions can be part of all of your content, even if it isn't a story.

There is nothing more B2B than global shipping. The largest shipping company in the world is Maersk, headquartered in Copenhagen. Maersk could convey a heavy, industrial brand message—"We rule the waves" or something like that—but instead they focus on the impact of their work, rather than just the nuts and bolts.[67]

Figure 55. Maersk Line Facebook header

Maersk is very active on social media with multiple accounts on Facebook, Twitter, and other platforms. And it uses stories throughout its marketing.

They tell stories about their customers. "These are not just simple boxes. These are the start of the dream!"

Figure 56. Picture of Maersk Line customer

They tell stories about the people manning their ships—the seafarers.

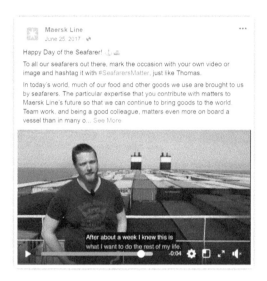

Figure 57. Maersk Line Facebook post about seafarers

Maersk has over 500 ships, yet it still celebrates the launch of a new one.

Figure 58. Maersk Line Facebook post about a new ship launch

Even people who aren't going to ship anything can understand the impact of Maersk's business, the appeal of the work to the sailors and the beauty of the vessels. That is storytelling. That is brand building.

Maersk Line focuses on lead generation results, as I'll describe in chapter 17. Maersk Group is more concerned with brand building. Alex McNab, their Digital Media Manager, says, "Between all the Maersk brands and channels, we reach around six million people on social media, most of who are professionals or managers. When we asked them last year, three-quarters of our followers said that social media improved their overall perception of Maersk. Our target in AP Moller Maersk (Group) is to heighten our brand reputation, and support the individual businesses where possible."[68]

Which is more memorable? This photo[69]?

Figure 59. Photo of chocolate brownies

Or this definition?

Chocolate (noun): a preparation of the seeds of cacao, roasted, husked, and ground, often sweetened and flavored, as with vanilla.[70]

Right. So use images. Use music. Use storytelling and emotion.

People often point to the American Express OPEN community as a great example of content marketing. It's full of countless articles and videos about how to make a small business more successful. (See fig. 60)

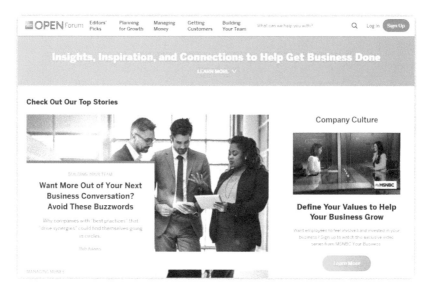

Figure 60. AmEx OPEN Forum community site

Not coincidentally the OPEN Forum is reportedly the top source of new business credit card sign-ups for AmEx.

You could say that the Tour de France is the ultimate content marketing. Every year an estimated 3-4 *billion people* worldwide see hours of beautiful images of the French countryside on TV without anyone ever saying "book your flight now!"—but many of those people ultimately will. France is the world's top tourist destination.

What can you do if you don't have a global brand or a 100-year old bike race to piggyback on? Plenty!

Herschel Supply Company, a lifestyle brand that sells backpacks, duffles, and many other products, has grown very rapidly in less than 10 years because it gets a lot right about its marketing. Twice a year it publishes The Journal[71], a "collection of seasonally inspired stories that celebrate design and travel." It's a physical publication, and then they re-use the articles on their website. Storytelling is at the heart of its content.

Figure 61. Herschel Supply Company Journal

You have one type of content that's utterly unique to you, that no competitor can copy: what's going on inside your company. How do you work with your customers to develop your products? What's going on in the personal lives of your people? How is your team working to get ready for your next conference? Your customers and prospects will probably be very interested in it if you make it useful and customer-centric.

I love "how it was made" stories in any format. A lot of your customers do, too.

Or do an AMA (Ask Me Anything) webinar with your CEO.

Be creative!

Awesome infographics

People are visual: they remember information in images more than text. (A picture is worth how many words?) So make your infographics work for you.

Make great infographics for your company like the ones from Scott Brinker and Gini Dietrich in this book's Introduction; they both do excellent jobs of making complex business ideas clear.

Edward Tufte is a statistician, computer scientist, and writer of several books about conveying information and data visually. His favorite data visualization is a French graphic created by Charles Minard in 1869. It illustrates Napoleon's attack on Russia. The brown line shows the invasion, with the width representing the number of troops in Napoleon's army—which was half the invading size by the time they arrived in Moscow. After they were defeated there, they started their long retreat. As you see the army dwindle down to just a handful of men by the time they leave the country, on the bottom you can see the falling Russian winter temperatures they experienced.

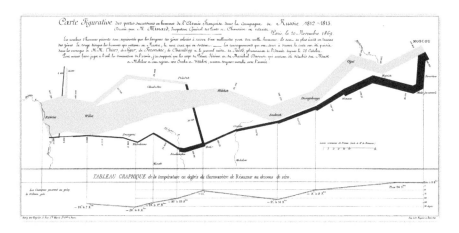

Figure 62. Infographic of Napolean's attack on Russia

Has any graphic communicated more human suffering without even a single image of a person? It is heartbreaking.

This infographic by Mauro Martino[72] illustrates the rise of partisanship in the U.S. House of Representatives from 1949 to the present. The trend is crystal clear.

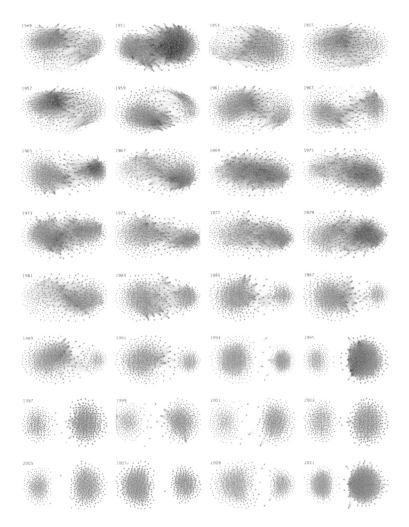

Figure 63. Partisanship infographic

This infographic, created by Hannah Ritchie and Max Roser at Our World in Data[73], illustrates that humans are second only to mosquitos for deaths caused (and way more dangerous than sharks). (See fig. 64)

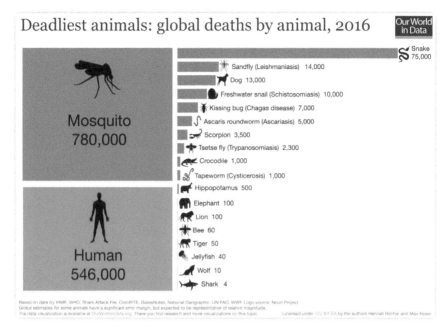

Figure 64. Deadliest animals infographic

In all of these, one or two clear messages are conveyed very effectively. If designers can do that for business and war and politics and social policy, surely you can do it for your company.

On the other hand, you only have to search for "bad infographics" to see many that are cluttered with countless different messages, are hard to read, or full of numbers and percentages that don't add up.

Bad business infographics are often veeeeeerrrrrrryyyyyyyy long, scrolling affairs full of text that can't be easily read on a computer, are horrible on a phone, and lack any visual punch. We have data that shows that people don't scroll far down long web pages; is it any more likely that they're scrolling long infographics?

When it comes to infographics, keep them simple and to the point.

Content strategy

The first step in your content marketing is to create a content strategy.

And the first step in developing your content strategy is defining your goals. As with many of these marketing programs, you're likely to have tactical/campaign goals and business goals. Tactical goals may include views, average time spent with the piece of content, shares, and comments, all of which can help you determine what kind of content your customers most value and engage with, and which you should create in the future. Business goals can include increasing:

- brand awareness
- branded traffic to your website
- new contacts in target demographics/companies
- new leads/opportunities
- velocity of deals through the pipeline
- customer retention, including selling more to existing customers

In your strategy define key messages that you want to communicate. Some of these are brand messages: we are innovative, trendy, traditional, inexpensive, high-end, healthy, smart, fun, or whatever your brand attributes happen to be. How will you reinforce these with your content?

This shows the different stages of the tech customer's journey and what they may be interested in in each:

	Sales enters conversation		
Awareness	Consideration	Purchase	Post Purchase
General industry info	Solutions	Confirmation	Success
Thought leadership, industry direction, white papers, blogs, social media, Top 10 lists, tip sheets, FAQs, educational webinars	Buying criteria, industry-specific information, analyst evaluations, case studies, spec sheets, demos, references, product webinar	ROI calculator, reviews, testimonials	Onboarding, Implementation guides, deeper tech info, best practices, replacement parts

Figure 65. Content preferences by tech buying stage

In your content strategy you also define which channels you will focus on. Is your audience on Facebook? YouTube? Twitter? Pinterest? LinkedIn? Reddit? In some industry forums? Offline? At trade shows? Can you entice them to come to your site and read your blog? How will you get them to download your infographic or attend your webinar? Will you send them physical publications? Newsletters? Later, in the content marketing plan, you'll get really detailed about those tactics, but initially you need to be defining who you're talking to, your messages, and how you'll reach them.

When you define your audiences—because you're almost certain to have more than one—also define the buying stages and the type of content that they need in each stage. Later you'll plan how to produce all of those discreet messages and pieces of content.

Conduct a content audit

Before you start developing new content, first catalog all of the content that you already have. Quite often companies have a large amount of very valuable content sitting around barely being used. You might call that "an existing marketing asset."

Right off the bat you'll be faced with finding all of your content. In many companies it's spread across the website, multiple corporate repositories (physical servers, Google Drive, Box, Dropbox, etc.), individual hard drives and personal cloud services, SharePoint—even emails.

There is no one way to do a content audit. In a small company, it may be done with a spreadsheet with such columns as:

- name of item
- type (web page, image, video, interactive, white paper, etc.)
- description
- meta data (topics, tags, how it fits into taxonomy)
- location/URL
- date last updated
- owner

- target personas
- target buying stages
- how to re-use
- copyright status/restrictions
- whatever else would be useful for you

Even in a small company, when you include web pages, you may find that you have hundreds of assets. After all, a single web page may have text, images, video and other elements each of which needs to be cataloged. If you're using a content management system for your website, it may be able to create an initial content audit of web pages and assets for you. In a mid-sized or large company, the content audit can be a daunting task requiring several departments working together.

Once you have completed the content audit, you are likely to see some holes: some important personas that don't have much content for them, or stages of the buying cycle with insufficient content. It's not unusual for companies to have a lot of top of funnel content intended to attract new prospects but not enough content for sales-people to use in closing deals in later buying stages. All of this research can help drive your content plan.

Interview with Ann Handley: Why every company needs to do content marketing

Ann Handley is the Chief Content Officer of MarketingProfs. As far as she knows she was the first person in the universe with the title Chief Content Officer. She is the co-author of *Content Rules* and the author of *Everybody Writes*.

Ann: A lot of people—a lot of companies and individuals—have embraced the notion that they need to consider content as a cornerstone of their marketing. They know that they have to be creating content consistently. But I think a lot of companies are struggling with a few things.

First, how do we do that consistently? How to create content that is not a one-and-done campaign, but is a long-term effort. That's one challenge. The second challenge is creating the kind of content that their customers want. The default for many companies is still to talk about themselves. They tend to favor corporate-centric content rather than customer-centric content.

Our world is a noisy world. So you've got to be creating content that is truly helpful to the people that you want to speak to. It's got to be very useful for them, and you've got to look at the world through their eyes, their point of view. One of the things that I talk about in my book *Everybody Writes* is, "Would your customers *thank you* for that content?"

Louis: A huge amount of content is being produced. More and more every day. Can people continue to affordably create original, high-quality content?

Ann: That's a good question. I don't think we have a choice. All of us as brands, as companies, as individuals need to be creating the kind of content that fundamentally has value for the customer. So that means answering their questions, first and foremost.

Just because it's been said before is not a reason to not do it. The key is to offer your particular take on something. Say it better. Say it in a way that creates more value for the people that you're trying to reach. So I'm not sure that I really buy that argument that there's a lot of content out there, so why should we be creating more content?

Louis: At MarketingProfs, what metrics do you look at? What are most important for you?

Ann: As the Chief Content Officer, I look at a couple things. Time on site is really important to me. I look at all the typical things like traffic, and where our members are going, what's interesting to them and what isn't. But I look at time on site to see how valuable our content is to them. How long are they sticking around? What's their path to conversion?

The other thing that I look at more to get a sense of what resonates on social is to look at our sharing metrics. It's easy to just discount them as not being very meaningful. But I've been watching them for years now, so I have a really good sense just from looking at those numbers whether something has resonated in the social space or not. Because as marketing trainers and educators, it's one way to get a sense of what our subscribers need from us.

Louis: Are there any technologies that you think are important to content marketing? Or that you use or that you see out there that you think are essential to good content marketing? Do you use much beyond a word processor, a CMS, and a good analytics program?

Ann: In a lot of ways, I tend to be allergic to much of the technology out there, because I think sometimes people—marketers included— think technology is a kind of magic bullet that can transform their content marketing. There is no magic bullet. Technology can help create efficiencies in your content. It can help you manage it and market it. But still you need the fundamentals: A great strategy. A solid plan. A whip-smart chief content officer. And a lot of grit.

Create a content plan

Once you have created a content strategy, and have audited your content, you are ready to create a content plan.

A content plan is a detailed description of

- what you're going to produce (text, videos, infographics, etc.) including message, target personas and buying stages
- who is responsible for it
- when it is due
- how you will distribute and amplify it
- what campaigns you will use it in

Broadening your reach and the awareness of your company and offerings, to ultimately generate more business, is the whole point of

Phase 3. While there's much you can do to promote and amplify your content, the process of getting a large audience for it starts before you create it.

- In your search marketing work in Phases 2 and 3, you will research the important keywords for your industry, and which you have a chance to rank high for organically. In your content plan, you plan the content that you'll create to go after your long tail opportunities. (The long tail is described in chapter 15.)
- Think about how you can aggregate and disaggregate content. When you aggregate content you re-use it by bringing different pieces together to create a new asset, such as collecting some case studies into one new ebook. When you disaggregate, you split up an asset into many smaller pieces and publish and promote them, such as taking sections of an ebook and re-using them as blog posts and social media posts.
- Most companies find that a few pieces of content create a large proportion of their traffic and leads. Often those are longer pieces, as various studies[74] have shown that longer blog posts—and by longer I mean over 3,000 words even—get higher readership and shares. Your showcase content may be an ebook, elaborate video, interactive marketing game, or something else.
- What are the hot topics in your industry? How can you use content to break into the conversation and get recognition? Sometimes directly challenging an industry leader with your own, contrarian point of view and ruffling a few feathers is the best way to get noticed.
- Some content strategists recommend what they call the "skyscraper technique". In this you search for some of the most popular content in your industry and then you "build" on it, creating an even better/more useful piece of content on the same subject.

An important part of your plan is cadence. People should be able to expect regular content from you whether it's in the form of ~10 tweets a day (or, initially, three a day), or daily emails, or twice weekly blog posts, or monthly newsletters—or whatever cadence you decide works for you. Of course, you'll also have other, irregular content, such as for short-term campaigns, but the foundation of your content marketing should be regular content that people can count on.

And then organize your content plan with a content calendar.

To gate or not to gate

Gating content is when you require people to give you some identifying information, at least an email address, to download or view a piece of your content. Fewer people are likely to see your content if it's gated, but you will get that contact information from those who do sign up for it. A constant debate among marketers is when, or even if, content should be gated.

Pro: You build up your database of contacts and can market to them.

Con: Fewer people will see your content, and the information they give you may not be accurate anyway (BugsBunny@loonytunes.com).

Some prominent companies have adopted the strategy of never gating their content, even something as valuable as a 100-plus page ebook. They feel that, as a result, they get far more downloads of their content, it gets distributed more, more people link to their site, and the people who do provide their contact information are legit and higher quality.

For some companies it takes 200-400 new inbound contacts to generate a single deal, so they are pivoting from that to fewer, more highly qualified contacts and leads.

It's worth considering.

Can HubSpot afford to do inbound marketing anymore? Can you?

In just a few years the customer acquisition cost (CAC) for marketing automation software company HubSpot more than doubled.

Could your company afford to spend more than twice as much to acquire each new customer?

The CAC is the average cost for each new customer. It is one of the most important metrics for a company and a marketing organization. You need to keep your CAC below the lifetime profits from a customer—their lifetime value (LTV)—or you're losing money on each customer.

HubSpot wrote in its annual report for 2014, "We believe that customer acquisition cost, or CAC, is an indicator of the efficiency of our sales and marketing programs in acquiring new customers."

And, based on their public financial statements and research that I did[75], from 2011 to 2016 HubSpot's CAC more than doubled from $6,671 to over $15,000.

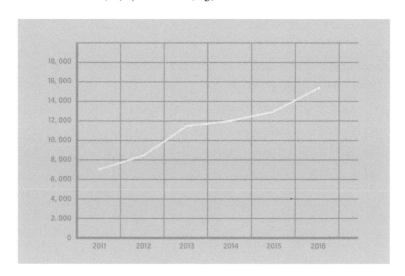

Figure 66. The rise of HubSpot's customer acquisition costs

HubSpot is a very important company to marketers because it created and evangelized the inbound marketing approach. Inbound is based on the idea that rather than "interrupting" people's content consumption with ads and other marketing, companies can most cost-effectively and considerately generate leads by publishing lots of content that draws people to it and induces them to contact the company when they're ready to buy. HubSpot is so identified with inbound that it calls its annual customer conference Inbound. They describe inbound as a movement, "the inbound movement."

If the CAC for the company most expert in inbound marketing keeps going up so rapidly, that suggests that the inbound channel can be exhausted. They've picked the low hanging fruit, or too many competitors are now replicating the tactic, and it's going to get more and more expensive for them to acquire future customers.

Results from each marketing channel will be different for each company depending on their customers, competition, and other factors. Maybe inbound will be cost effective for your company. Only considerable effort and time will tell.

The power of choice

At the heart of the buyer experience today is choice. Content marketing puts choice at the center of the company's promotions, too.

Quite simply, people prefer content and experiences that they choose over those which are forced on them, like ads.

In one study[76] a group was split in half. One half was told that they had to watch a movie trailer and then were asked to rate it. The other part of the group was given the choice of two movie trailers—which were both actually the same trailer that the first group had seen—and asked to rate it. The second part of the group gave the movie trailer—an ad—a higher rating simply because they had chosen which to watch. There was a doubling of likeability and many other ad-related metrics, like recall, were much higher, too.

Many other studies have produced similar results. Unlike an ad that interrupts what the person is reading or watching, content is what the person was looking for: what they chose to consume.

Choice is a major reason why content marketing can be so powerful.

Publish and amplify your content

Once you've published your content on your blog, or YouTube channel, or website for download, or wherever, who's going to see it? How are you going to expand your circle of awareness? That, after all, is a key purpose of Phase 3 Bullseye Marketing—building awareness of your company to a wider circle of people potentially interested in your offerings.

Of course, you want to take care of the basics. Use the SEO tactics that are described in the next chapter so Google and Bing have as many cues as possible about the nature of your content. Add social media and email share buttons to your blog and other content. Use "tweet this" callouts in blog posts that make it easy for people to share your most important points and a link back to the full piece.

Beyond that, though, you need to decide which content you will make a special effort on. Try though you may, some of your content will be better and more important than other. You want to promote the content that (1) organically generates more interest and engagement on its own, so you know that efforts to promote it are likely to show a good return, and (2) is especially important to building your brand or generating leads. In the case of #1 you're being opportunistic; in the case of #2, you're being strategic. Focus your efforts on these two cases to have the greatest impact.

You can use unpaid and paid means to amplify your content. The primary unpaid methods are through email, social media, and influencers.

In your regular emails to your house list, promote your important content.

Post to your social media accounts. To expand the reach beyond your current followers, use Twitter and Instagram hashtags for your business (#marketing, #fashion, #SMB), general categories (#summer, #travel, #food) and, if it's relevant, location (#Houston). You can post one content asset many times to social media, and try different images and messages to see which performs best. Posts with images generally get much higher readership and engagement.

Create your own social media posse. At a company, you can notify employees active on social media when a new post goes live and ask them to share, comment on and like it. Or you might create a mutual admiration society of 10 or 20 people who agree to do that for one another's posts.

Participate in online communities and forums related to your business and post links to your content there. Do try to engage with other members, too, and don't just use the community to post your content; that's not very neighborly.

Industry influencers can help to greatly expand the awareness of your content. Every industry has influencers. They can include reporters, bloggers, analysts, venture capitalists, and others. Social media influencers—people with lots of social media followers—can make many more people aware of your best content. Check out chapter 18 on PR and influencer marketing for a deeper dive on how to use this to amplify your content.

After you've exhausted the free opportunities, use paid ads to get broader exposure and readership for content that meets one of the two (tactical or strategic) goals I described above. Yes, now we're getting into spending more money, but that's why this is in Phase 3.

Other options include:

- Promote your content to your current customers and website visitors by using remarketing, a Phase 1 program.
- With Google, broaden your remarketing reach to other people like the ones who have visited your website using their "similar audiences" feature.

- Or narrow your targeting by uploading the emails of your customers, prospects and/or contacts to Facebook and Twitter and target ads to just those people.
- Target promoted posts on Facebook, Instagram and Twitter using interests and other factors.
- If you're after a professional audience, try ads or promoted content on LinkedIn.

You may offer up your content using paid search ads, especially if it is content that answers questions that people are searching on. If it doesn't, and you try to shoehorn it into the search results of people who are looking for something other than content, Google is likely to give you a poor Quality Score and not show your ads much, if at all.

There are many other places to run ads to promote your content, of course, including industry websites, newsletters, and so forth. The ones I mention here are a few that you can do for just a few hundred dollars.

If your content is good and valuable, you should start to see shares and likes that get your content in front of an even wider audience. And then you can decide if you should continue or end the amplification of that content.

Tools for content marketing

As Ann Handley said in her interview above, you don't need a lot of tools to create great content. Word, Google Docs, PhotoShop and similar tools are at the heart of creating great content.

Excel and Google Sheets are useful for a content audit.

Ceralytics provides content analytics and competitive intelligence.

Easel.ly, Canva, and Piktochart can be helpful in designing an infographic.

Final Cut Pro, Premiere Pro, Movie Maker, Animoto, and Filmora are useful video editing software.

Chapter 15

SEARCH ENGINE OPTIMIZATION

MOST PEOPLE START THE BUYING process with a search on the Web. As sales and marketing analysts SiriusDecisions puts it, "Our research shows that online searches are executives' first course of action (just like everyone else)."[77]

Search engines are the everyday technology miracle that we quickly have come to take for granted. Billions of times every day people conduct searches on Google, Bing and other search engines. The most direct way to reach new people interested in buying your products and services is by getting in front of the people who are searching for them. While some of them may be in a research phase, many will be looking to buy soon. They have essentially pre-qualified themselves as interested in your offerings. If you work hard enough, and are fortunate, they will find you.

While in the early days of the Internet people might have looked through two, three or more pages of search results before clicking on a link, today the majority of search clicks happen on just the first three links on the first search engine results page (SERP). By the ninth or tenth positions on page one, click-through rates are down to just one percent or less; very few people go to page two anymore.

In a few, nascent categories it may be possible to quickly grab and maintain high organic rankings. In more mature industries it is next to impossible. A study from Ahrefs found that only 5.7% of newly published pages even get ranked anywhere on Google's page one within a year, and that the average age of the page with #1 ranking is close to three years.[78] High organic search rankings can be difficult to achieve but, once achieved, can provide a steady stream of traffic to your website and other benefits such as branding and reputation management.

Paid search ads, which I discussed in chapter 11, are a valuable supplement even if you do achieve high organic rankings. Paid ads in combination with high rankings can increase organic clicks considerably.

And all of this is changing. As people do more and more searches on smartphones, where so few of the search results display, the ads and top links will be even more important. And audio search, such as on Google Home and Alexa, may produce only one result.

Like chapter 11 on search ads, this will be a more detailed, specific chapter than most in this book. I guess search just brings that out in me.

Understanding the power of the long tail

Before getting into the specifics of search engine optimization, I want to introduce the idea of the long tail because it's important in so many marketing areas, including search. (See fig. 67)

Here's an example of the long tail: Amazon Prime Video has over 18,000 movies and Netflix over 4,500.[79] How many of those are rented at least once a month? Although neither company publicly discloses its rental stats, the answer is the vast majority of them. The latest blockbusters get millions of views, and last year's blockbusters get thousands, and then there are some movies that get hundreds of views, and dozens, until finally you're at the far end of the tail where a documentary from the '90s still gets one or two views a month.

Figure 67. Long tail

The same concept applies to marketing and search.

The "head terms" for an industry are the one- or two-word general phrases such as "insurance," "software" or "airfares." You may not be able to rank for those. But as you get into multiple word searches, you can start to exploit the power of the long tail and find a much more useful and profitable audience. Long-tail phrases in those three industries could be:

- Chicago car insurance agent
- open source AI software
- cheap airfares Dublin Ireland

You have a much better chance of getting high rankings for long-tail terms. And the people searching for those terms are a much narrower, better-qualified set of people to be talking with.

I once did work with a local investment banking firm. They wanted to rank high on Google's page one SERP for the search phrase "investment banking," but that would be impossible. Page one listings were dominated by huge firms like Goldman Sachs and Morgan Stanley. There was nothing that this little regional firm could do to break into those page one listings.

However, they could be successful with longer-tail terms such as "Boston investment bank" or "technology investment bank" or "technology investment bank case studies".

If you have a local business, like a restaurant, retail shop or professional services practice, you're in luck. When people do searches with related phrases, Google assumes that they're looking for a local business and prioritizes those on page one, often with a map.

Figure 68. Local Google SERP for Thai restaurants, with map

In the U.S. about 60% of searches are on one- or two-word "head" phrases, but another 40% are people making long-tail searches. So you have lots of opportunity in the long tail. If page one search results for the head terms in your industry are locked down and can't be easily broken into, you may find greater success by focusing on long-tail terms.

How to get high search rankings

Some search experts have estimated that Google uses over 200 factors when—in less than a second!—it generates and ranks its search results from billions of Web pages. Others dispute that figure.[80] The exact number doesn't matter; it's obviously a complex algorithm. And Google doesn't say what those ranking factors are, or how they're weighted. If they did it would encourage people to game their system.

Google does say that it tweaks its algorithm virtually every day, and it usually releases one or more major, named upgrades to its search algorithm every year. Given this, and changes that you're making to your website, changes on external sites linking to yours, and activity from competitors and others in your industry, you're likely to see your rankings bounce up and down over time. SEO is never done.

Those algorithm changes are the details. What's important for you to know is that Google is primarily and increasingly focused on generating the most useful results and links for the person searching. It ranks and promotes useful content, and demotes what it sees as low-quality content or spam.

Choosing target search phrases

Google's semantic analysis keeps improving. Google uses it to understand what searchers actually are interested in when they type in a search phrase, and what a page is about. So in some sense keywords are less important than they once were. Nonetheless, keywords probably are the best way to focus your SEO efforts.

Remember to optimize for how your customers speak, not how you may talk within your organization. I've done a lot of marketing work with private schools. They often refer to themselves as "independent schools"; their organization is the National Association of Independent Schools. And some of them organize themselves with British labels of Lower, Middle and Upper school rather than elementary, middle, and high school. But few parents are searching for an "independent upper school," they're looking for a "private high school." Google doesn't handle these as synonyms; the search results for the two phrases are very different.

You can use the AdWords Keyword Planner, discussed in chapter 11, to identify keywords that could be valuable to rank for; third-party software can help you discover what keyword phrases your competitors are ranking for. Before you get to work, though, you not only have to figure out popular search phrases but *winnable* ones. If the top positions have been locked up by other companies for some time, it may be hard to break in.

SEO tool Ahrefs provides this example[81] showing the top positions for "search engine optimization." You can see that the top three positions are locked in with only a bit of bouncing around between them in more than six months, and the same is true for positions four and five. So even other SEO Jedi can't overcome the positions these pages have achieved. If that is the case for some of the keyword phrases that you're planning to work on, you may want to consider how long it will take to be successful. You may want to focus on long-tail terms that you can succeed with faster instead.

Figure 69. Example of impenetrable top search results position

Every two years Moz surveys about 150 of the best search engine optimizers, and runs its own correlations to try to determine which are the most important factors affecting search ranking.[82] (Remember: these are correlations, not causations, but it's the best that we have to go on.) Two major categories of components that can affect your search ranking dominate the results: on-page factors and off-page factors. Let's look at each.

On-page factors

On-page, or on-site, factors are the easiest and quickest for you to affect. So even if they rank slightly below off-page factors in power, they are likely to produce your fastest results. And in our Bullseye approach time-to-results is a critical factor.

Conducting a content-to-keyword audit can be valuable for SEO purposes. This is easier than the content audit described in chapter 14 because you're only reviewing keywords and web pages, not all of your content. In this audit, or map as it's sometimes called, you have columns for such factors as:

Keyword	URLs	Search Volume	Organic Traffic	Rank	Title Quality	Content Quality	Internal Links	External Links	Etc.

Figure 70. Content-to-keyword audit form

In your audit, you may identify keywords with no content, or multiple pages of content. You may find pages related to high-volume keywords with poor Title tags or content and no internal links. And so on.

The most important on-page factor is the quality of the content. Using a few keywords in your content is important, but don't use so many that Google thinks that you're trying to spam it. Content, including keywords, near the top of the page is more important than that farther down.

Add on-page tags

Various meta tags can communicate to Google what you think this page is about, and what you think it should rank for.

Title Tag: After the actual content itself, perhaps the most important on-page element is the page Title tag. When you're looking at a page, the Title tag is the text that displays in that page's browser tab and when you hover your cursor over the tab. Having a keyword-rich Title tag can do a lot to improve a page's ranking. On the other hand, when I go to a website and see that the Title tag on the homepage is "home" or just the name of the company or, even worse, the site URL, I know that they haven't done any serious SEO work on that site.

For SEO purposes, a set of keywords is a better use of the home page Title tag than a tagline.

Figure 71. Home page title tags

Google will use about 50-60 characters from your Title tag, even if there isn't enough room in the browser tab to display them all, with the earliest words being the most important.

Description: The Description tag may or may not be a ranking factor, but it usually appears on the SERP, so that can affect click-throughs to your site. Unlike the Title tag, which should be keyword phrases, the Description tag should be a readable sentence or two that includes a few keywords. You can use up to 155 characters.

H1, H2, etc.: If your text is somewhat lengthy—and it should be, longer text tends to rank higher—break it up with keyword-rich headlines and subheads and use the H1, H2, etc. tags, to reinforce their importance.

The Title and Description tags are hidden in the page's code. You usually can edit the header tags while creating the page's content.

High-quality content, Title, Description and header tags should be primary focuses of your SEO efforts.

Technical site audit

These are some of the more technical aspects of optimizing a site for Google:

- *Set up Google Analytics*: If you're one of the few companies that isn't already using Google Analytics on your website, set it up. GA isn't just a tool for you: it gives Google detailed information on how many people are coming to your site, how long they spend on each page, and so on. All of these could affect their rankings of pages.
- *Make sure Google is indexing your site*: An easy way to do this is to go to Google and use the Site: command in the Google search engine. For example, go to Google and search for site:mydomain. com (replace "mydomain" with your domain, of course). See if Google displays your site's pages. You can also use Google's Search Console to make sure your site is being indexed.
- *Manage your robots.txt file*: Make sure that your robots.txt file, which controls what search engines can index on your site, isn't excluding sections that you want public. Sometimes a robots. txt file inadvertently gets left on when a new site launches. Your robots.txt file is found at www.mydomain.com/robots.txt. If it says this, then search engines would ignore everything on your site:

    User-agent: *
    Disallow: /

- *Improve your site speed*: Google cares about not just high-quality content but a good user experience. It penalizes pages that load slowly. You can test the site's loading speed with Google's tool at https://developers.google.com/speed/pagespeed/insights/

- *Provide a mobile version*: Worldwide over half of Google searches are on mobile. So Google thinks mobile first and penalizes sites that don't have a mobile-friendly version. This will typically—and ideally for SEO purposes—be done with a responsive website design, although you could instead have an m. site.
- *Create SEO-friendly URLs*:
  - Keep your page URLs short, using keywords and hyphens instead of underlines.
  - If you change the URLs of existing pages, be sure to use 301 redirects so that people looking for the old URL will automatically be redirected to the new one, and no SEO juice will be lost.
- If you have a large site, make it easy for Google to find every page on it with an XML sitemap. For small sites, just clear, easy navigation should suffice.

Optimize Images and Videos

Google's Universal SERPs may include links, maps, snippets of information, summaries of Wikipedia listings, image previews, videos, etc. Getting an image included in the top image search results can be very valuable. (See fig. 72)

Provide a descriptive alt tag and file name for each image (don't have an image file name like image9392.jpg).

To improve the searchability—and accessibility—of your videos, include a transcript for each video.

All of this on-site SEO activity can have a dramatic impact on your search ranking over the course of just a few months. You need to apply it retroactively to existing website pages and assets, and to everything that you add to your site going forward.

But remember that it all starts with creating content that people want to read, view, share and link to.

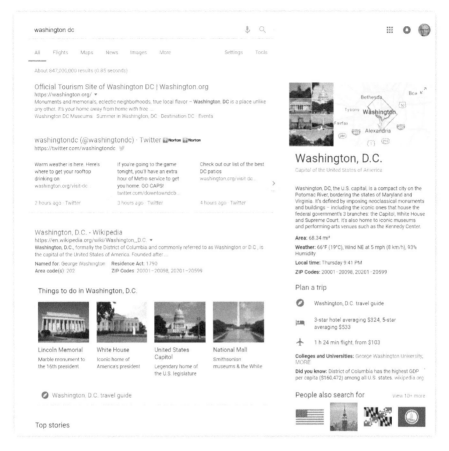

Figure 72. Google universal search results page

Off-page factors

The original, breakthrough idea of Google founders Larry Page and Sergey Brin was that links to a site or page were a kind of vote from the rest of the Internet on the value of their content. According to the Moz ranking factors report, SEOs still consider external links to be the most important factor in Google's ranking of a page.

If you consistently produce high-quality content and amplify it, over time it should naturally generate links. We're going to look at a few other ways to produce links.

Link Building

Guest blogging on high-quality sites can be a very effective way to get quality links to your site (and raise the visibility of yourself and your company). While they won't usually pay, many industry blogs are looking for content. If you have something intelligent, well-written and reasonably new to say, you can likely find a home for it on an industry blog. It may not be accepted by the first blog that you contact, but even those rejections may lead to contacts and insights that lead to them publishing your future guest posts.

The process is pretty simple. First, make a list of the major blogs in your industry that get a lot of traffic. Look at what they're publishing and would be likely to be interested in.

It's usually easy to find out who the editor of the blog is. Send them your post in a short email; I never just send ideas. They may accept it, they may reject it, or they may say that they'd be interested if you made certain changes. If they reject it and don't tell you why, you could politely ask why. And if I don't hear from them in two or three weeks I politely remind them of my submission; at the least they'll probably then tell me when they expect to be able to review it.

When you write a guest blog, you're unlikely to get paid. From an SEO point of view your payment is a link from your author description back to your website. Before submitting a post for consideration, make sure that the site provides that. Check the site's page source to be sure that they provide "follow" links back to the contributor site. A follow link shares that site's SEO juice with your site. A "no follow" link tells Google not to follow that link to the other site and doesn't help your search ranking.

You'll have to look at the page source to make sure that the site provides a follow link. This is what a follow link looks like:

Louis Gudema is the president of <a href="http://revenueassoci-ates.biz/">revenue + associates</a>

If it were a nofollow link, it would look like this:

Louis Gudema is the president of <a rel = "nofollow" href="http://revenueassociates.biz/">revenue + associates</a>

Why is there such a thing as a nofollow tag? It's usually automatically used for any URL put into a comment to prevent comment spam.

I find that typically only about two percent of people who read a guest post will go to the author's site, but the follow link passes important SEO fairy dust whether it's clicked on or not.

When approaching blogs that you want to write for, don't give up if the first, or first 10, don't accept your submission—even *Harry Potter* was turned down by a dozen publishers. You never know what a blog might be looking for. One time I wanted to publish an interview I had done about the brain science of content marketing. I approached a major blog that had published several of my pieces before, but they told me that they had an ironclad rule against publishing interviews except when done by someone on their staff; they had found that outsiders were using interviews to promote their clients. Even though my interview was with a person at another agency—a competitor, if anything, and certainly not a client—they would not budge. So I approached another blog, and their editor said that they had just been talking about how they wanted to publish more interviews and they were happy to use it. You. Never. Know.

Finding a home for your guest blog posts gets easier as you go along since you can start to say in your cover email, "I've already been published by X, Y and Z blogs; I hope you will find this a good fit for yours."

When your guest post is published, be sure that you share that in your social media channels. One hand washes the other. The editor may remember it next time you submit a guest post.

Manual link building is a valuable, if time-consuming, activity. And, no, there's no way to fully automate this.

First, use Google to find the mentions of your company on other sites.

Be prepared: you may find some very depressing mentions of your company, including on spammy sites that have nothing to do with your industry, and may have even stolen your content. However, that's not our primary concern, yet.

You want to work on the high-quality sites first. You could use the Domain Authority tool in Moz Pro, Ahref's Domain Rating, look for how much traffic the site gets relative to yours on Alexa, the SEO Review Tools website authority checker, or some other tools. Look for sites ranked equal to or higher than yours.

If the mention of your company has a link to your site, great—you can move on to the next one. If there is a mention of you but no link you need to contact the webmaster of the site and ask them to please add a link from the mention to your site, or to the particular content that they referenced. Make it easy for them: give them the URL of the specific page that your mention is on. If they do it, great: thank them. If they don't, you might ask a second time after a few days, but there's not much you can do about it, so move on.

You'll likely be more successful with recent mentions so you should also create an alert for your company name with Google Alerts or a similar tool and then reach out to sites that newly mention you but don't have a link to your site.

Competitive link analysis: The next step in your link building is to use third-party SEO software to analyze the backlinks to the sites of your competitors, and then try to get links to yours from the quality sites that you're not already linked from. Maybe they're getting a backlink from a blog that you could guest write for. Or they're mentioned in a list of vendors that you should be included in. Or they're in an online directory that you should add yourself to.

Social Media: Social media is a Phase 3 Bullseye technique for customer acquisition, and it probably only has a modest impact on search ranking. Do be sure to post your new blog posts, videos, etc., to social media—you've taken hours to create them, you can take 60 seconds to post them. Ones that get many shares and links may see a ranking boost from it. Tweets are included in search results, a professional's LinkedIn profile is often one of the top links on a search for their name, and Facebook pages can show up in SERPs, too.

These on- and off-page techniques are some of the most effective ways to improve your search rankings—and way more than most sites are doing. If you want to do even more to improve your site's search ranking, you could also:

- look up Schema for tags to improve how your page is described on the SERPs
- use canonical URLs to deal with duplicate content on big sites
- look into Google's Disavow tool for eliminating spammy site links to your site

You might even go after that most elusive of SEO unicorns: the Google snippet that displays the answer on the top of some SERPs. Interestingly the snippet doesn't always come from the top-ranked page.

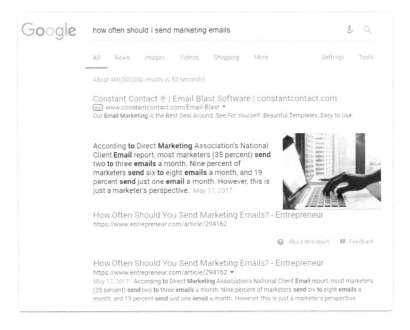

Figure 73. Google snippet

Also consider a strategic case for extra SEO love: a page that's ranking 4-10 on a page one Google SERP. If you rewrite it to improve the content and make it fresh (Google likes more recent content), create internal site links to it, work to get a few external links, and do everything else that I recommended above, you may be able to move it up into one of the coveted top three spots. Even if you don't get into the top three positions, moving from 7th to 4th could double your search traffic to the page. Similarly, you could work to move up pages that are at the top of page two results onto the bottom of page one and get more traffic from them.

Oh, and if you haven't already, create a Google+ page for your company and link it to your website. After all, it is Google. Use their tools.

SEO is a marathon, not a sprint. Follow these recommendations conscientiously over time—especially the creation of valuable content part—and you should see steady improvements.

What SEO dominance looks like

Many companies with good website SEO get a few links in those critical, top three positions, and then a long tail of additional links on page two and beyond that don't drive much traffic. This is a typical chart for a large site produced with SEMrush.

Figure 74. Typical organic search distribution

But this is what the breakdown is for Amazon:

Figure 75. Amazon's organic search distribution

And for the country's largest supermarket chain, Kroger:

Figure 76. Kroger's organic search distribution

Both Amazon and Kroger have many more pages ranked on page one than is typical. SEMrush reports that those companies get the equivalent of hundreds of millions of dollars a year in "free" website traffic from search.

Of course, it's not truly free. They have invested heavily over many years to dominate their industry search rankings in this way. The value of the search traffic that you're generating to your site may be part of your case to senior management for the ROI of search.

Beware SEO con men

Now that you know the most important practices for producing high search rankings, you and your team can manage them yourselves. If you decide that you need a consultant or agency to manage them for you, or to implement more advanced techniques, then choose carefully. I can't tell you the number of times that, in talking with a prospective client for the first time, I've said, "It looks like you haven't done any serious SEO work to your website" and they have replied, "You're kidding. We paid someone $25,000 just a few months ago to optimize it."

However, I can see that no real work was done because of the lack of the most elementary SEO practices that I described.

No area of marketing has a higher number of disreputable vendors than SEO—what are sometimes called "black hat" vendors. Just think of how many times you've gotten emails promising you #1 Google search rankings.

I assume this problem exists because few clients know how to evaluate the work of a search engine optimizer. And even when done right, SEO efforts can take a few months to show results, by which time the black hat SEO vendor has long ago cashed the check and ridden off into the sunset.

Google AdWords, by comparison, can be set up very quickly. You can see the ads appearing on the SERPs, and you can start working with the vendor to measure results and continuously optimize after just a few weeks. That doesn't make it better; it just makes it easier to evaluate what—if anything—is being done.

A sure tip-off that an SEO con man is approaching you is if they *guarantee* you results, especially #1 Google ranking. Check out the SEO's site: does it display the practices that I described? Do they rank high when you search for vendors in their city? How are their references? Google has a whole page of tips about selecting a reputable, white hat SEO.

SEO goals

The three primary ways to monitor the success of your search engine optimization efforts are:

- higher rankings on Google's search results pages for your target search phrases
- more organic search traffic to your website
- more qualified leads and sales from organic search traffic

When working on improving your search results, the first metric will be the campaign one: improvements in search ranking. Are you being successful in getting links high on page one of Google search results? That's where all the action is.

While high rankings don't guarantee more traffic to your site, they do have at least two inherent benefits themselves. They can improve awareness of your brand and build your brand equity. And they're useful for reputation management; you want the highest ranked pages about you to be positive.

As you get more highly ranked pages, you should get more search generated traffic to your site, too. If you aren't, then there may be a problem with your page Descriptions, or even your brand.

Finally, if your rankings and organic search traffic are rising, but your leads aren't, then it may be time to look at the conversion experience on your website.

Other goals can include the distribution of your content and building of your brand. But in the long run that has to produce increased leads and sales or it isn't worth much.

PS: There are other search engines

There are other search engines besides Google, and I don't mean Bing—although Bing may broaden your visibility and organic search traffic by 10% or more.

Amazon is a retail search engine; it's estimated that more retail searches are done on Amazon than Google.[83] Yelp is a search engine for restaurants and other local service businesses. Airbnb is a search engine for short-term rentals. TripAdvisor is a search engine for local attractions, restaurants, and hotels. Capterra and G2 Crowd are search engines for software. There are countless others.

If your business fits naturally into one of these other search engines, then you need to look into how to get top rankings on it. Yelp, for example, has several filters including price and distance. One of the most important, though, is ratings—not surprisingly, studies have shown that the restaurants with the highest ratings get a significant revenue boost. So Job One is looking after the quality of your offerings and service, and the experience of your customers.

This book isn't big enough to cover all of those industry-specific search engines, but in many cases you will find explanations online for best practices for getting high rankings on them. Tend to it.

 ## Tools for search engine optimization

Google Search Console and Google PageSpeed.

Ahrefs and Moz Pro provide a range of useful SEO tools.

SEMrush and SpyFu provide keyword research and competitive analysis.

Screaming Frog is a free website SEO crawler that will help you identify broken links, analyze page Titles, generate an XML sitemap, and deal with other SEO matters.

Excel and Google Sheets for SEO audit.

Chapter 16

VIDEO, TV, AND PODCASTS, OH MY!

FOR DECADES TV WAS THE #1 advertising medium due to the ability of TV ads to create strong emotional and brand connections. TV ad campaigns also have a long impact; in a study of TV ads for consumer packaged goods (CPG) companies, additional purchases *after* the month in which people saw the ads were typically at least double of that first month.[84]

The use of online video by marketers is increasing rapidly because of its great impact and recall, too. Only recently has digital advertising (in all its forms) surpassed the money spent on TV, and more and more of that money is being spent on video ads.

Video has a greater impact than image ads and animated GIFs. People may glance at or ignore an image ad, but they are more likely to get pulled into a video ad. Twitter wrote, "Across 406 Nielsen Brand Effect studies, those who saw video ads on Twitter were 50% more likely to be aware of the advertiser's brand, feel 14% more favorable about the brand, and had 18% higher purchase intent (versus those not exposed to video ads)."[85]

Radio and podcasts, on the other hand, have tremendous reach because of the time we spend in cars and listening to radio in the home when doing other tasks like cooking—even if radio doesn't have the emotional impact of TV. The average person spends a dozen hours or more a week listening to radio, and a third of people now regularly listen to podcasts.[86]

And you have something that very few advertisers had in the past: the ability to inexpensively have your own TV and radio channels online.

Video

I spent much of the first half of my career producing marketing videos for IBM, The Boston Globe, and many other companies. We pitched them on the idea that video is especially good for communicating emotion—the enthusiasm of the speaker and the gleam in their eyes during a customer testimonial is worth more than the words. Video is also good for demonstrating a process.

Many people have found that it's easier to watch a video than read on their smartphone. Mobile viewing may be especially important for consumer companies, but 86% of business videos are still viewed on the desktop.[87] Video content not only has a much longer recall and impact than text, but it also has a longer shelf life than other social media: most tweets get attention for about 30 minutes, a Facebook or LinkedIn post may be seen for a few days, but a video on YouTube can get views for years.

Here are a few ways you can take advantage of video:

- Live video events are especially popular. Use Facebook, YouTube, and other *free* services to reach a live global audience at no cost. All you need is a smartphone to stream talks by your people at an event.
- In short, promotional, online videos get your message into the first few seconds because many people won't watch to the end.

- In customer testimonials, tell stories and convey emotions.
- Create how-to videos that answer questions people are searching on.
- Use humor.
- Create video blog posts that include the full transcript so people can watch or read it, and you'll get maximum search engine optimization.
- Use large, stylish text on your videos as "subtitles" so they can be watched with the sound off—because 85% of the time on mobile they will be.[88]

Figure 77. Video with large subtitles for mobile

- Test adding videos to your landing pages—they can dramatically increase conversions.
- Run video ads.
- Create video in different formats for different channels. Videos for Instagram can be square, whereas on Facebook they're typically horizontal. When Snapchat signed a deal with Time Warner[89] for 10 shows, they announced that each episode would only be three to five minutes long because Snapchat users expect short content.
- Your sales people can use video emails as door openers; many companies experience higher engagement and numbers of appointments from these.

Create a video hub on your website so that people find and view your videos there, and it increases your web traffic and conversions.

While YouTube is free and well-known, and the videos can be shown on a corporate site, many companies use other services to host their website videos. The primary reasons for using other services are (1) YouTube is so wide open that people are easily pulled into viewing videos on other topics, (2) brands may not want their videos and ads associated with some of the content on YouTube, and (3) the other platforms provide superior marketing tools including branded video players and integrations with marketing software and analytics.

This is an example of a video hub for *Variety's* Power of Women event[90]:

Figure 78. Variety's Power of Women video hub

And the hub of video platform Vidyard:

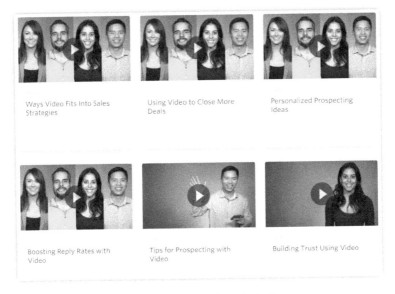

Figure 79. Vidyard's video hub

Variety also has a branded channel with over 2,000 videos on YouTube, and Vidyard's YouTube channel has over 150 videos.

How to target TV and radio ads

If you're reading this book you likely aren't running, or in the position to run, a big national TV or radio campaign, but local and regional campaigns may be within reach. You can place an ad on some local cable shows for as little as $10 per minute. Of course, you have production costs on top of that, and you'll need to run the ad more than once to be effective. But imagine having your ad running twice during each episode of a daily show for a month with a media spend well under $1,000; in some markets on some shows that's possible.

The number of TV and radio advertising options are far too many to cover, and they're changing so rapidly that if I did try to write about them all it would be woefully out of date before you read it.

But before we get into the particulars, we need to settle on terminology. For the rest of this chapter, I'll refer to "video" rather than

TV because an increasing proportion of video is watched on a device other than a TV. In fact, Millennials and those younger (Gen Z) watch a majority of their video on non-TV devices like phones, tablets, and laptops. "Radio" also is often listened to on those devices whether it's over the air, via channels like iTunes, or in the form of a podcast. I'll call it audio.

The number of video and audio options is incredible including major network channels, hundreds of cable channels, Hulu, Video on Demand, and in-stream ads for video watched on phones, tablets, gaming consoles, and PCs.

Of course, the first step is to figure out where your audience is. They may be watching shows beyond the obvious; for example, business owners and execs may be watching sports and not just the business reports. (This is why IBM has sponsored The Masters Golf Tournament TV broadcast for decades.) The media sellers from the various cable operators will be happy to help you with that, but you may want to work with your own media planner and buyer.

Video advertising

Can't afford to advertise on TV? No worries: in a survey of 120 ad agencies, 72% said that online video ads are as, if not more, effective than TV.[91]

As with many other online ad options, you can get into online video advertising with a very small spend, target your ads very narrowly and—much more easily than on TV or cable—measure their results. AdWords and Facebook are fine places to start.

To produce a full motion video ad may take experience on both the creative and production side, but the tools are way less expensive than in the past. Professionals are shooting and editing short professional-quality videos on iPhones, replacing equipment that would have cost tens of thousands of dollars in the past. And many services make it easy to create online marketing videos with pre-built templates.

You don't need to shoot from scratch. You can use video and still images from online stock image libraries. Or hire an animator through an online service to create a short, animated video. Or take still images of your company and products and create a "slideshow" style video.

The Judge Judy Election

David Axelrod, who served as Chief Strategist for both of Barack Obama's presidential campaigns, is now director of the University of Chicago's Institute of Politics. He hosts a podcast of interviews, many of which are with people in politics. In an interview with Ron Brownstein, senior political correspondent and demographer, the two of them talked about how political TV ads could be hyper-targeted in unexpected ways.[92]

Axelrod: "I can tell you that what we discovered when I was doing President Obama's campaigns was that the marginal voter wasn't watching the evening news. And the people who were watching the evening news knew who they were for. You weren't going to sway them because they were highly informed voters. So one of the revelations that came from the analytics work that we did was that the marginal voters, and there weren't that many of them, weren't paying attention to the evening news. And so we bought 64 cable networks. And while the Romney campaign was buying the news, we were buying reruns of *Andy of Mayberry* at three in the morning, which seemed insane except the data suggested that that's where we were going to find the marginal voters."

Brownstein: "A friend of mine who worked on the Romney campaign said that if they lost Ohio, which of course they did, he was going to blame it on Judge Judy. He called it 'the Judge Judy election': all the Obama ads on *Judge Judy* aimed at blue-collar white women, especially stay-at-home moms."

How to produce a podcast

If you're doing an interview-style podcast, you don't need to over-complicate it. It's pretty easy to produce.

You can decide if you want to provide questions for your guests in advance. As an interviewer I rarely do, and I've rarely had them provided to me when being interviewed. In his interview below, James Carbary explains how he essentially has his guests create the questions for him.

Jay Baer says that he uses GoToMeeting to record his podcasts.[93] I've had good results with UberConference. You could use Audacity to record and edit. Keep your edits to a minimum in an interview to maintain the feel of the exchanges.

For a few dollars a month you can use a podcast hosting platform which will also distribute your episodes to iTunes and Android players. And, voila—now you have your own "radio station."

Alternatively, you could do a lot of this by hand: create a podcast-only RSS feed on your site, and submit that to iTunes Connect and various Android apps, and they'll update automatically in the future from your RSS feed.

And then promote and amplify your content as you would any other, including asking your guests to post about them.

Interview with James Carbary: Podcasts that feature your ideal customer

James Carbary is the Founder of Sweet Fish Media and co-host of the B2B Growth Show podcast.

Louis: James, do you know how many people are listening to your B2B Growth Show podcast?

James: We are getting anywhere from 40,000 to 45,000 downloads a month. So each episode is getting downloaded anywhere from 1,200 to 1,500 times over an 8-week period, and then the downloads tend to trickle in after that 8-week mark.

Louis: That's great. I am surprised it lasts even eight weeks; that's a terrific length of time.

What do you see as the opportunity with podcasts? And is it different or greater than what companies can do with blogging or YouTube videos or other content?

James: I think that the unique thing about podcasting, which has been my thesis from the time we started the agency, is that a podcast is just one way for you to become the media company. And when you are the media company—be that through your blog, be that through your podcast, be that through publication that you write for—when you are the media company you can create very strategic relationships with a wide range of people. So if you are looking for referral partners, instead of saying, "You want to refer a business my way?" You can say, "I'd love to feature you on my podcast." Instead of saying, "You want to buy my product?" You can say, "I'd love to have you on my podcast." Instead of saying, "Can you feature me on your podcast?" You can say, "I'd love to feature you on my podcast." And so a podcast to me is just a very tangible way to add value first to the people that you are ultimately trying to work with in some way, shape or form.

Podcasting is not the only way that you can do that. There are several ways that you can do that.

So for the example of B2B Growth, Jonathan, my co-host and myself, we didn't know anything about B2B marketing when we started the show. But we knew that our buyers were B2B marketers, and so we started reaching out to them asking to feature them on our podcast by having conversations with them about topics of their choosing. A couple of things happened. One, we built really strategic relationships with those potential buyers and several of those people have now purchased our service from us. So that's I think a massive benefit. But then also we learned B2B marketing from experts by having these conversations. And so it positioned us as thought leaders in the space by creating the platform that distributed that type of content from these experts.

Louis: One of the big issues for any B2B marketing is getting in front of the right audience. If you are having 1,200, 1,800 or more downloads of your podcast, how do you know it's the right audience? Not just you but for someone who is creating a podcast: how are they going to get the right audience to listen to them?

James: That's a great question. I think that the way that we've done it is we've just been very, very targeted and specific in the type of content that we create. So in order to attract our audience essentially we feature their peers on our show. And so if we are featuring a lot of VPs of marketing at companies with more than 50 employees that are B2B companies, we know that the content that they are talking about isn't going to be relevant to everybody. So not everybody is going to want to listen to it. But it is going to be hyper-relevant to the exact type of people that we want to reach.

Louis: What do you think are effective promotional or amplification strategies that you've seen companies use, perhaps with podcasts that you produced for them, to get their content in front of the right audience?

James: One thing that I have recently started doing is setting up co-promotions with other podcasts in my space. So The Marketing Book Podcast, I went to Douglas Burdett and I said, Hey, I will talk about your show for 20 to 30 seconds at the beginning of our show for a few episodes. Would you be willing to do the same for me and in that way we will expose both of our audiences to each other's podcasts? He said yes, and so we are doing a co-promotion together. And I've structured similar deals with five or six other shows that are reaching B2B marketers.

Louis: You release a podcast every day, every business day. Do you think that's necessary for podcasting success? What do you think is the best cadence for a business podcast not necessarily for a marketer?

James: That's another great question. With our clients, we do weekly shows. So that's the cadence that we advocate for. But you know again, it comes down to your goals. And so with us, the reason we do a daily show is we are a young business, and we need as many relationships as we can possibly get.

Louis: You talk about who you want on your podcasts, you want potential customers or referral partners on your podcasts. For your customers who are businesses not necessarily in marketing services, or marketing technology companies who are outside of the marketing field, what kind of guests do they have?

James: So we've got one show called The CLO Show, and so it's a software company that has built a learning management system, an LMS, and they traditionally sold to the government. And with this new product, they wanted to sell to chief learning officers. And so for this particular client, we branded a show called The CLO Show and they ended up adding $250,000 to their sales pipeline within the first six episodes. They had somebody on episode six that happened to be very interested in their product and so it started—put a legitimate opportunity into their pipeline. So that's a tangible example of something outside of our own show.

Louis: So do you have a formula for most interesting questions? You've done over 500 interviews now, and presumably learned some things along the way. Are there ways that people who are doing a podcast for the first time that they should phrase the questions? Or the kinds of things that they should ask?

James: We have a lot of people that ask us for, "Hey, can you send me over the questions that you will be asking?" And we actually don't do scripted questions. Instead, what we do is, with each guest that we ask to come on the show, we allow our guests to choose the specific topic of the episode so long as it's helpful for whatever the audience is. In our case so long as the content is helpful for a B2B marketing leader, it's fair game. And then we give them the very clear directive that basically says that the more granular that you can get with the topics, the better. So at that point they come back to us and say, What if we talk about this? I did an interview this morning about creating a demand generation strategy for a skeptical buyer. I didn't come up with that topic. My guest did. And so as soon as she came up with that topic, I said, during our pre-interview, we will talk through 3 to 5 talking points that you want to make sure that we touch on so that you cover everything that you want to cover as it relates to the topic you chose. And what you are doing is, your guest is essentially coming up with your outline for you. I didn't have to do any question prep. I had to do very little prep for the guest.

Louis: Okay. So anything else that I should have asked?

James: I think that the biggest thing is strategy. If they have a smart strategy and they understand the audience they are trying to serve they are going to win. If you brand a show around your buyers persona, and you feature the people that you want to ultimately sell your service to as a guest on your show, I am just convinced that that's a smart strategy.

 ## Tools for video and audio

YouTube is the 500-pound gorilla of video hosting, and it's free.

Vimeo (kind of the classy YouTube), Brightcove, Kaltura, VidYard, and Wistia are leading video hosts, and some of them include video for salespeople emails.

Impossible Software provides mass customization of marketing videos at scale with personalized images, text, customer names and other custom content.

Buzzsprout, Podbean, and Libsyn are leading podcast hosting platforms.

Chapter 17

SOCIAL MEDIA

YOU HAVE PROBABLY NOTICED BY now that I'm a skeptic about using organic social media for acquiring new customers. Here are some of my reasons:

- It takes a lot of time and effort to build a following of any significant size. Devoting that effort to other activities is likely to produce faster and better results. (That's a major reason why social media is a Phase 3 activity.)
- Many of the people who follow an account are not potential customers. Consider the Twitter account of one of the largest tech companies in the world. They have hundreds of thousands of Twitter followers, but profiles with no photo and/or no description don't look like enterprise buyers to me. (See fig. 80)
- An estimated 40% or more of followers on Twitter aren't even humans; they're bots. You can use Twitteraudit.com to see how many fake followers an account has. The last time I checked I had 17% and Starbucks had 50% fake followers.

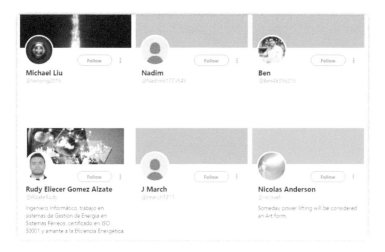

Figure 80. Sample of corporate Twitter followers

- The major social channels (Facebook, Twitter, etc.) have modified their algorithms over the past few years so that now a typical brand's organic (unpaid) post is only seen by two or three percent of their followers. For every 1,000 followers, typically only 20-30 will even see a brand's post unless it gets a lot of engagement. Late in 2017, Facebook announced that they would be accelerating that trend.

- Brand engagement rates (likes, shares, and comments) are very low. In part because few followers even see them, a typical brand post is only engaged with by less than .1% of their followers (less than 1 out of every 1,000).

- The number one reason[94] that consumers follow brands on social media is to get discounts and promotions. Is that your most desirable customer?

Although I have several thousand followers on social media, and am active, I don't think I've ever gotten a job from them. Other channels have brought me lots of work.

However! Social media is the most popular online activity. And while it takes time and effort, there are no media fees. So we would be foolish to completely ignore the channel.

Let's see if we can make this work.

What is social media?

What are we even talking about when we say "social media"? What makes something a social network? Social media networks are characterized by user generated content (UGC); social networks provide *platforms* for members to post, comment, share, etc., rather than the site creating most of the content itself. Also important are the ability for members to make connections, to share with selected individuals, and comment on their postings. There are far more social networks than Facebook, Instagram, LinkedIn, Twitter and Pinterest. Yelp is a social network, as are Snapchat, NextDoor, Reddit, YouTube, Flickr, Tumblr and many, many more.

There are also private social networks which I'll talk about in the Rent versus Owned section. And there may be important online communities that are exclusive to your industry, or your city or neighborhood.

Choose your channels

The first social media marketing question that you need to answer is: are there social networks that you can use to engage with your customers and produce business results?

Consider the profiles of the major services:

Facebook

In 2017, Facebook crossed the two billion monthly active user line.[95] More than one in every four people on earth uses Facebook at least once a month. Over half of Facebook members use it daily. That is astonishing.

Contrary to rumors that millennials have given up on Facebook, it's still the most-used social network by them.[96] It skews slightly toward those who are more educated, but also includes lower-income people. Everyone is on Facebook, especially in the U.S.

But the question for you is what are they doing there? And what kind of content do they want to engage with?

Entertainers have large, active (by social media standards) followings.

Many consumer companies have large followings on Facebook. Amazon, with over 28 million followers, uses it to offer deals, provide a look inside the company (video: "How to Pack a Prime Plane"), and encourage entrepreneurs to open businesses on Amazon.

Apple has close to 11 million likes on Facebook but doesn't post. Ever. Apple Music, with about 4 million likes, though, is active.

Tech and other B2B companies tend to have much smaller followings on Facebook, but they can engage in conversations on their technology.

Maersk Line, which I wrote about in chapter 14, has a very aggressive program on Facebook with over two million followers across multiple accounts. The creator of their program, Davina Rapaport, has said[97] that their customers consume 10.4 pieces of content "before even picking up the phone and calling a shipping company." Maersk uses social to make sure that their content is heavily represented in that content. The social media team may be concerned with campaign metrics, but Rapaport reports that ultimately the executives measure the program on business results: leads and revenue. "As a B2B brand, LinkedIn is an important platform for us to reach key decision makers when they're in the right mindset," said Rapaport. "Facebook is too big to ignore and an important channel for us to reinforce our message in a more subtle way."

Instagram

A few years ago Instagram + Snapchat was the young person's alternative to Facebook. But since Mark Zuckerberg acquired Instagram and integrated it with Facebook, it's grown tremendously beyond just young people.

Demographically Instagram users are somewhat more female than male, more urban, and younger. But with over 800 million users as of the fall of 2017 and an accelerating rate of growth, both consumer and B2B companies are likely to find an audience there. I've seen a business software ad with over 100,000 likes and 1,300 comments.

LinkedIn

LinkedIn is THE professional social media network. Owned by Microsoft, it reports over 500 million members but doesn't say[98] how many use it each month, or how many are paying customers. LinkedIn is a great way for people to build their brand by commenting on the posts of others and by posting professional content either as LinkedIn articles, links to their content on other sites, or articles and videos from others that they think are interesting.

Posts that encourage interaction, such as ones that ask a question or ask people to vote on something, can gain considerable traction.

LinkedIn groups may be useful for some professions, although sometimes groups become dominated by service providers and the actual customers then stay away. In those cases, decision-makers may be hanging out in a private group.

We'll discuss below how LinkedIn is especially good for targeted B2B ads.

Twitter

Twitter has over 300 million monthly active users but also probably suffers from the biggest harassment and troll population. People can make up account names, and if Twitter bans them they can just create another fake account and keep on.

Many people come to Twitter for headlines and the latest news. Many business leaders post to Twitter (as do an increasing number of politicians, you may have heard); a handful also engage with the people who respond to their tweets.

Many companies use Twitter as part of their customer support. Even Snapchat has a support account on Twitter.

Pinterest

At this writing Pinterest is closing in on 200 million monthly active users. A highly visual platform, Pinterest users have always skewed strongly female.

Because of its strong visual appeal, Pinterest may be especially useful for consumer companies. Target has over half a million followers and has created dozens of boards for Back to School, Swim Trends, Skin Care, and many other categories.

Snapchat

Snapchat also has close to 200 million daily users, and over 300 million monthly active users. Seventy percent of Snapchat users are female.

Over 75% of people 12-24 use it, but it drops off quickly from there. In the 35 to 44 age group, fewer than 20% of people do.

Those are just six of the more popular social networks, but there are countless others. Where are the people that you need to reach? Maybe a mass social media site isn't the best place to reach your customers.

Listen and engage!

In most consumer markets, and some B2B markets, there is an active online conversation about the products, services, and vendors. At the very least you need to be aware of what people are saying about you and your competitors. Listen in: you might be surprised.

Basic social media monitoring tools will let you track conversations on several major social networks. The most advanced, and expensive, tools monitor conversations in dozens of language, across millions of global networks and blogs, and include sophisticated sentiment analysis to tell you if messages are trending positive, negative or neutral.

However, if you're a B2B company the most important conversations about your industry may not be on the public social media networks. You may need to listen more informally within private industry communities. And it can be well worth it: listening to the conversation about your industry is critical to understanding your customers' ever-changing attitudes and needs.

Social media can help you gauge the impact of your marketing campaigns. Note upticks in mentions during campaigns to see how, and how much, people are reacting.

Listening can provide important competitive intelligence. Learn what your competitors are up to, what new products and services they're releasing, what people are saying about them, and the marketing that they're doing.

Listen: it's Job One.

And go beyond listening. Be a member of the community and engage with others. Like the best content of others, comment on it, and if it's really good share it.

Social media can also help your customer support team. Your team could reach out to people who are posting negative comments about you, even if they aren't asking for help—or they could wait to see if others come to your defense online. Thank people for favorable comments that they post about your company. Take actual support conversations offline as quickly as possible.

Figure 81. Sygnify walk-by social media command center

Some companies have created social media command centers. These typically take one of two forms:

Physical command centers where the social media team works together to react in real time to comments and posts about the company and trending industry topics.

Walk-by command centers, like the one shown in figure 81 from Sygnify[99], that display real-time data and posts to not just the social media team, but anyone in the company who comes by.

Given that many social media teams are distributed, and most social media tools provide apps that let you monitor and manage your social media through them, either of these may be options for your company depending on your situation.

And either should let you react quickly if a major social media issue flares up around your company or industry.

Tailor your content to the channel

Once you find your social communities, engage with them on their terms. Don't post LinkedIn content to Instagram, or vice versa.

A great example of a campaign[100] that's unique to a network is a fundraiser that was done on Tinder, of all places, for Kenya's Ol Pejeta Conservancy. Tinder is a dating app where you swipe right on a person's photo to show that you're interested in them.

Posts by Sudan, the last remaining northern white rhino male, appeared on Tinder with a pretty compelling come on: "I'm one of a kind. No, seriously, I'm the last male white rhino on the planet earth. I don't mean to be too forward, but the fate of my species literally depends on us getting together."

This was part of a fundraising campaign for the Conservancy to raise money to protect the very few remaining white rhinos and possibly use artificial insemination to preserve the species. In a month they raised over $100,000.

Interview with Evan Kirstel: Using social media for enterprise B2B marketing

Evan Kirstel is Social Media Business Strategist at UCStrategies. He is a Top 50 social media influencer with a rapidly-growing following of over 200,000 people on Twitter, and even more when you include other channels. He is especially focused on serving B2B telecomm companies.

Evan: I'm essentially a one-man social media marketing agency for B2B tech companies, although I do have collaborators. My clients are vendors and service providers in the enterprise telecomm, cloud, mobile world. From big companies like CenturyLink and Qualcomm to quite a few startups and early-stage companies. It's extending their reach and coverage and capacity to engage on social media, which increasingly is where their customers are spending time, where their partners are, where the events are, where analysts and journalists are.

Louis: So what are the biggest challenges?

Evan: There are still questions about the ROI of social, the measurability of social. There were a lot of skeptics and question marks. And there still is, to a degree, on the value of social in real lead generation, and how do you measure and monetize those activities. But when you look at where people are spending their time, in terms of where customers are, where your analysts and influencers and thought leaders are, increasingly there's no doubt that they're just spending more time on social media. And you need to go where they are in this new attention economy. So that's less of an issue now than in the early days. I think now with analytics you can measure things like click-throughs and website visits. The marketing analytics tools that are available can easily track opportunities and deal flow even, leadgen and top of funnel activities.

Louis: And you're talking about organic social, not paid social?

Evan: Most of my clients do both. The organic social is critical. They're mutually supportive. And then paid campaigns can help, too. But in terms of engaging those CIOs [chief information officers], engaging analysts, that really has to happen, in my opinion, organically. People are kind of numb to ads and to paid promotion these days, whereas nothing beats real interaction.

Louis: Have you found those people? Are CIOs on Twitter?

Evan: Yes, increasingly they are. And some of them do it as a sort of career advancing self-promotional thing as well. They have a point of view. And not just social, also blogging, content creation, videos, and interviews. And the ones that are in the forefront of this are becoming pretty social creatures and are getting out front of the industry, and they're seen as a thought leader.

Louis: I've told you some of my reservations about social media marketing. Thoughts?

Evan: I think the earlier comment of paid versus earned social, I think that requires context. I'm focused on very specific niches, very specific industries. I'm using very targeted hashtags and keywords. If I do occasionally have a strategy of following certain people, it's based on very specific keywords, combinations of keywords. I'm using very complex hashtags; if someone is tweeting around Cisco DevNet Congress, that's a pretty targeted event. So I'm not worried about stray cats and dogs that I may pick up, who may follow me back. So I think that if I were in B2C marketing like Nike, I might agree with that. But if you're in a very niche market, a very targeted market, an industrial market, you're hunting with a rifle, not a shotgun.

Louis: Good point.

Evan: Secondly, you go for relationships. For me, the value of Twitter and LinkedIn is in that initial awareness, visibility and engagement and turning it into something else: turning it into a face-to-face meeting, a call, a sign-up, a webinar, getting a content view, going to an event. This is all very top of funnel stuff, not some independent thing unlinked to everything else that you're doing in marketing. So that's the second thing.

And I think the goal of social is to create and build relationships. There's this entire watercooler out there, and you're participating in conversation around the watercooler in a very targeted way. And when I get into a conversation around the Internet of Things, there's a very targeted community of vendors, of consultants, of analysts, of suppliers talking about that. I'm not interested in the macro; I'm very focused on the micro of those conversations.

Use a big seed

Everyone who uses social media for business hopes that some of their social media posts will go viral and be seen by millions of people. But it's very, very, rare. After all, the competition is immense. Facebook users post four petabytes (four million gigabytes) of new information every day. Hundreds of hours of video are uploaded to YouTube *every minute*. Thousands of tweets are posted *every second*. The odds of your post going viral are infinitesimal, and even more so if it's not about cute children, pets, or a trending news story like the Academy Awards or Super Bowl.

Usually, a social media post needs a "big seed" to go viral, which is another way of saying it needs help. For example, the ALS Ice Bucket Challenge—arguably the most successful social media campaign ever—only took off after it was featured on *The Today Show*.

You can attempt to create a big seed with paid ads, or the use of influencers with large followings (or many micro-influencers), or piggybacking on a popular hashtag, or timing your campaign to coincide with another, related event—or some combination of all of these and more.

Organic versus Paid

My major issue with social media as a demand generation channel is with organic social media, although as Evan explained above it can be useful for connecting with industry influencers and leaders one-to-one.

Social media can also be a very good channel for paid ads.

Paid social media are the paid ads and promoted posts. These can be effective because of how well you can target based on the demographics and interests of people. Sites such as Facebook, LinkedIn, Instagram and Snapchat have gathered massive amounts of data about their members; you can use it to target ads very well.

These are some of the ad targeting options for major social platforms.

- Facebook and Instagram
  - demographics: location, age, gender, education, job titles, relationship status
  - interests
  - behaviors: purchases, device usage
  - custom audiences based on uploaded email lists, people using your mobile app
  - look-alike audiences: people similar to those of your custom lists
  - remarketing to website visitors

- LinkedIn
  - demographics: location, title, seniority
  - specified companies, and companies based on industry, number of employees and other factors
  - custom audiences based on uploaded email lists
  - look-alike audiences
  - remarketing to website visitors

- Twitter
  - demographics: location, age, platform, device
  - keywords, followers of your account, people similar to followers of your account, lists
  - tailored audiences based on emails uploaded
  - remarketing to website visitors

Those are some great targeting options and are one of the real strengths of advertising on social media.

Rent versus Owned

When you're considering building an online community you need to make a fundamental choice: will you own it or rent it?

You own a community if, for example, it's on your website. American Express owns the OPEN community, perhaps the largest private business site that incorporates elements of social media. Many other companies and industry associations host their own, private communities.

But if you're relying on company pages on Facebook or LinkedIn, then you're renting them, even if you're not paying actual money to rent.

It may be faster and easier to build a following when renting. You can piggyback on the huge numbers of users that the large social media sites have accumulated. It would take a lot of time and money to attract people to your community site.

But if you're renting, you're at the mercy of the landlord. Initially, companies thought it was pretty cool how they could reach tens of millions of customers with a Facebook page—until around 2013 when Facebook changed their algorithms so that brand posts displayed to far fewer of the people who had liked the company's page. Now only two to three percent of those people see a typical post. Facebook makes you pay to promote your post if you want more to see it.

Meetup is a social media site that's used by organizations to promote events. It makes it easy to grow a group from its millions of members. Meetup does not, however, share the email addresses of members, so you can never communicate with "your members" outside of Meetup. And it doesn't share metrics for emails sent through its system. You have no idea how many people opened one of your messages or clicked on a link to see more, or which Subject lines were most effective. That's part of what you don't get as a renter.

And social media landlords can change the rules anytime they want.

The best approach may be a combination of the two: use large social media accounts (and other channels) to drive people to your own, private community.

There's no easy answer to this, and a lot to consider.

You may be dealing with the effects of your decision for a long time.

How often should you post?

People who are relatively new to corporate social media, as opposed to their personal use, may be afraid that if they post too much it will come off as spam.

But remember: on most social media networks only two to three percent of followers will see a post. While people who engage with your posts are likely to see them more often than the average, you could post 40-50 times before other followers see even one of your posts.

Large consumer brands like Starbucks, Walmart and Target only post to Facebook or Twitter a few times a day. Marketing experts/ authors, with followings in the hundreds of thousands, typically tweet a few times an hour. They may post a very different kind of more personal content to Facebook, and less frequently. Check out some of your favorite accounts and see what they do.

Given that the half-life of a tweet is probably 30 minutes whereas a Facebook post can circulate for a day or two, posting more frequently to Twitter would make sense. Content on YouTube is evergreen and is watched for years.

Just as you need to choose the social media channels that work for your business, you need to experiment and find out what content and frequency of posting works for you.

Tools for social media

Buffer, Hootsuite, Social Oomph, and Sprout Social are tools for small and mid-sized business social media posting and monitoring.

Brandwatch, Sysomos, Synthesio, Sprinklr, Crimson Hexagon, Digimind and tools incorporated in major marketing cloud platforms from Adobe, Salesforce and other companies are suited to mid-sized and large companies.

Marketing automation programs have built-in social media tools.

Tailwind is an Instagram and Pinterest manager.

BuzzSumo is useful for ranking the most shared content and identifying influencers.

Hashtagify is useful for identifying top hashtags.

Chapter 18

PR AND INFLUENCER MARKETING

PEOPLE DON'T TRUST ADVERTISEMENTS LIKE they used to. They trust the recommendations of people they know.

They also trust some third party validators. So, for example, if a publication that they trust runs an article about your company, some people will lend more credence to what the reporter writes than if your company was to say the same thing about itself.

A common image of the role of public relations, or PR, is managing media relations to generate those positive mentions in news outlets. But that's far from the entire function.

What is PR?
Some people say that the difference between PR and advertising is money: PR works to get free or earned mentions, whereas you pay for advertising.

It may be easier to define PR by what it does. Among the activities of PR professionals are:

- Collaborate on the defining of a company's message and communicate it to their customers, prospects and the general public.
- Strategize around which company activities are likely to engender significant media attention, and how to create new ones that will.
- Speech writing, writing thought leadership guest blogs (especially for senior executives), and arranging for company leaders to appear on shows, podcasts, at events, etc.
- Cultivate relationships with journalists and editors to better understand what they want to cover, and pitch them on new story ideas in the manner that they prefer—which may be via email, phone, social media, Pony Express, or other means, depending on the person. If you're in the lucky position where you have more interest from the media than you can handle, your PR people will handle media relations and decide who should have what kind of access.
- Write and distribute press releases, and answer follow up questions from reporters.
- Develop a crisis and communication strategy in case a crisis comes up.

Some PR consultants and agencies go far beyond this, as Gini Dietrich explains in her interview later this chapter, and may be almost indistinguishable from other marketers who are generating and promoting content in various ways.

In larger companies, PR may be part of the corporate communications group rather than marketing. On the other hand, as experienced a businessperson as Mark Cuban says that startups and small companies shouldn't hire a PR person[101] (internally or externally) because the founders are the best spokespeople, they know the key writers and can speak for the company better than anyone else.

Maybe. But, frankly, not all founders and presidents are comfortable in this role. They may not understand what reporters want or need, may be paranoid about what a writer will write, and may feel that their time is better spent in other areas of the company.

What reporters and editors want

The news business has changed dramatically in the past 10-20 years. You need to understand that to appreciate what editors and reporters are looking for today.

While formerly newspapers put out one or more editions each day, and the TV news was heard perhaps three times a day, now news is a 24/7 activity. Stories are released and reported on throughout the day. Headlines and links to full stories are available for free via sources as diverse as Google News and Twitter. People can easily follow breaking news about their interests and industry.

Many newspapers have folded, and others are financially challenged. Most have much smaller staffs than before.

But on the other hand, there are far more news outlets than before. Thirty years ago there were three major TV networks; now there are countless cable, YouTube and other channels. HuffPost, Buzzfeed, Fox News, and aggregators such as Reddit, Google News, and Yahoo News have tens of millions of online readers. Anyone can publish news via the Internet, and stream video on Facebook and YouTube and podcasts and other channels at very low cost.

Reporters and editors now receive exponentially more news pitches and tips than a decade ago. A major challenge for them is filtering out the few good stories that they have the resources and space to cover.

- In 1995, launching a website was newsworthy, but today it likely wouldn't be unless that site introduces a new type of business or has significant investors.
- Most new product releases don't have the value that they had in the past, but if you're Amazon introducing the grocery store of the future it does.

- Want a mention of your $1.5 million funding round? Sorry, in some cities those are a dime a dozen. Maybe if you raised $10 million. But in others cities the business press would cover a $1.5 million funding round.

Look at what people are writing about in the outlets that will reach your audience.

Ideally, reporters want to be the first to break a story—they don't want to do one more story about something that was first reported by another outlet. They want something that's new—news! If you can guarantee an exclusive, you may be able to nab coverage in a larger outlet. And if you, or your PR person, has developed relationships over time with the reporters covering your industry you have that much better of a chance of getting their attention when you have a worthwhile story.

Keep in mind that if you have a big story, it may touch on more than one part of the news organizations. A major headquarters move or opening could interest the business reporters, real estate, HR, and other departments.

If you do hire a PR professional, it should be a person with contacts in your industry. A restaurant doesn't need a PR person who specializes in medical devices. Contacts are one of a PR person or agency's most important assets.

A good David versus Goliath story

A group of high school students in Boston showed how to attract the interest of the media. Wanting to raise money for a new ice skating rink for their neighborhood, they uncovered an agreement from 24 years earlier for TD Garden, where the Boston Celtics and Bruins play, to hold three fundraisers a year and donate the funds for neighborhood recreational facilities. But they had never held even a single fundraiser. The students now wanted what TD Garden should have raised to be allocated for their rink.

They held a news conference, with nicely designed graphics, to call out TD Garden. Now that's a David versus Goliath story that got a lot of coverage! And they received over $2 million from TD Garden and the state for their rink.

Give the media what they want, and they'll give you what you want: coverage.

Writing press releases

Are press releases dead? Maybe for some news organizations. But you can go to the Apple website and see their archive of press releases about quarterly earnings, important executive hires, major new product releases, and some of their other activities. And you'll find similar press release archives on most major corporate sites; check out the leaders in your industry.

As I mentioned before, many news organizations have significantly fewer staff people than before. The upside for you is that smaller newspapers may be very receptive to not just getting your press release but running it as an article with few if any changes.

So study those press release examples available on corporate sites. Then write your press release like a news story. Don't fill it with PR puffery that your CEO would like. Make it something that an editor could easily use.

An archive of press releases on your website may also help with your search engine optimization, as will copies of your press releases on other sites with links back to yours. There are web services that can help you distribute press releases beyond your known universe of publications.

Some companies have also found that a visit to the website press release archive is one of the last stops that customers make when doing their final due diligence on them as a new vendor.

Opportunistic and scheduled PR

You have a special opportunity to grab media attention when a topic is hot and in the news. David Meerman Scott calls this "newsjacking" and wrote an entire book on it.[102]

The idea of newsjacking is that if you can jump on a major news event and get out a media statement, blog post, live stream video, social media post or other communication in real time, you may achieve media attention—including high search rankings for the day or so while the topic is hot and people are searching on it.

Of course, you may or may not be able to break into a national conversation unless your website or people at your company already have significant authority. If you or your PR person has cultivated relationships with key reporters, you may be able to capitalize on them at moments like that. After all, for every tweet about a major story that goes viral, thousands don't. But you may be able to get local or regional attention that could be very valuable.

Let's say that tests of autonomous vehicles are announced in your city, and your company has something to do with the cars, automotive safety, autonomous vehicles or a related area. (Sometimes the relationship can be humorous.) Contacting a reporter, getting out a press release or doing something even more creative may gain you significant media attention; make sure you have a good spokesperson available.

In England, a TV personality punched a producer when he learned at the end of a long day of shooting that no food was available. Snickers, capitalizing on its "hangry" campaign, immediately sent a box of Snickers to the personality with a note on top, "You're not you when you're hungry." And Snickers tweeted it, of course, and made sure the image got out; the tweet alone garnered over 8,000 retweets and likes.

Digital security firms have a PR opportunity every time that there's a major data breach or similar incident.

Many PR opportunities last longer than a few hours. When a sports team is in the World Series or Super Bowl, the local mayors and governors often bet a local specialty, such as New England clam chowder or New York bagels, on the outcome. Being the restaurant that provides that is sure to get mentions.

And PR can be done on a scheduled basis. ADP handles payroll for hundreds of thousands of companies and millions of people. Based on that unique dataset, each month ADP puts out its employment report just a couple days before the federal unemployment report. That ADP report typically gets significant media attention.

What unique research or insights could you provide to news outlets to get free coverage for your company?

Does the PR department do these? Social media? Marketing? All of the above?

How these responsibilities are divided up will be different in every company. What matters is that you're set up to do it.

Interview with Gini Dietrich: What is PR today?

Gini Deitrich is the CEO of Arment Dietrich and the author of *Spin Sucks*.

Louis: What is PR today and how is it different than in the past?

Gini: I believe in the **PESO model** which is Paid, Earned, Shared and Owned media. So you have your traditional **earned** media which is media relations, publicity, working with influencers, brand ambassadors, things like that. You've got **shared** which is social. **Owned** which is content, content marketing. And then **paid,** although not from the perspective that we are going to go out and create these gorgeous ads and then put them on the Super Bowl. No, it's more like take the content that we are creating and then amplify it through paid social or through email marketing. So it all works together from an integration standpoint, and that's what we do. So, we really look at communications as an integrated model. A lot of people think of PR and they think of publicity. They think, you know, you're getting on the front page of The New York Times. And that's just one teeny-tiny part of it. We really look at it holistically.

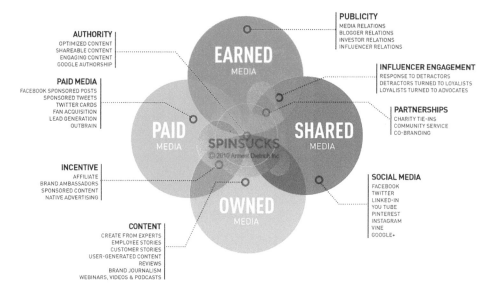

AUTHORITY
OPTIMIZED CONTENT
SHAREABLE CONTENT
ENGAGING CONTENT
GOOGLE AUTHORSHIP

PAID MEDIA
FACEBOOK SPONSORED POSTS
SPONSORED TWEETS
TWITTER CARDS
FAN ACQUISITION
LEAD GENERATION
OUTBRAIN

INCENTIVE
AFFILIATE
BRAND AMBASSADORS
SPONSORED CONTENT
NATIVE ADVERTISING

PUBLICITY
MEDIA RELATIONS
BLOGGER RELATIONS
INVESTOR RELATIONS
INFLUENCER RELATIONS

INFLUENCER ENGAGEMENT
RESPONSE TO DETRACTORS
DETRACTORS TURNED TO LOYALISTS
LOYALISTS TURNED TO ADVOCATES

PARTNERSHIPS
CHARITY TIE-INS
COMMUNITY SERVICE
CO-BRANDING

SOCIAL MEDIA
FACEBOOK
TWITTER
LINKED-IN
YOU TUBE
PINTEREST
INSTAGRAM
VINE
GOOGLE+

CONTENT
CREATE FROM EXPERTS
EMPLOYEE STORIES
CUSTOMER STORIES
USER-GENERATED CONTENT
REVIEWS
BRAND JOURNALISM
WEBINARS, VIDEOS & PODCASTS

EARNED MEDIA
PAID MEDIA
SHARED MEDIA
OWNED MEDIA
SPINSUCKS
© 2010 Arment Dietrich Inc

Figure 82. Spin Sucks PESO Model

Louis: So I think of PR as traditionally being the earned media part of the PESO model. You know: the publicity, the media relations, influencers and so forth. How then is a PR agency today different from a marketing agency?

Gini: Well, it's probably not in some cases. There are certainly some digital agencies that are trying to do everything that a PR agency would do as well. Typically what I find marketing agencies do better at is branding, product development, that kind of stuff versus communicating externally and internally.

Louis: Is there an area of the PESO model that you think is most important to your work as a PR professional?

Gini: I think content is where it starts, because without content, you don't have earned. Without content, you have nothing to share on social. Without content, you have nothing to share in email or amplify on paid. So, I think that's where it all starts. I think you are right in that most PR professionals and most executives expect that you should start with earned, but you can't start with earned if you don't have anything to share.

Louis: Yes. Well, content is central to everything today, like you've said. So, what about influencer relations now? You know, that's kind of at the heart of the earned part of it.

Gini: Yes.

Louis: So, do you do that for your clients and if you do, how do you go about doing it?

Gini: We do. And actually, we take a different approach because I've had the whole experience of working with celebrities. And I used to do food PR, which I really miss, and I've done everything with celebrity chefs. And I have gone that whole route but what we find is that that's great for awareness but not for sales conversions. And because we do so much work with B2B organizations, awareness is great but clients aren't happy if you are not helping them convert sales. So we find that micro-influencers are actually much more effective because they may have 100 followers but all 100 are avid fans of everything that influencer says and if that influencer believes in and is passionate about a product and they talk about it, all 100 of those people are going to actually buy. Whereas if you are Tiger Woods and you are touting a new watch, millions of people will see that but how many people will buy? I would rather have 100% of 100 people than 0.0001% of a million.

Louis: Yeah, that's a great point, and I have heard that from some other people who are involved in social media influencer outreach. They might focus on influencers—more like a couple of thousand followers rather than a hundred. But you don't need someone with Kim Kardashian levels of followers.

Gini: No. You do not.

Louis: So how much of that time when you are working with influencers are they doing it because they love what you're doing and how much of the time is it because you're paying them in some form?

Gini: With the micro-influencers, we try to find people who are already using the products or have a passion for the products or the industry or maybe have worked with the competitor. So we try to find those kinds of people. For someone like me who works on both sides because I'm also an influencer, I will not work with an organization unless I've used their product and believe in it. And I want to have used it on my own, paid for it, all of that before I even consider it.

How Eataly uses PR to open new stores

When Boston's Eataly opened, it was immediately crazy busy. This was the 16th store of this Italian food emporium. Their success is built almost entirely on PR and word of mouth; they do very little advertising.

Eataly uses PR aggressively and effectively. The Boston Globe had over two dozen articles before and around the opening; they were reporting about a possible Boston Eataly a couple of years ahead of the opening—before it had even signed a lease. This is an example of their breathless coverage a month before the opening, "Eataly Boston will open its doors Nov. 29, but you can almost smell the food cooking already."

A 45,000 square foot set of stores and restaurants led by celebrity chef Mario Batali in one of the city's prime commercial locations does get attention.

Boston Mayor Walsh attended the Boston opening and performed a ribbon cutting. It's a tradition: when Eataly opened in New York, Mayor Bloomberg did a pasta ribbon cutting. Their PR agency claims that their New York media and consumer events produced over 80 million media impressions.

You can't expect that kind of coverage for a me-too product. But if you have something that is truly newsworthy, and as colorful and inviting as Italian food, it's hard to beat good old-fashioned PR and free media for building interest.

Influencer marketing

Influencer marketing is a sometimes-free, often-times-paid form of promotion.

Getting Kim Kardashian West, with her 100 million-plus social media followers, to carry your brand's handbag into an event is an example of influencer marketing. In some markets, the top influencers may only have tens of thousands, or hundreds of thousands, of followers.

But on the other hand, you may not want to deal with the influencers with millions of followers. As Gini Dietrich said, it may not be believable to their followers that they're involved with your brand. Many consumer brands have found that it's better to engage many "mommy bloggers" and other micro-influencers with modest followings instead of one big name.

Here are three ways to get influencers to promote your product:

Do something for them

A few years ago I did a series of interviews with marketing and sales leaders. They were open to being interviewed because the interviews would appear on the IDG Connect Marketer blog—in other words, they were getting something out of it beyond what I could have provided if the interviews had only been on my blog. I later aggregated 10 of these interviews into an ebook. I used excerpts from some of those interviews in this book. When I posted the original interviews, and again when the ebook came out, the interview subjects were very active in tweeting about it.

Sometimes all it takes is free samples. Under FTC regulations influencers are supposed to identify when they received payment in any form, including free products, in exchange for a mention or endorsement. In these situations in a tweet you may see the hashtag #ad.

Influencers are just like the rest of us. They're thinking, "What's in it for me?" How can you help them?

Pay them

Lord & Taylor paid 50 fashion influencers on Instagram $1,000 to $4,000 each to wear the same dress on the same weekend. Their posts reached 11.4 million people and produced 328,000 engagements on the Lord & Taylor Instagram account. That 2.8% engagement rate is at least 20 times higher than the rate for the typical social media post;

that's the power of influencers.[103] The dress quickly sold out. If you do the math, Lord & Taylor paid influencers a total of about $100,000-150,000 for the campaign, with a CPM of $70-110. The CPM is high, but the cost per action was only 45 cents each. And, with a sellout, the campaign met its goals. (However, Lord & Taylor didn't properly attribute the posts—which they reviewed and approved—as #ads. And they ran a native ad that looked like an article on a site without identifying it as a paid placement, either. As a result, they had to pay a fine to the Federal Trade Commission.)

There is no standard rate. The deal for each influencer will be different. Influencers with tens of millions of followers may be paid hundreds of thousands of dollars for involvement in a campaign. It's not just the number of followers, but how many are real and see a post. One study[104] found that the worst-managed influencer campaign was paying for 78% fake followers; the best-managed campaigns, though, had remarkably low $2-3 CPMs.

As discussed in the chapter on social media, typically only a couple percent of an account's followers see a single post. You want to pay for actual views, or actions, not the 98% of their followers who aren't seeing your content. To boost that, an influencer deal may include multiple postings, and even in-person appearances and other involvement.

Engage with them and get lucky

Sometimes the influencer will just be interested in what you're doing, especially if it is truly pathbreaking and important in their field. If they are open to engaging with you (some are, some aren't), and your content interests them, they may share it with others. Or they may share or respond to a tweet to them. You never know. Influencers are people, too, and most of us don't do everything for lucre.

You should know many of the influencers in your field, and by using social media tools it usually isn't hard to discover others. Some agencies can put together influencer campaigns for you, and negotiate deals with bigger celebs.

Tools for PR and influencer marketing

HARO (Help a Reporter Out) is a free service that three times a day sends out dozens of requests from reporters for comments on stories they're working on.

Business Wire, Cision PR Newswire, Newswire, PR.com, and EIN Newsdesk are press release distribution and analytics services.

Mention, Brand24, AirPR, and TrendKite are monitoring and analytics tools, in addition to the tools listed in chapter 17.

Followerwonk is useful for influencer identification.

Chapter 19

EVENTS AND TRADE SHOWS

WHEN DONE WELL, EVENTS CAN outperform virtually any other marketing activity. Many marketers consider them to be the most effective marketing tool they have after their website.[105]

It's not hard to understand why. What's more memorable: a tweet, a TV commercial, or an in-person experience that lasts an hour or two? Or a day or two? Almost certainly it will be the event.

And events combine that experience and information with the opportunity for you and your salespeople to meet customers and prospects in person.

Just consider all the types of events companies use:

- grand opening for a new office or facility
- breakfast, lunch or dinner seminar for 10-20 prime prospects; you see financial service advisors hosting these all the time
- thought-leadership series of speakers on industry topics
- conferences for hundreds or thousands of customers and prospects
- golf tournaments and ski days

- press conferences
- product launches
- professional networking event
- food/wine tastings
- auctions, including non-profit fundraisers

And if you create a good enough event, you can get people to pay to attend.

"Chiefmartec" Scott Brinker, who is interviewed in chapter 24, started with blogging and speaking and then he created his own highly successful semi-annual event, the Martech Conference. Ann Handley, the Chief Content Officer of MarketingProfs, who was interviewed in chapter 13, heads up content development for MarketingProfs' many live and online events.

Professional advisors charge hundreds or thousands of dollars for people to attend their workshops.

Variety, the entertainment industry business publication, hosts a large number of paid events on topics ranging from Sports & Entertainment to Entertainment & Technology.

Software companies typically charge their customers over $1,000 to attend their users conference.

So some of these events are money-makers themselves, some are to gain leads and advance opportunities through the sales pipeline, some are customer success focused, and some are brand building. And some are All of The Above. What are you doing your event for? What will be your metric for success?

What is your event about?

Once you have established the purpose and goals of your event, you can start to plan the event's content and, more importantly, the entire experience.

For example, conferences typically have a schedule of speakers established and promoted well in advance. However, at an "uncon-ference" only the theme is established and on the morning of the conference attendees spend the first hour volunteering to lead sessions on related areas of expertise. The experience of an unconference is very different and, when done well, has much higher energy. Comic Con is utterly different from a financial services conference!

When we opened a new office for my then-agency, we held a welcome party. I hired the jazz combo of one of the employees to provide the music. A wall in our new open conference space was painted with chalkboard paint, so we hired the late Sidewalk Sam, a well-known Boston area sidewalk chalk artist, to draw pictures all evening. We had terrific food. None of those were terribly expensive, but I remember one attendee called it the best opening party they had ever attended.

As Maya Angelou said, "People will forget what you said, people will forget what you did, but people will never forget how you made them feel."

Some events have:

- woken up the attendees by starting the day with a drumline from a local college
- fed attendees from food trucks; each attendee got a ticket good for a meal from one of the dozen or so trucks they arranged to pull up outside
- closed with a talk by Oprah (no one left early)

Think this has to be expensive? I'm part of the executive committee for Boston's Sales and Marketing Innovators Meetup. Such outstanding speakers as Larry Kim, founder of WordStream and MobileMonkey; Chiefmartech Scott Brinker; and David Rose (then at the MIT Media Lab, later VP of Vision Technology at Warby Parker) have all spoken for no charge. All we did was ask. (We've also been turned down. Next.) Who are the stars in your area?

So what experience do you want for your event? How can you make it reflect your brand, and achieve your objectives?

Where and when

Where you hold your event is critical if it's not going to be at your business.

- Is the location convenient for people? Will they go there for your event? Depending on the transportation logistics, some people may not want to travel too far or to particular towns or areas.
- Is your facility convenient to public transportation? Is there a place to park for people who drive? Are you offering parking validation?
- Is the facility on-brand? Does it have the right kind of image for your organization?
- What is their support for Wi-Fi? Often Wi-Fi is a very expensive add-on; don't assume that they're providing it for free.
- Have a list of all of the things that you'll need and find out which are included and which will be an add-on.
- Go to the place! Don't believe the beautiful photos on their website. I visited one potential conference hotel, had lunch in their restaurant and was staring at a dumpster right outside the window; they didn't show *that* in their online photos!

You want to schedule your event far enough in advance that you can get it organized and people can get it onto their calendar. There are some other considerations to keep in mind:

- What time of day is most likely to attract people in your audience and area? Many business people like early morning or after-work events so they don't take time out of their work day. But if you're doing an event for people who have to get kids off to school, early morning isn't likely to be a successful time. A professional mixer for people in their 20s is an evening activity.
- Don't schedule an event on a holiday unless it's related to the holiday. Be aware of religious holidays, too, including ones like Jewish holidays that you might otherwise not be thinking of.

- If a major sports team in your area has a chance to make the playoffs, don't counter-schedule against a playoff game.
- Be aware of possible weather issues. At my agency, we held an annual conference for users of our website content management software. The first year we scheduled it in February. What was I thinking??? Attendees in Boston were greeted by a major snowstorm. We had to adjust accommodations, a planned dinner in the city was scrapped (the bus couldn't make it up the drive of the conference facility to pick up people), and the conference center graciously got together dinner for 40 almost overnight (they were great). It was a mess. So we then polled our customers and asked when they would prefer future conferences to be: April, mid-summer, or October? They voted for April, and we had successful spring conferences going forward.

BTW, if you're the kind of organization that could have a users conference for your customers, but never has, you definitely should. At my agency, it was the highlight of the year *for the staff*. They loved being able to get together in person with people that they typically only interacted with on the phone or by email. And while people who have never hosted a users conference might fear all of their most negative customers using it to gang up on them, in fact, they don't usually show up. It's really a love fest. Do it!

How to get people to attend

How you promote your events depends on who you want to attend.

If this is an event for your customers, then using your customer email list is perfect and inexpensive. You can supplement it with direct mail, ads targeted to your list via Facebook and LinkedIn, and you could also use remarketing ads that show to people who visit customer-only pages of your website.

You can use all of the other techniques we've described in this book to reach new people, such as paid and organic social media, highly targeted display and video ads, direct mail, and posting on community calendars.

Get your speakers to help promote the event. Encourage them to post to their social media followers where they're going to be speaking. You can also offer them a discount code to share.

You'll want to use offers in your promotions. If you're hosting a paid event, you can offer early-bird discounts (often these are in the form of earliest bird, early bird, and regular).

You may also want to partner with other organizations, and offer them a discount for their members if they help promote your event.

Keep in mind that there's a difference between who registers to attend and who actually shows up. If you're hosting a free event, you may have 50%—or more—no-shows. Companies frequently over-book free events for that very reason. If you're charging anything at all, even just $10 to $15, you are likely to get a much higher rate of people who registered attending. In my experience, with any payment the attendance rate goes up to over 90%. For a very important/expensive event, like a conference, it may be over 95%. So you don't want to overbook that!

You could do a joint event with one or two or more other companies. Some B2B companies do multi-city tours with several related vendors. With several companies combining to do an event, you have a bigger email list and network to promote it through. Make sure that the commitments of each company are clear and in writing before joining up.

Even if you're the only host, if your event is going to attract a large enough attendance other companies may be willing to pay for exhibitor space or sponsorships.

The day of

The job of event manager is one of the most stressful jobs in business[106] because there are no second chances. If something goes wrong, and usually *something* will, you need to deal with it in real time. You don't have the opportunity to sleep on it, talk it over with your team, and make a decision sometime in the next few days or weeks. You need to act now.

Ideally you'll be working with an experienced event manager who knows what to expect, how to arrange to take care of the usual details and handle the unexpected.

- Do people need to show identification to get into your building? If yes, do they know that?
- Who will handle signing in people who registered in advance? Can people pay onsite? What are you going to do if someone claims that they registered, but you don't have them signed up?
- Are you offering parking validation? Who's handling that?
- Do you have name tags? Materials to hand out?
- Are refreshments arranged?
- What will you do if a major speaker can't attend at the last minute? (Family emergencies and other matters do come up.)

There are a million details.

You may want different people on your staff to handle the program and the logistics of the facility.

Provide digital support for physical events

Attendees can amplify the impact of your physical events via social media if you do just these three things:

1. Provide Wi-Fi so people can be online with their tablets and computers when at your event. If your event is deep inside a hotel or conference facility, even smartphones may need Wi-Fi to get online.
2. Make the Wi-Fi login information prominently available. It should be on screen when people enter the event rooms. You may also want to include it in your physical event handouts.
3. Create an event hashtag and promote it aggressively. Again, you can have the hashtag on screen when people enter rooms. Some conferences have speakers put it at the bottom of every presentation slide.

When you start the first session and welcome people you should point out the Wi-Fi login and hashtag information.

Providing the Wi-Fi may cost you (a lot of) money. Making the Wi-Fi login information readily available and promoting the hashtag costs you nothing. But if you do this not only will people at the event be able to easily see the comments of others, and learn about the best sessions, but many people not at the event will learn about it and what you're talking about, too.

Post-event follow up

The event does not end when the last person leaves. You should continue to exploit it for weeks or months to come.

You may want to send out an email or even launch a web microsite with some of the event highlights. Consider posting people's presentations, and even videos of entire talks.

Add new contacts generated through the event to your email lists. And update existing contact records in your CRM and marketing automation program with the fact that they attended. Perhaps you'll set up a community site on your website, or on LinkedIn or another social platform, for people to continue to engage and exchange ideas.

If this is an event to generate leads, you should have ones that you'll need to get to sales for timely follow-up.

Trade shows

With a trade show, you're not managing the event, but there are many ways that you can take advantage of one to grow your business.

Trade show success requires tight cooperation between sales and marketing. The benefits that come out of a trade show often are attributed as much, or more, to sales than marketing. They include:

- Gaining new leads
- Meeting in person with current prospects that, until the show, you may have only had remote conversations with
- Re-connecting with current customers
- Building your brand

Trade shows can be very expensive if you create an elaborate booth, have a glitzy prize for a drawing, have to ship heavy product samples, or have to travel a long way for it. And that's in addition to the exhibitor and sponsor fees you'll pay, and staff time invested.

If you're starting out, you may want to keep your booth simple. Look at photos to see what is typical at that event, but entry-level exhibitor spaces in the U.S. are usually 10' by 10' areas. You may get a table and a couple of chairs, but may have to pay for a lot of extras—even carpeting sometimes. Trade show extras like electricity, furniture, and wastebaskets can be very expensive; you may pay close to the full value of the item to use it for a few days. To plan your budget, check over everything in advance to understand what you're getting, what will be extra, and what the extras will cost.

A booth with a tablecloth with your logo on it over an eight-foot table, one or two banner stands, and some brochures on the table may be enough for your first few events. Add a monitor with looping presentation and you're really rolling!

An inexpensive way to get more out of a trade show is to arrange in advance to meet with customers and prospects there. You're both probably going to be there for several days and regardless of how good the program is there are some weak spots in it in which they will be happy to skip out of the scheduled sessions and meet with you. Salespeople have a rare opportunity for real face-to-face time, so take advantage of it by planning ahead. Top sales and business development executives typically have meetings scheduled back-to-back for the entire length of an event.

Email all of your contacts to let them know that you'll be at the show and encourage them to come by your booth. Some shows give exhibitors or sponsors access to lists of attendees in advance, and you can send messages to them, too.

Will you have a special trade show offer? Companies often offer 10% to 20% off as an event special if they're selling something that can be bought by show attendees like food, personal items, and small electronics. You may want to have a drawing for a special prize; these can be a terrific way to gather the contact information of attendees.

At one trade show, my agency gave away a $2,000 bike—or any combination that added up to that (two $1,000 bikes for a family, for example). We did this in partnership with a local bike shop, so it only cost us $1,400. They let us take a bike to the show to display and when we wheeled it into the exhibition hall in the morning one person we passed said, "Now THAT'S a giveaway!" We asked people to complete an entry form with several business questions, and they were lined up to do so. Since one deal would easily be worth at least 20 times the cost, it was well worth it. The revenue we gained in new business alone made it worth it, plus the new contacts and awareness.

On the other hand, things can happen. For one trade show, a major software vendor sent out in advance to all attendees a nice mailer with a key. They were giving away a Harley Davidson and inviting people to come to their booth to see if they had the winning key that would start the motorcycle. Great idea! One little problem: at the show IBM showed up with a giveaway of a bright, yellow Corvette. (IBM can afford that kind of thing.) So the Harley giveaway no doubt was successful, but the buzz was all about the Corvette. And lucky IBM: the winner of the car couldn't accept it because his company had rules forbidding accepting gifts worth over $100 from a vendor.

On the other hand, some companies have moved away from giveaways and enticements altogether. They don't want people who are interested in them only to win a prize; they want conversations with fewer, higher quality leads.

Make sure you plan with sales on the post-show follow up to all of your new contacts and leads. Having spent the money and considerable time to gain them, you need to take full advantage.

Webinars

We now turn our attention away from physical events to online ones. Online events don't have the same in-person touchy/feely benefit of physical events, but can be a very effective part of a B2B marketing media mix, and perhaps a few B2C ones, too, such as financial services.

The logistics are much simpler for a 30-60 minute webinar than a physical event, and you don't need to worry about weather. There are a variety of webinar hosting services that, depending on the level of service, can include sign-up pages, webinars for dozens to thousands of people, recording of the webinar, and other features.

Given how busy people are these days I've found promoting "15-minute" webinars to be an effective hook. In a 15-minute webinar, you're promising to get across all of your content in just 15 minutes. You can provide another 15 minutes (or more) for questions and answers.

Just as with a physical webinar, you'll want to schedule high visibility presenters if possible. At one agency where I did business development, we were Google partners; I arranged for a Google representative to do a webinar with us on the latest in search marketing once a quarter. Attendance was very strong and it was good for our brand, too.

With a webinar, the various presenters can be in remote locations. You will want to make sure that all are in places with no background noise and a good microphone; if you're going to be streaming their video, they will need a good backdrop and camera, too.

Be sure to rehearse. A key purpose of the rehearsal is to make sure that all of the presenters know how to use the technology and have their presentations ready. If you have multiple presenters, you may be passing off the presenter role on the webinar from person to person, and they need to be comfortable doing that, too. You may want to have a moderator who will screen and present the questions that come in during the webinar during the Q&A session.

During a webinar, you can use online polls to survey your audience. This can be a good way to increase engagement. Some companies have had success with asking a question or two as part of their registration process and urging people to attend the webinar in which their questions will be answered. The reason for needing this kind of encouragement for attending is because it's common for 40% to 50%

or more of the people who register for a free webinar to not attend. A few may watch the video later, but quite a few don't.

Your email list, and that of co-sponsors, will be a key promotional tool for the webinar. You typically can send three or four emails to your list encouraging people to sign up. Ideally, your email system is sophisticated enough that once a person has signed up you won't send them more solicitations, but do be sure to send a reminder email 24 hours in advance to everyone who has registered, as well as another reminder on the morning of the webinar.

I recommend recording the webinar, posting it to YouTube and your website with a transcript, and sending out the link to the recording asap after the webinar to everyone who signed up, whether they attended or not.

Be sure to also have an exit survey at the end of the webinar. It can be as simple as three questions:

1. How would you rate this webinar (1-5)?
2. What is the reason for your rating? [open text answer]
3. What topics would you like to see us cover in future webinars?

And don't forget your hashtag for people to tweet about the webinar as it's going on.

Virtual conferences

A virtual conference is a kind of webinar on steroids. A virtual conference may be two or three days long with dozens of sessions in multiple tracks. People have a choice of which sessions to attend, just like in a physical conference. You also can setup virtual exhibitor spaces and rooms for real-time chat.

A virtual conference is a much, much bigger logistical challenge than a single webinar. You need to arrange dozens of speakers, prominent keynotes, and co-sponsors and exhibitors.

Event planners for virtual conferences typically pre-record a significant number of the presentations. In an event with so many moving parts, and such a possibility for technical problems—as well as last minute conflicts for speakers—having many sessions pre-recorded takes a lot of risk and anxiety out of the event.

Whether you're doing a webinar or a virtual conference, check the analytics afterward. The platforms will tell you how many people attended a session, how long they stayed, if they had another program open on top of the conference software (i.e., weren't paying attention), and so forth. It's a great way to find out how interested and engaged people were in your content, and to decide what to do events and other content about in the future.

 ## Tools for events

Eventbrite, Eventzilla, etouches and, for organizations, Meetup are event registration tools.

Cvent is useful for event management.

GoToWebinar, Zoom, and Webex are leading webinar platforms.

Communique and vFAIRS are two virtual trade show platforms.

Chapter 20

ONLINE DISPLAY ADS

YOU SEE DISPLAY ADS ALL over the Internet: on news sites, blogs and social media. Big ads spanning across the left, top and right of the IMDB.com home page for the movie opening that weekend. Home page takeovers of news sites that slide down for a few seconds, and ginormous banners on the top of SportsIllustrated.com that slide down the entire page. Little ads at the bottom of your mobile screen. And ads embedded in the middle of your social media stream. They are everywhere.

Display ads have very low click-through rates[107]: just .05% on average—only five out of every 10,000 views of an ad will result in a click on it. Some ad formats, industries, or countries have higher—or lower—click-through rates, but that's an approximate average.

So their branding value is likely to be greater than their direct response value.

You're likely to get the best results if you combine your display ads with other programs as part of an omni-channel approach. Remember, remarketing ads are display ads. They typically get much higher CTRs and can lift search advertising program results by 50% or more.

Give your ads punch

Even if your ads won't have great CTRs, follow the same Bullseye principles you would with search and other advertising. Target narrowly (see below), make a compelling offer, and support it with clear creative.

Make sure that your design makes your message clear, and that your text and logo stand out—even if you're using an image in the ad. These ads do this well.

Figure 83. CNN online display ad[108]

Figure 84. Cambridge Savings Bank online display ad[109]

Many of your display ads will be seen in their smaller formats, so keep that in mind when designing them.

It doesn't take a lot of money to get your display ad designs right. A company of any size can compete in creativity.

Google also has a tool to create simple responsive ads for you, although results vary. If yours don't look good, you may need to create custom ads in the several formats needed.

Where and how to advertise

Combined, the "duopoly" of Facebook and Google account for just over half of the online display ad market.[110] But close to half is still elsewhere—you have many opportunities to reach your audience.

The critical questions are where is your audience, and what context do you want your ads to appear in?

Facebook

Remember: your list or audience is your most important direct response, and Bullseye Marketing, success factor. Facebook has a lot of information about its two billion members, and you can use it to target your Facebook display ads, as discussed in the chapter on social media.

Facebook also offers a retargeting service similar to Google's. You put the Facebook tracking code, what they call the Facebook Pixel, on your website. Facebook will build a list of people who visited particular pages or took particular actions. You can then target subject-specific ads to people based on which pages they visited, or what they did. The Pixel also helps you measure the results of your ads by providing conversion tracking.

Google

An estimated 90% of Internet users see the ads that appear on the two million-plus websites on the Google Display Network. So clearly you can reach your audience there, too.

Google provides you with a ton of targeting options, such as on specific websites, websites based on keywords, individuals based on their interests and, of course, geography. Google's Customer Match is similar to Facebook's Custom Audiences; you can upload data that includes name, email, physical address and phone number. Of course, you can retarget your website visitors, which can be especially powerful if you retarget people who came to a particular landing page through a search campaign.

Bullseye marketers may be especially interested in Google's intent data based on people whose behavior tells Google that they are in-market now for a particular product or service. This is actually a Phase 2 program since it's based on intent data. When creating a display campaign, you can specify a custom intent audience in the Audiences section of the AdWords manager.

A concern for many companies is the sites that their ads will display on: they don't want their ads to appear with objectionable material. You can use Google's AdWords Display Targeting report to see which sites your ads are showing on, and how effective they are. Then if you find sites that you want to exclude, you can do that in the AdWords Manager.

Advertising on the Google Display Network is more complex than advertising on Facebook. But then on Facebook you're only advertising on one site (with two billion users) whereas on the Google Display Network you're advertising on over two million sites (also with billions of users).

Experiment with both and track and measure to make each work for you.

Advertising on other sites

Even with their enormous reach, you may decide that you want to target additional customers, or can target better, by advertising beyond Facebooks and the sites that Google serves.

Advertising on other social media sites, and taking advantage of their rich targeting options, is a natural. Consider Instagram, LinkedIn, Twitter, Snapchat, Yelp, Reddit, and others.

Retailers may want to advertise on Amazon.

B2B advertisers may find industry-specific sites to be especially useful to advertise on. TechTarget runs over 140 high tech websites with millions of monthly visitors; they provide many marketing options including ads. ThomasNet is based on the 120-year-old register of American manufacturers. World Pumps is a site, and publication, about industrial pumps. Go where your customers are.

If you search for "largest advertising networks" you'll find many other ways to place ads on sites as different as NPR.org, HuffPost, and BuzzFeed.

You may sometimes have the opportunity to bundle your online advertising with other opportunities that the publisher offers such as emails, magazines, newsletters, social media posts, and "native advertising"—an ad that looks like an article, although it is marked as an advertisement. If you negotiate you may find that a publisher will throw in ads in their newsletter for "free"—or a review of your product, or social media posts—for a sizeable enough online ad buy, or some other package of services.

You can also negotiate rates and packages based on performance (if you get X results you'll advertise more), or your commitment to a long-term deal.

You'll want to find out what they consider an impression (how much of the ad is visible for how long) and how they track that.

Media planners and buyers are experts in figuring out what online and offline publishers would be best for you to advertise with, and will negotiate terms with them. Many marketing agencies provide this service, but if you're starting out small, you may want to engage an individual contractor. You could find some on LinkedIn—maybe one at an agency would like to make some extra money moonlighting—or on freelance contractor sites like Upwork and Guru.

Ad buying and placement is increasingly programmatic

In the previous two sections of this chapter, I laid out two different approaches to buying online ads: the highly automated process of targeting and buying ads on Facebook and Google, and a fairly manual process involving person-to-person negotiations.

You probably won't be surprised to hear that the future is automated.

Programmatic ad buying and placements or just, as it's usually called, "programmatic," is taking over the online ad buying world, and for good reason.

With programmatic, advertisers can inform their buying and placements with a tremendous amount of data and show the right ad—even personalized ads—to the right person at the right time.

Programmatic takes advantage of real-time bidding, the science fiction-like technology that in milliseconds can choose between millions of ad options and choose the one that is best for that page based on who is viewing the page, and potentially thousands of other factors.

Think back again to how you can target display ads on the Google Display Network. You have broad options such as age, gender, location, and interests—as well as retargeting to recent site visitors. But with programmatic, advertisers add first-party data, such as what the person has bought from them and their activity on the company's website, and purchased third party data about potentially thousands of other purchases and behaviors of the person.

As a result, people see more relevant ads, advertisers get their messages to the right people, and publishers may make more money.

For these reasons programmatic is rapidly taking over the online advertising world. In 2012 it was about 13% of online ad buying, but by 2017 it was close to 80%.[111]

And programmatic is moving into other areas like ad buying for TV and print. They may not be as targetable as online, but over time they are likely to become increasingly so.

If you go deeply into display advertising and programmatic, you will soon encounter a whole new lexicon and set of acronyms such as:

DMP	Data Management Platform
DSP	Demand Side Platform
I/O	Insertion Order
ROAS	Return on Ad Spend
RTB	Real-Time Bidding
SSP	Supply Side Platform

Currently programmatic is mostly used by large companies because of the complexity of the technology and amount of data needed. There are an increasing number of programmatic tools geared towards the needs of small- and mid-sized businesses, too.

Display ad formats

Online ads come in many formats including, but hardly limited to, video, simple animated GIFs, complex HTML5 ads, carousels, ads with sound, and ads with augmented reality on smartphones.

The Interactive Advertising Bureau (IAB) sets industry-wide standards for size and format of online ads that advertisers can feel confident using across millions of sites. In 2017, after months of industry input, IAB released a new set of responsive ad formats that includes new maximum file sizes and support for experiences as varied as virtual reality and 360-degree video, too. The responsive display ads are designed to work on desktop computers, tablets and smartphones. The entire set of guidelines is 36 pages long.

AdWords supports over 20 ad sizes including 250 x 250 pixel squares, 120 x 600 skyscrapers, 468 x 60 banners, 930 x 180 top banners, and several mobile sizes. Uploading fixed size ads gives you maximum creative control, and you should also create responsive ads to accommodate sizes other than what you uploaded.

Facebook's large newsfeed ad is 1,200 x 628, plus a headline, text, and link. It has smaller ads to the right of the newsfeed, but they don't perform very well. Its expanding mobile Canvas ads have more complex specs.

First, decide where you want to advertise—based on how to best reach your audience—then research the ad formats that they support.

Determine the formats that can best promote your company's offerings. Then you can look into how to create them.

Native advertising

Native advertising is advertising that looks like a site's or publication's editorial content but is sponsored, and it's labeled as an ad.

In a strategic use of native advertising, from 1985 to 2000 Mobil ran 819 paid op-ed pieces, sometimes called "advertorials", in The New York Times. These pieces, which included the Mobil logo, were a weekly feature aimed to move the thinking of opinion leaders who read The Times.

Native advertising can take the form of an article, a video, or even an infographic—any content that you'd expect to see on a site or in a publication.

Spending on native advertising is rising rapidly. Given their usually larger format, and required coordination with the publisher, native ads can cost tens of thousands of dollars or more, although they can be far less in local or industry websites and publications with smaller readerships.[112]

How to pay—CPC or CPM?

You often have the option of paying for your ads on a cost per click basis (CPC) or by CPM (cost per 1,000 impressions). If you're paying by the click, and your CTR is very low (.05% or 5 in 10,000) you might think of those 9,995 impressions when people aren't clicking as free. But you wouldn't get them if you weren't paying for the five clicks.

If you have the choice, such as on sites with self-service ad platforms (Facebook, LinkedIn, Google, etc.), after running your ads for a while you can calculate which would be cheaper to do, CPC or CPM. Let's say that you run a CPC campaign and your ads generate 10,000 impressions and 10 clicks at a cost of $16.50. Dividing the $16.50 by 10 (since you had ten thousand impressions) you find that your CPM is a very low $1.65. If you ran it on a CPM basis would it be cheaper or more expensive?

Your click through rate—and, therefore, your costs in a CPC campaign—also may vary considerably depending on the nature of your ad. If you have an ad with no call to action, you're not likely to get as many clicks. If you have an ad with a strong call to action and a timely offer, you may get far more clicks and a CPC campaign will be more expensive.

When you have a limited budget, you may deliberately not want to have a strong call to action to keep down your click rate and the expense of your campaign, and just take advantage of the impressions and low CPM. With a low click-through rate and, therefore, low income to the ad platform, though, over time they may not show your ads to as many people.

 ## Tools for online display ads

Facebook and Google AdWords are the places to start with online ads for most companies.

Pathmatics, AdBeat, Advault, and WhatRunsWhere provide digital ad competitive intelligence.

Moat provides advanced analytics around viewability, including whether ads are being seen by humans or bots, the effectiveness of ads, and other metrics.

Chapter 21

DIRECT MAIL

DIRECT MAIL IS ONE OF the classic marketing channels. Since it costs so much more than email to design, manage and send, it took a serious hit in the early 2000s. But around 2009 use of it stopped declining, and from 2009 through 2016 (the lastest available data) about 80 billion pieces were sent annually.[113] 80 *billion*! For many people, it may seem that the use of direct mail has increased because while its volume was flat, the number of first class letters continued to steadily decline, so direct mail is making up more and more of the mail that we receive.

Why is direct mail in Phase 3? Why isn't it in the center of the Bullseye? It is, after all, based on an existing asset: our house list. (I'll discuss bought prospect lists later in this chapter.) Direct mail could be a Phase 1 program for a company, but it's the relative cost of direct mail that's putting it into Phase 3 for many.

Even the least expensive type of direct mail—a 4.25" x 6" postcard—will cost several thousand dollars to print and send to 10,000 people. On the other hand, for less than $100/month you can manage 10,000 contacts and send unlimited emails through an email service.

(If your list has hundreds of records, instead of thousands, the difference will still be roughly 10x.) If you're just starting to scale up a marketing program, I know which I'm going to begin my tests with.

The direct mail industry is where the hierarchy of list-offer-creative that I've referred to many times began. Large-scale consumer direct mail programs continue to send pieces to tens of millions of customers. In those cases, a test may be sent to 100,000 or more people. Very large B2B companies, with millions of customers and prospects globally, may also be using direct mail at that scale.

Will your audience open it?

Some direct mail vendors continue to make extravagant claims, such as that it's more effective than digital messages, or has a bigger impact on branding.

The reality, of course, is that it depends on those list-offer-creative factors. For example, you may find direct mail more effective with retirees, who have more time on their hands, than with millennials.

The Data & Marketing Association claims an average 3.7% response rate from a house list and 1% response rate from a prospect list.[114] But industry benchmarks are meaningless. The brand equity of the sender, the offer on the direct mail piece, and the creative will have a huge impact on how many people open it, let alone respond. Direct mail is an ideal field for experiments with offers and creative. I know of a large, B2C company with deep direct mail experience that sends out 100,000 test pieces to get 300 responses: a .3% response rate. Then they send the winning pieces to millions. It's expensive, but the value of a new customer makes that worth it to them.

Direct mail can provide a larger canvas for image-rich messages, such as this piece promoting the upcoming season of a theater. It opens up to detailed descriptions of the planned productions and ticket package options.[115]

Figure 85. Direct mail piece for theater company

Industry veterans describe the three-second rule: most people will look at your direct mail piece for only the three seconds that it takes to decide to throw it in the trash, and very few will open it, so to get maximum benefit everyone better at least get a brand impression in those three seconds.

Figure 86. Direct mail envelope

Some direct mail campaigns test the opposite approach: they deliberately look like a personal letter in the belief that more people will open that. So in those cases, there is no brand impression if the person doesn't open it.

People's RFM score will drive which envelope to send to current customers. I'm a donor to WBUR. But I'm not a customer of this auto insurance company, so they put the offer right on the front and don't identify themselves on the front or back, hoping that the offer will be enough to entice me to open it.

Figure 87. Direct mail envelope with offer

Will a nickel, or personalized return address stickers, showing through a window on the envelope increase opens and, more importantly, conversions? Or a frightening headline? Or a 20% off offer?

If you are selling a service or something else that's not inherently visual, you don't have to develop real elaborate creative for your first mailings. You can start with something as simple—and inexpensive—as a regular letters to customers and follow up with calls and see if that produces results.

Use direct mail in integrated programs

Direct mail can most profitably be part of integrated, omni-channel marketing programs. A clothing company, for example, may market to their house list with a combination of:

- Direct mail catalogs
- Emails
- Direct mail postcards with sale offers
- Targeting customers on Facebook with a Custom Audiences list created with customer email addresses

A B2B cold calling program is likely to have more success if the prospects are warmed up a bit first. A sequence for that might be:

- Send direct mail piece of value: a report or eye-catching dimensional mailer
- Send email with content
- Phone attempt
- Email attempt
- Another email with content
- Phone attempt
- Etc.

Catalogs

While the use of direct mail in general has plateaued, companies continue to slowly cut back on catalogs. They are down almost 50% from their peak in 2007, but 10 billion catalogs a year are still being sent out. (See fig. 88)

Catalogs are at the center of multi-channel marketing for many retailers year round. They are sent out in such large numbers because they still work. Many people enjoy the tactile feel of paper and browsing through large, colorful displays of products. Large retailers may have dozens of different targeted versions of their catalog. Various retailers have found that customers who receive catalogs spend more. Retailers can track that when they send out catalogs their online sales increase. And when the catalog drives people to the website the company can then retarget them if they don't buy.

Figure 88. Print catalogs with offers

Obviously catalogs are a lot more expensive to write, design, print and send than a postcard or envelope, so they need to produce a much higher increase in sales to hit their needed ROI. The mailman's bag tends to get much heavier with catalogs in the last couple of months leading up to Christmas when so much of the annual retail spending happens.

Some companies are using catalogs—and their cousins, corporate magazines—as brand building mechanisms, complete with storytelling and emotional appeals. (See fig. 89)

Advanced omni-channel campaigns, like REI's "Force of Nature" campaign aimed at women, combined an editorial catalog[116] with paid media, social media, influencer strategies and over 1,000 in-store and outdoors events.

Figure 89. REI Force of Nature catalog two-page spread

Dimensional mailers

Around Christmas it's not uncommon for companies to send consumers small product samples in the mail. And if you've ever owned a business, you've probably gotten sample company pens from promo companies. Done more creatively, dimensional direct mail is a good way to get the attention of a prospect who has otherwise been ignoring your marketing.

Voice recognition leader Nuance wanted to open C-suite doors for its sales reps to sell their documentation artificial intelligence solutions into new hospitals and other healthcare organizations. Their agency, King Fish Media[34], created this very cool 3D interactive mailer that included a role-specific brochure (for chief financial officers, chief information officers, and chief medical information officers—three different personas), an interactive book with video clips… and a drone! The personalized letter included a link to an account-specific URL. This package resulted in a lot of appointments. (See fig. 90 on next page)

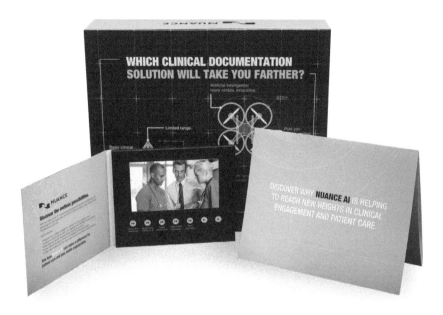

Figure 90. Interactive mailer

A few other examples of successful dimensional direct mail:

- Staples sent desktop gumball machines to prospects which cut through the clutter and produced many appointments for Staples sales reps.
- A direct marketing firm sent actual mailboxes with personalized messages inside to prospects. How many people aren't going to open a mailbox that they receive?

Some of these mailers can cost a few hundred dollars each to send out, so you'd only send them to large accounts that are worth the investment.

But good ideas can sometimes be inexpensive, too: the same firm that sent the mailboxes sent out cocktail napkins with hand-written notes before a conference inviting people to stop by for a "drink" at their booth. (It was a bottle of water.) This also worked well.

Okay, now you can buy a list

Many companies buy lists. Oh, the shame.

The inbound mantra is to build opt-in lists only. A bought list is not going to perform as well as a list that you build, but building a list that covers all potential customers may not even be possible in large markets. You may need to buy lists to hit the level of growth that your company wants.

List vendors tout databases of 300 million consumers in over 100 million households, and well over 10 million businesses. They offer dozens of ways to customize your list including location, birth month, number of children, interests and so on.

Companies typically supplement this first pass with consumer, or business, data from multiple third-party data brokers and use analytics to create segments and predict those most likely to buy.

Personalize

Every direct mail piece is personalized. You're printing a unique name and address on every envelope, and using the first name of the recipient in your direct mail is table stakes.

You can improve results, though, with highly personalized messages using Variable Data Printing (VDP).

With VDP you can personalize your mail with messages like:

- You bought X from us before, and this would go with it great! [Photo of suggested item]
- We appreciate that you donated $X in [month], but with the recent hurricanes we have to reach out and ask your support again. Could you please donate $Y now to support our disaster relief efforts? We'd really appreciate it.
- Thank you for signing up for information about our service. Here's a map to the service center in [city] closest to you [map of location]
- Here's your new membership card! [With the person's name, member since, and other data, and a membership renewal response card]

You could also personalize the envelope, making it much more likely that the person will open it. And pre-populate the response reply card with the person's information, making it faster and easier for them to respond to your offer.

Some retailers have gone as far as using their customers' buying history to create personalized brochures. Companies often use personalized landing pages and personalized URLs (PURLs) in their B2B programs.

To use VDP you supply your direct mail fulfillment house with a CSV file (comma separated value file exported from a spreadsheet) of information to plug into dynamic fields in your direct mail, and the supporting files, like images. You have to be careful to test the longest dynamic data that you're putting into your piece to make sure it fits and everything wraps properly.

If you're new to using VDP, talk it through with your direct mail house; they'll be happy to help you.

Using direct mail in politics

Direct mail has not declined in politics and cause marketing in the same way that it has in the catalog business; in fact, some estimates say that its use continues to increase. Perhaps this is because older people are the most reliable voters and avid consumers of direct mail.

Local politicians often send out visibility postcards that are little more than mailed yard signs, but better funded and more sophisticated campaigns use targeting and tactics that rival the largest retailers and credit card companies. The campaigns use all sorts of data related to demographics, psychographics, past voting behavior, occupation, magazines that they subscribe to, and so on to micro-target individuals who are likely to be supporters or persuadable, and save money by not targeting those unlikely to vote for their candidate or issue.

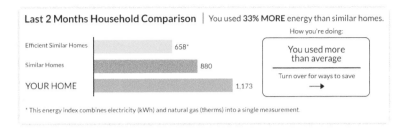

Last 2 Months Household Comparison │ You used **33% MORE** energy than similar homes.

How you're doing:

Efficient Similar Homes	658*
Similar Homes	880
YOUR HOME	1,173

You used more
than average

Turn over for ways to save
⟶

* This energy index combines electricity (kWh) and natural gas (therms) into a single measurement.

Figure 91. Utility bill with personalized social pressure

Like the electric company, campaigns have also found it effective to use personalized social pressure. Some send letters in plain envelopes (so they don't look like a fancy marketing campaign) to supporters, thanking them for voting in the past and encouraging them to do so again this year.

Tools for direct mail

Rather than managing your own tools, as you might with email, for direct mail you will probably want to work with a local printer and direct mail fulfillment firm.

Chapter 22

PRINT AND OUT OF HOME (OOH)

PRINT PUBLICATIONS HAVE TAKEN A tremendous hit over the past 20 years. Nonetheless, print continues to be an important part of many people's media diet in such forms as physical newspapers, magazines, newsletters, journals, theater playbills—even the program for the nearby high school musical (which could be good for promoting a local business). In fact, the number of magazines in the U.S. is more than 10% higher than in the early 2000s and near an all-time high.[117] (And many of these have digital versions, too.)

Print has a particular appeal for many people because it is tactile in a way that a tablet or smartphone is not. Images used in ads can be very high quality—higher resolution than on a screen—and the competition is not a click away.

The big rap on print advertising is that it's too expensive relative to the number of people that you reach. And it is not personally targetable or as trackable as digital, although as I'll discuss later it can be used for direct response advertising.

Unlike digital advertising, which is often programmatic, much of print is still bought directly. You may want to work with an experienced media buyer who can help you identify the best properties on which to advertise, and also has experience negotiating package deals and discounts. How do free ads in the digital newsletter in addition to your magazine ads sound to you?

Great print ad creative

Print advertising can be eye catching and thought provoking in a way that digital advertising still rarely is. And it can be used for direct response, similar to online ads. Here are some examples of great print creative. You don't need a big budget to be creative.

The Dallas Farmers Market played off of the look of the well-known McDonald's French fries to promote its fresh fruits and vegetables.[118]

Figure 92. Dallas Farmers Market branding print ad

The American Red Cross used a similarly simple, compelling image to encourage blood donors.

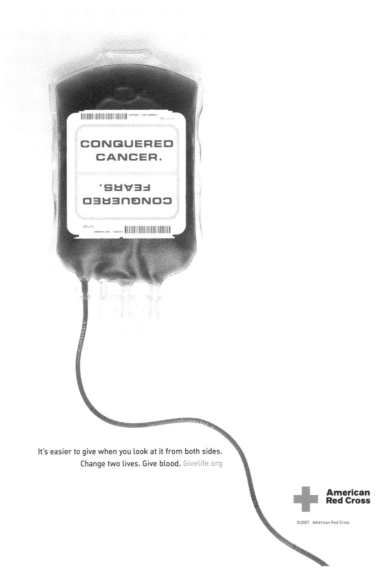

Figure 93. American Red Cross blood donor ad[119]

This ad from the Tufts Medical Center effectively uses storytelling to engage the audience in the work of the hospital.

Figure 94. Tufts Medical Center branding print ad

Not all ads are for branding, though. For decades print ads have been used for direct response, too. This ad from Cambridge Savings Bank promoting their retirement accounts with an offer of up to $700, part of an omni-channel campaign, is a good example.

Figure 95. Cambridge Savings Bank direct response print ad

Out of home advertising

Out of home (OOH) advertising includes billboards, ads on bus shelters, screens in elevators, wrapped buses, and transit ads (inside and outside buses, subways, and taxis).

While you can't target for intent or psychographics, you can often effectively target based on demographics. Certainly the demographics of people seeing a wrapped bus on 125th Street in Harlem (aka Martin Luther King Jr. Boulevard) are different from the people who see one in midtown Manhattan.

You may be able to create effective cross-channel messages by using OOH ads in the vicinity of an important trade show or other event.

Audi did a clever ad at the 2016 New York Auto Show when it provided free Wi-Fi access on a network named "328 reasons to choose A4".

Figure 96. Reebok interactive outdoor ad

Swedish agency Animal created an interactive outdoor ad for Reebok in Stockholm. Whoever ran past it at the pace of 17 kilometers per hour (roughly 10.5 miles per hour) or faster got a code for a free pair of running shoes.[120]

More and more OOH ads are digital, with a whole succession of ads running on a single billboard or other device. Consider the creative options for that!

One-to-one billboard advertising

Early in 2017 P&G Chief Brand Officer Marc Pritchard called out the digital advertising industry.

He wanted to know if half of P&G's ad dollars were going to ads being viewed by bots. And did the industry count a quarter of an ad showing as an impression? Half? For how long?

He wanted to know what's real in digital advertising.

He gave them until the end of 2017 to clean up issues around viewability or P&G, the largest advertiser in the world, would stop running digital ads.

Lamar Advertising, which has 325,000 billboards and other out of home displays in the U.S., responded with a billboard across the street from P&G's headquarters that said, in very large letters: HEY MARC, THIS AD IS REAL.

It was a response to Pritchard, and it was part of the OOH industry Feel The Real campaign[121] to promote the targetability and effectiveness of outdoor advertising.

Fun.

But 1:1 billboards are coming. In fact, they've arrived.

A few years ago Coca-Cola ran a campaign in Israel where people could download an app, put in some information, and then nearby electronic billboards would display personalized messages to them. Mini has also used personalized digital billboards.

In the future, billboard companies are likely to use cameras that quickly read license plates to identify cars and drivers and then, a block or two up the road, hit them with a personalized message.

Fearless Girl confronts the bull

In March, 2017, to mark International Woman's Day and promote its index fund of companies with gender-diverse senior leadership, State Street Global Advisors installed a statue of a "fearless girl" in a most iconic location—confronting the charging bull statue on Wall Street. SSGA also promoted the Fearless Girl with ads and social media posts, but more importantly the statue went viral on social and free media. A New York Times video report on Facebook had five million views in one day.

Figure 97. Fearless Girl statue facing Charging Bull [122]

This is what the volume of Google searches for SSGA that week looked like.

Figure 98. Google Trends for State Street Global Advisors

This was a huge PR windfall for SSGA, while also promoting their corporate cause. (The value was somewhat diminished a few months later when SSGA paid $5 million to settle a salary discrimination suit brought against it by women employees.[123])

Originally the statue only had a one week permit, but it was extended to a full year. In 2018 it is being moved to permanently face the New York Stock Exchange building.[124]

The charging bull statue itself was originally a work of guerilla art; the 7,100 pound statue was installed on December 15, 1989, and proved so popular that the city allowed it to remain.

Chapter 23

ANALYTICS AND ATTRIBUTION

"Without data, you're just another person with an opinion."

– W. Edwards Deming

IF YOU'RE NEW TO DIGITAL marketing, you'll likely be amazed at the amount of data that the tools collect and the analytics that they provide to help you optimize their performance.

In fact, it can quickly overwhelm you.

Consider just a few of the sources of data:

- website usage data from Google Analytics
- search ad data from Google AdWords and Bing
- email performance data
- landing page conversion data
- social media channel analytics
- ecommerce data

- cross-channel analytics and attribution models
- predictive analytics based on the above, and possibly thousands of third-party data sources

Now add in data from traditional marketing channels such as direct mail, call centers, print, TV and radio.

To use this tsunami of data and analytics tools effectively you need to focus on what's important and how to achieve it.

Campaign versus business goals

For most companies the primary business goals will be tied to top line revenue such as increases in qualified leads, opportunities and sales. Those are things that CEOs and CFOs usually care about.

To achieve those, though, as marketers you'll also have campaign metrics that you're optimizing, such as conversion rates and website page views. The C-suite likely won't be very interested in those, and they shouldn't be.

Consider, for example, the hierarchy of email marketing metrics:

1. Increased email opens and shares
2. Increased traffic to your website from email
3. More qualified leads from that email traffic
4. Increased revenue from leads that originated from email

The first two are campaign goals, the last two are business goals.

Increased email opens may indicate you have better Subject lines and content, and you're building a strong following for your emails, but if that doesn't produce more traffic to your website then perhaps you don't have enough, or the right, calls to action in the emails.

If the increased traffic doesn't produce more qualified leads then you, again, may have an issue with your offers or calls to action, or the website conversion experience.

If you're getting more qualified leads but that doesn't produce a good increase in revenue, then you may have an issue with the handoff of leads from marketing to sales, or the sales team may not have the content it needs to close the deals.

In the process of using your tools you'll have countless opportunities to optimize results. The important thing is to stay focused on what really is driving business results.

How to use data

At the top level you may have goals for your company's growth: you want to grow 5, 10, 20 or whatever percent in the next year. (People who write down their goals tend to be more successful in reaching them.)

With those sales goals in hand you can then work backwards to figure out your marketing goals and plans. Create an upside-down funnel:

- What is your sales team's close rate? If your sales team closes one in three proposals, then they need three times as many opportunities as final sales. What percentage of opportunities is marketing responsible for generating, and what percentage is sales responsible for?
- Continue that calculation back through your funnel:
  - How many of your sales qualified leads become opportunities?
  - How many of your marketing qualified leads become sales qualified leads?
  - How many new leads are qualified?
  - How many new marketing generated contacts become leads?

From this data you should be able to determine how many new contacts and leads marketing needs to generate to hit corporate sales goals.

You can make a similar calculation for ecommerce sites, and for B2C and retail companies.

Once you have these target funnel numbers you can work on the programs that will generate those new contacts and leads, move them through the pipeline, and help sales close them.

You may start with a hypothesis: Email generated X new quali-fied leads last year. We need X plus 25% from email this year. We can achieve that by (1) increasing our list size, (2) changing the frequency of the emails, (3) having more effective offers and calls to action, (4) improving the landing page and conversion experience, or (5) some combination of those and other factors (subject lines, email copy, etc.). Then you can test each of these to reach your goals.

Sometimes you will find that a particular channel or campaign simply isn't going to produce the results that you need. That is valu-able information, too; everything is an experiment. Thomas Edison's team tested 10,000 materials before finding the one that would work for the light bulb filament. He said, "I have not failed. I have just found 10,000 ways that won't work."

Persist. Keep experimenting. Keep track of everything. And if you have a valuable product or service, you will find the best channels for generating new business for it.

Marketing attribution

In this omni-channel world where you need to connect with your customers throughout their buying experience, attribution models help you determine the relative importance of the various marketing channels toward the final sale.

There are many marketing attribution models. Let's look at the pros and cons of three.[125]

Last click/interaction

Let's say that a person clicks on one of your search ads, comes to your website, and buys something. With the last click model, you give 100% credit for the sale to the search ads.

However, this is probably not very accurate. The person may have had several interactions with your brand before actually buying. They may have visited the website a few times, read reviews of your prod-ucts on review sites, watched videos on YouTube, and so on. They may have been interested in your product for years. But with the last click model, none of that counts.

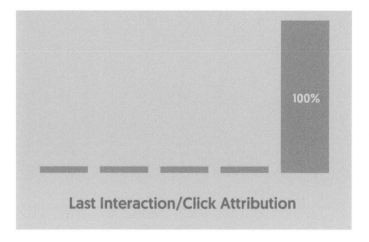

Figure 99. Last click attribution

Despite these problems, the last click model is the most commonly used for one simple reason: it's the easiest. Companies may have the data for a last click attribution; it's much more difficult to track an individual through all of their interactions with your brand on multiple devices that lead up to a sale.

First click/interaction
The first click model gives credit to marketing or sales for their contribution of qualified leads to the pipeline. This may be an especially useful model in B2B companies with a long sales cycle and many members on the buying team in which the sales team will be ultimately responsible for closing the deal. (See fig. 100 on next page)

First click may also be the only option for a company that sells through distributors or dealers and doesn't have insight into which leads are eventually closed and turn into revenue.

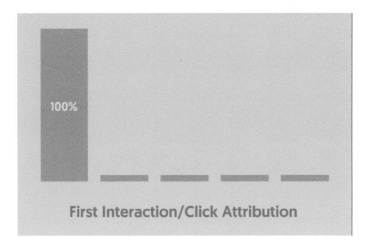

Figure 100. First click attribution

Multi-channel attribution

Multi-channel attribution models are the ideal. Time decay is one version of a multi-channel attribution model. It gives a larger weight to the most recent actions but doesn't entirely disregard earlier actions like the last click model does.

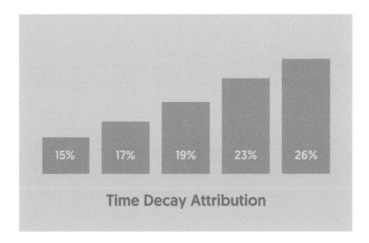

Figure 101. Time decay attribution

Multi-channel models present many challenges. The first is the question of identity: how to track individuals across many devices and interactions. You also need a large amount of data to be able to analyze it effectively and tease out actionable insights.

You may want to start with a simpler model and over time move toward a multi-channel model.

Geo-targeted testing

Geo-targeted testing is a different way to measure the effectiveness of particular channels and campaigns. A company operating nationally may test in just two or three cities and measure the increase in brand awareness and sales in those cities to decide if it's worth it to take the campaign national.

What's a lead or sale worth?

A key metric for marketers is the customer acquisition cost (CAC).

The CAC is easy to calculate. Simply take all of the sales and marketing costs and divide them by new customers. So on the most basic level if you spent $10,000 on sales and marketing and gained 10 new customers, your CAC would be $1,000.

It gets more complex when you start to calculate CAC by channel—remember the issue with the attribution models—and the value of those new customers.

CAC for direct sales, distributors, dealers and online channels may all vary.

And your margins will likely be different by channel, too. For example, a retailer may find that selling online is less expensive than selling in a traditional store. (Or the opposite may be true: in the store, there are little or no picking, packing, and shipping costs. And the building may have been paid for 20 years ago.) Software companies have certainly found that selling SaaS software that they deliver online is far less expensive than selling boxes at retail.

Finally, you need to consider if you need to make a profit on every purchase or if you will be basing your strategy on the lifetime value of the customer.

Reportedly the company that won the $2.68 billion contract to operate Boston's commuter rail system spent over $4 million to win the deal.[126] However, if the economic value of a customer is through a long string of follow-on sales, then you'll need to calculate the LTV over many years—or even a lifetime. The classic example is companies selling razors, as described in chapter 11.

SaaS companies typically calculate that they need a LTV of at least three times CAC to operate profitably. That LTV:CAC ratio will be different for every industry depending on some of the factors that I mentioned above.

Work with your executive team to establish acceptable CAC metrics for your company.

 Tools for analytics

Analytics tools are built into virtually all digital marketing platforms.

InsightSquared provides sales analytics based on CRM data.

Databox integrates data from dozens of sources and provides dashboards, alerts, and updates on performance relative to KPIs.

Adobe Analytics, Bizible, BrightFunnel, and Full Circle Insights provide attribution modeling.

Chapter 24

BUILDING YOUR TEAM

THERE IS PERHAPS NO MORE common saying in business than "our people are what make us great." That is certainly true when it comes to marketing. No matter how much marketing technology you implement, or data you acquire, the difference between failure, meh, and great success is always going to be who is using them and how.

The quill pen is one of the easiest writing devices to use, but it was how Shakespeare used it that made all the difference.

When I asked CMO Jeanne Hopkins, who was interviewed in chapter 3, "You've got all these issues around the search marketing channel, online advertising, social media marketing. And then you've got offline things: you've got print, and direct mail, and radio, TV, and everything. So where do you start?"

Without hesitation she answered, "So that is a phenomenal question. And I think you have to start with the team."

So invest the time and effort to hire the right people, and give them the support they need to succeed.

The skills needed

The marketing team today needs a wider range of skills than ever before. Many of the skills are new, but they don't replace earlier ones. They are additive.

Marketers have always needed to be good at:

1. Understanding the customer's motivators and emotions
2. Planning how to reach customers with messages
3. Writing and developing creative
4. Graphic design
5. Events
6. Project management

A modern marketing team also needs expertise (occasionally or always) in:

1. Website design and development
2. Conversion rate optimization
3. Email marketing
4. Marketing automation
5. Remarketing
6. Account based marketing
7. Online events
8. Analytics

And that's just for the center of the Bullseye!

In the second phase you'll need to add skills in search advertising and other intent-based programs. And in Phase 3 add skills in social media, deeper content marketing, display ads, events, other channels, and attribution modeling.

Some team members will come to marketing from the traditional creative-first side, whereas others will be much more comfortable and experienced with technology and data. It's important that you create an environment of mutual respect. Both have much to contribute, and for your marketing programs to succeed people with both backgrounds—and blends of the two—must feel comfortable and respected when contributing.

Staff, agency or consultants?

Unless you, or someone on your team, have very deep, modern marketing experience, it should be clear by now that you shouldn't attempt to do all this, or even lead all this, on your own. You don't want to spend months and months trying to learn what others have taken years to learn—and repeating their early mistakes. Hire either a head of marketing or an experienced marketing consultant to get you started.

It's common now for companies that are just ramping up their marketing programs to use an interim head of marketing for 6-12 months, or longer, to develop and begin to implement their strategy. This may not necessarily even be a full-time person. In a small company, a one-quarter or one-third time person may be able to produce results, build confidence in the program, and help hire a permanent person to head the effort.

Initially, you may not want to add many people to your headcount and so may want to use more part-time consultants. Many experienced consultants are available in most major cities. You also can find experienced people with marketing skills on Upwork, Guru, and similar sites. Be sure to go with people with excellent reviews by many clients; let others check out the newbies. You can ask people questions before you hire them, and how helpful they are in this stage may predict what they will be like to work with, too.

You may want to keep creative positions, especially writing, in-house so that the people doing them can learn more about your customers and offerings and improve their work over time. As your program scales, you may need full-time employees, contractors or agencies to manage specialized programs such as managing search ads or large scale email programs.

Build a great culture

Management guru Peter Drucker once wrote, "Culture eats strategy for breakfast." And it's true. The best plans will go nowhere if your people aren't behind them.

You may not be able to change your company culture overnight, but you should be able to help build a great culture in your group. Some of the elements of a great culture include:

Values

The company should have values beyond "make a profit." Let your people know why you exist and what you plan to achieve. Many people care more about the Why than the What.

For example, Apple is about more than creating computers or electronics. Steve Jobs' vision included developing tech products that are easier to use and more elegant. Walmart's Values include:

- Service to the Customer
- Respect for the Individual
- Strive for Excellence
- Act with Integrity[127]

These values should be incorporated into your marketing narrative, too.

Collaboration and Camaraderie

- Hire people who not just can work together, but enjoy working with others. I can remember just one time when I got a bad reference for a potential hire. I asked his former boss, "Would you hire him again?" and, after a pause, she said, "No, no we wouldn't." When I asked why, she said, "Because what he really wants to do is sit off by himself and write code all day, and we need people who can work in a team." So did I; I didn't hire him.
- This camaraderie isn't simply "let's play foosball" or "let's get a drink after work," although those have their place. I'm talking

about people who respect one another and work together to achieve common goals.

- Here are a few possible interview question:
  - ○ Describe a scenario where schedules shift and the applicant won't be able to meet all of their deadlines, then ask them what they would do in that situation. Don't accept "I'd work harder"; it's not going to be possible to get everything done. The answer that you're looking for is something like, "I'd go to my boss, explain the situation, and ask how they want to prioritize the work." That's the answer of a team player.
  - ○ Ask who was the best boss they ever had and why. Their answer to the "why" may tell you if they are going to work well with their boss at your company.
  - ○ Ask about the best workplace teamwork that they ever experienced, and what made that team successful.

Learning

All companies need people who are committed to life-long learning, and that's especially important in marketing. In your job interview, you could ask what they are studying and how they go about keeping up with advances in their field. Develop a culture in your team in which failure is not only accepted but expected—zero failures means that you're not trying anything new. But people need to learn from their failures; what isn't accepted is failing in the same way twice. Your company should also support learning with stipends to take courses or attend conferences.

Responsibility

You want people who take initiative and responsibility.

Here's a possible interview question related to responsibility: Ask the person to describe something that they did—in or out of work—that they're especially proud of. Then ask them to describe something they did that failed and why it failed. (Don't accept, "I can't think of a failure that I've had.") In their answer, they should describe, without you prompting it, what they did wrong to contribute to or produce that failure. If instead, they blame the failure on co-workers and clients, that's a bad sign.

Your company may have other values than these. Make sure that your policies and incentives align with your values, and that you look for people for your team who appreciate and support those values, too.

Interview with Scott Brinker: Assembling a modern marketing team

Scott Brinker is one of the leading proponents of the "chief marketing technologist" role in companies. He founded and heads up the MarTech Conference. He was co-founder and CTO at ion interactive at the time of this interview, and in 2017 became Vice President of Platform Ecosystem at HubSpot.

Scott: Marketers have a simple mission (laughs): we have to be where the audience is. We have to give the audience what they want. So, since customers have gone digital, marketers must too. And everything digital revolves around software. The web itself is software. Google, Facebook, Twitter—these are software programs, and marketers need to be adept at using them.

But then there's also a huge collection of dedicated marketing software—the software that marketers use inside their organizations to produce and deploy digital content and experiences and to listen to and measure activity in these digital channels. These tools give us tremendous power. They give us unprecedented visibility into our audience and let us leverage those insights to craft amazing customer experiences. If there's one fundamental way in which technology has changed the nature of marketing, it's this: marketing has shifted from the business of communications to the business of experiences.

Louis: I know a lot of people in marketing who think of this as utterly changing the way that 90% of marketers think. To be very technical *and* to be very analytical *and* to incorporate the data into your decision-making is not something that a lot of marketers are comfortable with.

Scott: I agree. There is a whole new set of skills that need to be incorporated into the marketing team. But I would stress that these are additive skills. They don't eliminate the need for traditional marketing skills such as a great eye for design and a great ear for copy. We still need inspired, creative talent to imagine and produce compelling content and experiences that really touch people. Use technology to deliver those experiences. Use data and analytics to learn which experiences resonate best. But at the same time, recognize that there has never been a greater opportunity for creative people to affect the world around them.

Louis: So how much tech does a traditional marketer need to learn, and how much data analysis, and so forth to work in this world?

Scott: It's a great question. We can think about it at two different levels: individuals and their personal career paths, and then the overall organization, the marketing department as a whole. For marketing as a whole, it's important that you collectively have all the necessary capabilities to be able to operate in the modern digital world. That means that you've got people who are producing great creative. You've got people who are leveraging technology to get that creative out in the world, in the right places at the right time. You've got data-savvy people who are analyzing those customer experiences and broader data sources from the market to help inform the evolution of the marketing strategy. So you need all of those capabilities in the aggregate.

However, I don't think that every single person needs to have high marks in every single one of those categories. It's just asking too much. The CMO's mission is to assemble a team that collectively covers all those bases and is effective in how they work together.

These are big changes. It's a very different kind of marketing organization and, frankly, a very different kind of business organization. Be prepared to evolve your organizational structure, your business processes, and even your culture. The technology itself is the easy part.

How Jeff Bezos changed the culture of The Washington Post

In October 2013, Jeff Bezos bought the unprofitable Washington Post.

Within three years its Web traffic had doubled, subscriptions were way up, and their smaller staff was posting far more online content than The New York Times and even BuzzFeed. And they were profitable. Licensing their new, speedy content management system to other newspapers was being considered as an auxiliary source of revenue, similar to how Amazon Web Services (AWS) produces revenue for Amazon.

Central to this turnaround was a change in the culture of The Post. It's very hard to change a culture.

CIO Shailesh Prakash and Director of Product Joey Marburger offered many insights into how the company changed in a Columbia Journalism Review interview.[128]

Culture: (Marburger) It's been three years since Jeff bought us. I'd say we'd probably be where we are maybe five to seven years from now. And who knows if we would've done half of what we've gotten done. But Jeff didn't just reach down to the newsroom and say here's a brand-new culture, here's a bunch of things you should do, here's what Amazon does, so you should copy it. The sheer thought of him spread throughout the company. Overnight, we thought there wasn't much we couldn't do.

Compensation: (Prakash) The number one criteria that grows our compensation used to be operating income. Did you or did you not hit the operating income target that was agreed upon at the beginning of the year? It was crystal clear whether you got your bonus or not. We were all in it together. When revenue was slowing and operating income is the target, then what do you do? You cut costs. There's no other way out.

When Jeff bought us, within about six months, he threw that out. Now there are three other criteria. It's basically: How fast do you move? It's very subjective. The second one is that there are no sacred cows, to push experimentation. The third thing is debate, but commit. So you can argue all you want, but once we agree, then there's no undermining. Those are the three things that now very subjectively drive the compensation.

Technology: (Prakash) It's been proven over and over again that speed matters. In some industries, the correlation is more direct, like in retail. You have a site and you change nothing except it becomes much faster, you see the sales change.

If you're used to a lot of other slow mobile sites out there, specifically news, and you come to us and it's significantly faster, you may be more likely to come to us on a regular basis. And you're more likely—which we see already in the data—to consume more content, hit the subscription meter faster, consume more ads, you name it.

User Experience: (Prakash) It was Bezos who brought this up. He said that when Amazon made the Kindle, they didn't think, 'Let's get rid of the book and come up with a new way to read books.' Their whole approach was, 'How can we keep everything that's fantastic about a book and also add in the gifts of digital?'

Market focus: (Prakash) We had for a very long time a tagline that said 'For and About Washington.' One of the big changes and explicit changes in strategy has been to go after a national and international audience. One of the things we've tried to do is to look at platforms we might be able to over-index on to get there faster. Take Facebook. One in seven humans visits Facebook every day. It's not possible to grow nationally and internationally if you say, 'I will send them 10 articles.' If we want to grow nationally and internationally it is really not an option to just ignore that platform.

Build a diverse team

I already mentioned the diverse skill set needed on a modern market-ing team. You should also strive to have a team that's diverse in other ways. If you're not fully taking advantage of the skills and potential contributions of women, people of color and older workers, you're missing out on well over half of the labor force. That's tying more than one arm behind your back.

When "blind" auditions were introduced for orchestras, where the performer sits behind a screen so their gender, race, and appearance are hidden, the number of women winning competitions for open seats dramatically increased.[129] In a study of thousands of compa-nies,[130] those with a significant number of women in top management tended to be much more profitable.

Diversity is likely to bring in knowledge and positive attitudes that a homogeneous culture doesn't, and is more likely to make a company better able to take advantage of what everyone can offer. A diverse workforce will have greater insights into the increasingly diverse cus-tomer base, too.

I once heard a simple formula for hiring. When you're hiring there are only three questions that you really need to answer:

- Can the person do the job? (Do they have the skills, experience, etc.?)
- Do they want to do the job? (Are they enthusiastic about this job and your company, or are they just looking for a paycheck?)
- Will they fit in?

And of the three, the last question is the most important.

The last question is the most important when it comes to diver-sity, too, because having a narrow definition of "fitting in" is the difference between a homogeneous and a diverse workforce.

If you consciously or unconsciously define "fitting in" as people of the same gender, race, class, and age—and similar non-work interests (Go Cubs!)—you will be severely limited in your hiring options. But if you define it as people who share your team's values and goals and skills, then the future is yours.

Hire slow, fire fast

At my marketing agency, I started out hiring fast and firing slowly. Over the dozen years that I ran it I learned to reverse that. Many business leaders believe in "hire slow, fire fast," too.

Take your time in hiring. Do multiple interviews including several people on your team. Check the applicant's references. Give them tests, if appropriate. Be thorough. Get it right. And admit your mistakes quickly when you get it wrong, terminate the person and get the right person in.

That doesn't mean that if the new hire makes one mistake they're out the door—unless it's a *really* bad mistake. You can give them two or three strikes before they're out. But explain to them if they do mess up how you do things at your company and what your expectations are. Also, praise what they're doing well. Famed UCLA basketball coach John Wooden said, "I can't begin to coach until the player does something right."

But if it's clear that they're not right for your company, then act fast. You don't have time for underperformers, and your team will appreciate it. A players want to work with other A players.

Chapter 25

THE AGILE MARKETING METHODOLOGY

IN THIS BOOK I'VE OUTLINED a whole new approach to marketing that wouldn't have made sense in the past when the Big Idea and big campaigns dominated marketing. Today we are much more focused on creating hundreds of small pieces of content—personalized emails, videos, blog posts, tweets, infographics, case studies, ROI calculators, website updates, and on and on. Then we need to continuously monitor this content and optimize these programs based on customer reactions, and be aware of—and possibly respond to—the moves that competitors are making. Often opportunities arise that we only have a few days or weeks to take advantage of.

We can't afford to take weeks to create a master plan and months to execute it. We need to be more agile.

In 2012, taking inspiration from the agile software development movement, a group of marketers led by John Cass and Jim Ewel (who is interviewed below) came together for what they called SprintZero and created the Agile Marketing Manifesto[131].

It read:

1. Validated learning over opinions and conventions
2. Customer focused collaboration over silos and hierarchy
3. Adaptive and iterative campaigns over Big-Bang campaigns
4. The process of customer discovery over static prediction
5. Flexible vs. rigid planning
6. Responding to change over following a plan
7. Many small experiments over a few large bets

It's worth stopping for a few minutes and reading each of those seven points again. Then read them again and take some time to consider how each can impact how you do marketing.

It's a manifesto that focuses on the customer– and feedback from them—at the center of marketing, data over opinion, a responsive and flexible attitude, and experimentation.

Agile intends to lower the risk in projects by increasing the ability of the team to respond to changes in the market and project requirements, and by being closer to the customer.

Many marketing teams who adopt agile marketing report being more productive: they increase throughput, get campaigns to market faster, and improve their business results. Employees also report improved job satisfaction with the agile method. It's perfectly suited for the Bullseye approach.

Agile marketing is a philosophy. Agile marketing practitioners have tended to adopt one of two methodologies for implementing it: Scrum or Kanban. Each method has certain practices and tools—the sprint, daily team stand-up meetings, and Kanban boards—but all of those are mutable. Or can be combined in unique ways. Just as all companies are different, each team needs to find or develop the form of agile that works best for it.

Scrum

Agile software development inspired the agile marketing movement, and Scrum has been adopted from the software world, as well. Some product development teams were using Scrum in the mid-1980s. (The term "scrum" comes from rugby; it is a means of restarting play in which a large number of players join closely together to try to move the ball.)

A key organizing unit for Scrum is a series of two-to-four week **sprints** in which the team works to achieve specific goals and tasks by the end of the sprint. The length of the sprint cannot be changed once it starts, nor can tasks be added to the sprint.

At the start of the sprint, the team holds a sprint planning meeting to determine the goals and the tasks for each team member for that sprint and to get buy-in from the team.

The team usually chooses the tasks from a product backlog of user stories. A **product owner** creates these user stories for the team; Scrum teams typically have one product owner, and this role is not combined with the Scrum master (below).

These user stories are customer-centric and include the Actor, Action and Achievement, such as:

- As a [particular persona] I want to be able to [learn specific information] to [understand product differentiators].
- As a potential end-user, I want to see a software product demo to understand how the user interface compares to other software.
- As a car buyer interested in sustainability I want to learn the carbon footprint of this automobile.
- As a person planning a trip to Croatia, I want to find the best seafood restaurants.

User stories also include context for the request and acceptance criteria for the task. Some criteria are objective—this landing page will increase leads by X%, or this blog post will get Y shares. Some criteria are more subjective.

The sprint planning meeting, and the entire sprint, is facilitated by a **Scrum master**. Unlike a traditional manager, though, the Scrum master is not ultimately responsible for the outcome of the sprint, the team is.

The Scrum master and product owner help the team decide which product backlog items to undertake for the upcoming sprint and identify what tasks are necessary to complete them.

During the sprint, Scrum teams start the day with 15-minute standing meetings. The three questions that each person answers in **the daily standup** are:

1. What did I do yesterday?
2. What will I do today?
3. Do I need help with anything that's blocking me from accomplishing today's tasks?

This keeps the team members focused on their goals for this sprint, and collaborating on how to achieve them.

At the end of each sprint, the team holds two meetings: the sprint review and retrospective.

In the **sprint review,** the completed work is presented to stakeholders, and the team and stakeholders review what they accomplished and discuss what should be worked on next.

In the **sprint retrospective,** the Scrum master and team review the last sprint and discuss how to improve their process going forward, and any changes in the process needed for the next sprint.

Wash, rinse and repeat.

Kanban

Kanban, which comes from the Japanese for "sign," originated in manufacturing at Toyota in the late 1940s and has been applied to many other industries since then.

Right from the get-go, Kanban is different from Scrum in that it does not have the start-stop rhythm of two-to-four week sprints.

Kanban is a continuous flow process, and when one item is completed the team member goes on to the next. Consequently, it also doesn't have the sprint planning, review, and retrospective meetings that are central to Scrum.

As in Scrum, Kanban tasks can be created as user stories which are then put into the backlog on a Kanban board. Kanban boards are central to the method and are also used by some Scrum teams. (There are physical and software Kanban boards.)

The simplest Kanban board has three columns or lists:

- To do
- Doing
- Done

More complex boards may have far more lists representing the stages of a process, such as this one for blog posts:

- Conceive
- Research
- Write
- Edit
- Design
- Post, amplify and promote

Cards aren't moved forward until they are considered as good as possible or, as would be said in manufacturing, error-free. In the blog post example, a writer would not move a post into editing unless they felt it was correct regarding content, spelling, and grammar—ready for publication.

And each list has a defined limit. For example, the editing list may only be able to accommodate four pieces at a time. If the list is already full, but another post is ready, it is not moved onto the edit list until one of those four already there is completed and moved on to design.

So Kanban is much less structured than Scrum, with fewer new roles and meetings. It is a process of continuous delivery, and the continuous improvement of an existing process. It may not be as radical of a change as Scrum is for most organizations.

These are short descriptions of two complex methodologies. Entire books have been written about each.

And teams don't necessarily need to choose between Scrum and Kanban. They can choose the aspects of each that work best for them. The important thing is to create a process that adheres to those agile principles that works for you.

Agile isn't necessarily applicable to everything. If you have a big product launch or website redesign, those may need more traditional "waterfall" or other planning approaches.

While agile may seem like a relatively simple process to implement with a small team, it actually affects relations throughout the company—such as with product managers and sales—who need to be involved in creating new user stories and reviewing marketing's work product. There may be some hiccups in transition, as there are with any change, but in the long run agile can help create smoother, more productive and successful working relationships.

Interview with Jim Ewel: How to implement agile marketing

Jim Ewel was one of the co-conveners of the inaugural agile marketing SprintZero in 2012. He is the president of AgileMarketing.net and provides agile training and coaching for companies. He is a former VP of Marketing at Microsoft and other companies, and a former CEO.

Louis: Agile can sometimes sound very reactive. Are you eschewing strategy and planning entirely? What's the balance?

Jim: It's a good point. That's one of the key things: the balance. Instead of writing yearly plans, the longest plans that any agile marketers use tend to be on the order of a quarter. They might say, "Okay, over the next two to three quarters here are some things that we think we're going to do. But you know how quickly things change, even over a year. The things that we forecast out over a year are our best guess right now, but we're going to re-examine those plans on a regular basis. At least once a quarter."

The second thing is we want to make plans that are relevant and drive action, not ones that get presented at meetings and then get stuck in a drawer the next day and then no one ever takes a look at them. What are plans that actually drive our priorities? They are shorter, more actionable, more user-centric and user-focused. And we need to be able to change those plans very quickly. The world just demands that anymore.

Louis: So we're talking in the second week of January. And this is the time of year when a lot of CEOs and the C-suites are saying, "These are our goals for the year. And marketing: we want to increase revenue by X percent. And we need to have your budget to do that." They have to do something beyond the quarter.

Jim: People say that. But the truth is that businesses all the time change their budgets within the year. If they don't make their number do they still spend as much as they were planning to do on the year's budget? Not most businesses that I know. If they totally exceed their revenue target or they do a merger, or things like that, do they modify their budget for that? Absolutely—they do. So what companies can do is to say, "Alright, we're going to have an approximate yearly budget that is based on this kind of revenue plan. But we are upfront declaring that we're going to re-examine this budget on a quarterly basis. And we're going to adjust it based on how we're doing to plan." Budgeting can be adjusted throughout the year.

Louis: In the past I kind of equated agile with Scrum, and standups and sprints. And now Kanban seems to be growing in popularity.

What do you see as the major differences between Scrum and Kanban?

Jim: In terms of what I see as the difference, I see Scrum as being particularly well-suited to marketing efforts where the team has a good ability to control their work on a scheduled basis. So the classic example is content production. Producing marketing content, anything from blog posts to videos to podcasts to whatever, is somewhat similar to producing software code. It's producing something. And Scrum is really well suited to doing content marketing, content production, on a calendar basis and so forth.

On the other hand, if you look at other groups where they don't have as much control over what comes through the door—like social media or events, because things happen in real time—they're better suited to Kanban. It's a more continuous flow of work, a continuous change in priorities. Someone finishes something and they go to the next task, whatever that is. They're optimizing for that steady flow of things.

I think most teams are figuring out what works for them and for their organization, and mixing and matching some of the practices within Scrum and Kanban. Whether you call that "Scrumban" or you just call that "I've just done my own thing," I don't particularly care. But that is what I see a lot of teams doing.

I teach them both. So I start with Kanban, and I do that because Kanban starts with where you are now. It doesn't require you to organize in different teams or that you have these roles like scrum master and product owner and all that. In some ways, it's the easiest transition. So I start with Kanban. Then I teach them Scrum.

Louis: What are the biggest issues that you see marketing groups having when they move to Agile?

Jim: There are two big issues. The first is management and how management learns to work in an Agile environment. So, in my opinion, no Agile project can succeed without management support. So I won't even go in and do an engagement unless management explicitly says, "Yes, we support this. We want this to happen." So that's the first thing that has to happen.

Louis: So that's the C-suite? What do you mean by management?

Jim: Depends on the size of the organization and what they're doing. So for small and medium-sized organizations, yes, I'd take that all the way up to the C-suite. For larger organizations, no; it's somewhere at the chief marketing officer/VP of marketing—that level.

So that's the first thing, but the second thing is the difference between doing Agile and being Agile. You can do Agile, and by that I mean that you're holding daily standups, running Sprints, writing user stories, and that will improve communication and it might improve throughput a little, and that's fine. You might see gains in productivity on the order of 20% or more. That's certainly nothing to sneeze at, but the greater gains come from being Agile. By that, I mean achieving an Agile mindset. You're constantly testing and learning, creating marketing that is focused on and personalized for customers, you're using marketing technology effectively, you're engaging employees, you're allowing people at every level to contribute. That can lead to gains on the order of 200% or more. Adopting that Agile mindset takes work and it takes change—changes both at the management level and at the individual team level.

Louis: What is the greatest success story that you've seen when a company adopts agile?

Jim: There are many. One that comes to mind is Northern Arizona University. I taught them Agile Marketing almost eight years ago. They published an article about their experience with Agile in one of the University publications, and they credited Agile with a 400% improvement in their marketing throughput. They were getting four times as much work done with the same people. They also said that it saved them money because they weren't having to hire contractors to get last minute work done.

Tools for agile marketing

Whiteboard and Post-It Notes: This is the basic version of a Kanban board.

Trello, Asana, and Mingle are Kanban board software.

Smartsheet is project management software with gantt, calendar and card (Kanban) views.

Wrike is project management software.

Chapter 26

CREATING AN OMNI-CHANNEL CUSTOMER EXPERIENCE

OMNI-CHANNEL MARKETING—BEING PRESENT ON ALL of the channels where your customers are hanging out– is critical today. In just the simplest example, product research often starts on mobile and then moves to desktop; people may move back and forth between mobile, desktop, tablets and in-person for some time. Or consider the retailer who has a customer in the store ready to buy, but that customer is going to do further research on their mobile phone before making that in-store purchase. Or the customer who is "showrooming"—looking at the item in the store before buying it online.

In more complex business purchases the customer may consume information on the vendor's website, social media, review sites, blogs, YouTube, trade shows, podcasts and other sources before making the purchase—a decision made in concert with several other people who are also consuming many pieces of information.

The omni-channel approach that Bullseye Marketing will lead you to ultimately provides for consistent experiences and messages across all channels and interactions with the customer. They can interact with the company in the way that is most convenient for them and know that what they do on one device will be reflected if they switch to another.

One version of the Domino's pizza home page lists many of the ways that you can order from them.

Figure 102. Domino's Pizza home page

Consider all of the potential media interactions that an airline could have with customers:

- TV ads to build brand awareness
- search ads when people are searching for airfares to/from cities that the airline flies to
- reservations website
- third-party reservation sites
- email and app reminders for an upcoming flight reservation
- digital check-in a day or two before the flight
- text notifications of flight delays or other significant news

- Eticket on app or phone
- in-flight entertainment and Wi-Fi
- in-flight magazine with articles promoting other locations that the airline flies to
- posting of the experience with the airline to social media, and how the airline responds to that

The full omni-channel customer experience with the airline goes far beyond those media interactions to include

- ticket/bag check kiosks and people
- boarding process at the gate
- flight attendants and how they handle the boarding and safety talk (Southwest uses humor)
- the in-flight drink and meal service
- on-time arrivals
- deplaning and getting bags (for those who checked them) at the destination
- how passengers are rebooked if a flight is canceled

Each of these is a customer touchpoint: a moment of interactions between the customer and the airline when the customer has an expectation and will come away from the touchpoint feeling delighted, satisfied, or annoyed. Some of these touchpoints are more critical than others and can make or break the relationship.

Over time you can build a rich omni-channel program that not only gets the right message to the right person at the right time, but also provides them with an excellent experience in all of their interactions with your company.

Nothing that I've written in this book should be taken to denigrate the Phase 3 programs. It's not that advertising or inbound or social media or content marketing are always ineffective; in the long run they may be tremendously valuable. Rather, the Bullseye approach outlines a way to prioritize the least expensive, fastest programs for a company to start with, to get quick wins, build support, and then move on to longer range programs.

Ultimately do everything that works for your business.

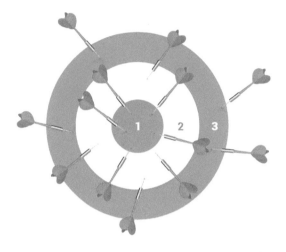

Figure 103. The omni-channel Bullseye approach

Chapter 27

EXECUTE!

"Genius is 1% inspiration and 99% perspiration."

– Thomas Edison

IT'S ONE THING TO CREATE a marketing strategy based on an understanding of your customer personas and touchpoints, an informed media mix, and constant optimization based on feedback and data. It's another thing entirely to execute on that.

Many marketing teams start off with the best of intentions but get distracted along the way by shiny objects, competitor efforts—or a simple lack of discipline.

It's easy to be creative and have new ideas, especially when we see so much inspiring creative around us every day. It's much harder to do the day-in-day-out work, stay focused, and make a marketing program successful.

When marketing programs fail, most often it is due to a lack of consistent, day-to-day execution.

So do your homework, plan, be creative, and then stick to it.

Execute.

Chapter 28

MIC DROP

Figure 104. Dropped mic[132]

DEVELOPING A 12-MONTH ACTION PLAN

YOU CAN USE THIS FORM to develop an action plan for your company. You may also decide that not all of these programs are appropriate for you. Focus and execute.

Program	Notes	Starting Month
Researching customers and developing personas		
Developing customer journey maps		
Improving your customer experience		
Selling more to existing customers		
Improving website experience		
Optimizing conversions		
Email marketing		
Remarketing		
Marketing and sales collaboration		
Search advertising		
Using third-party intent data		
Ramping up content marketing		
Tracking engagement with your content		

Program	Notes	Starting Month
Search engine optimization		
Video		
Social media		
PR and influencer marketing		
Events and trade shows		
Online display ads		
Direct mail		
Print and OOH		
Others		

ABOUT THE AUTHOR

LOUIS GUDEMA HELPS COMPANIES FROM MIT startups to the Global 2000 increase their revenue by focusing on the fastest, least expensive and most cost-effective programs to get more leads and sales. He is the founder and president of marketing consultancy **revenue & associates** and previously founded and grew a marketing agency into one of the top three or four in its national market before a successful exit. Between his two companies he was vice president of business development at two mid-sized marketing agencies, successfully closing many enterprise accounts.

Louis speaks frequently on marketing and business at regional and national events, and has written for such leading business sites as The Harvard Business Review, MarketingProfs, IDG Connect Marketer, Chiefmartec, TechTarget, VentureBeat, Content Marketing Institute, and Econsultancy.

ACKNOWLEDGEMENTS

LIKE ANYONE WRITING ABOUT MARKETING, I owe a debt to the countless people who have gone before to create and advance the profession, and I could not possibly list all that I have been influenced by over the years—including many outstanding clients. I do want to thank a few people who were especially helpful in the creation of this book.

Scott Brinker, Ann Handley, David Greenwood, Steve Lishansky, David Reske, Mari Ryan, and Bill Schley were generous in sharing their experiences as authors, especially around how to promote a book.

I appreciate the time that the interview subjects in this book took to be interviewed and to review and edit their transcripts: Scott Brinker and Ann Handley (again), James Carbary, Gini Dietrich, Jim Ewel, Evan Kirstel, Jeanne Hopkins, and Zorian Rotenberg.

Since the book is intended to educate those with less experience – whether in a class or working in the field—having examples is crucial. Many thanks to the dozens of companies who permitted me to use their materials, and I'm thanking in advance for their understanding those companies whose materials I used under fair use.

A shoutout to people who read and gave feedback on parts of the book as it was being developed, especially Geoff Bock and Greg Collins. I didn't follow all of your suggestions, but your ideas were very helpful.

Thanks to those people on the Advance Praise pages who provided promotional quotes—Ron Bloom, the enthusiastic David Maffei, the always-helpful Jeanne Hopkins and Jill Rowley, Michael Brenner, Peter Cohen, Kim Wallace, Mike Wittenstein, Mari Ryan, and Steve Lishansky. I want to thank my book launch team who have been so supportive in reading the book in advance, providing their online reviews—good, bad, and ugly—and promoting it via social media.

I wanted a book that looks terrific and I think I got that thanks to the outstanding book design of Adina Cucicov and cover design of Laeeq Hussain Arif, as well as the graphical contributions of Hassan Ahmmed, and Maria Lilibeth Mamon.

Finally, a very special thanks to my wife, Liz Minnis, who has been so patient and supportive in this, as in all of my other schemes.

ENDNOTES

All trademarks are the property of their respective owners.

The examples in this book were observed in 2017 and 2018. Since top digital marketers are constantly experimenting and trying to improve their results, if you look at the sites what you find the companies doing now may have changed

1   I did a study of 351 B2B companies with $10-100 million in revenue. Grading them with my 9-point digital marketing scorecard—which includes such programs as search ads, having a mobile-friendly website, and using a marketing automation program—I found that software companies are running a median of 7 of the 9 programs. Outside of the software industry, though, all other companies combined—in such fields as manufacturing, medical devices and professional services—are only using 2 of the 9 programs.
    And if you're not doing digital marketing in 2018, you're not doing marketing. Looking more deeply at those 85 software companies I found that those that scored at the high end of my scale were growing four to five times faster than those at the low end. Effective marketing can make that big of a difference.

2   "The Techsurance Marketing Revolution" study from Velocify. http://pages. velocify.com/techsurance-marketing-revolution-ty.html

3   2013 Annual Report, page 2; AFA Protective Systems, Inc.

4   https://spinsucks.com/communication/
    the-communicators-playbook-peso-model-program/

5   https://www.smartinsights.com/online-brand-strategy/
    multichannel-strategies/selectmarketing-channels/

6   https://chiefmartec.com/2017/05/
    marketing-technology-landscape-supergraphic-2017/

7   https://hbr.org/1986/09/hustle-as-strategy

8   https://twitter.com/tom_peters/status/964579885178957829

9   Marc Benioff and Carlye Adler, *Behind the Cloud*, Jossey-Bass, 2009.

10 http://www.slideshare.net/totango/5th-annual-saas-metrics-report

11 http://www.mckinsey.com/business-functions/marketing-and-sales/
    our-insights/why-marketers-should-keep-sending-you-emails

12 https://www.mediapost.com/publications/article/303978/email-still-the-
    king-of-roi-says-dma.html

13 http://www.nbcnews.com/id/36005036/ns/business-forbes_com/t/new-
    improved-failed/#.Vx8BGEf9nko

14 https://www.brandwatch.com/blog/
    top-10-free-social-media-monitoring-tools/

15 https://www.census.gov/quickfacts/table/PST045216/00

16 http://www.sbdcnet.org/small-business-research-reports/
    bakery-business-2014

17 http://www.forbes.com/sites/joemckendrick/2016/05/31/public-cloud-
    computing-growing-almost-50-percent-annually-cisco-says/#54fd6b112273

18 https://fredblog.stlouisfed.org/2017/02/the-economics-of-greeting-cards

19 https://www.nsf.gov/news/special_reports/i-corps/

20 http://tomtunguz.com/the-business-of-selling-promotions/

21 *Crossing the Chasm*, Geoffrey Moore, third edition, 2014, HarperCollins
    Publishers.

22 http://decisionmode.com/

23 http://www.babycenter.com/0_how-moms-and-dads-spend-money-
    differently_10371839.bc

24 https://hbr.org/2014/10/the-value-of-keeping-the-right-customers

25 https://en.wikipedia.org/wiki/Pareto_principle

26 https://hbr.org/2003/12/the-one-number-you-need-to-grow

27 Net Promoter, Net Promoter System, Net Promoter Score, NPS and the
    NPS-related emoticons are registered trademarks of Bain & Company, Inc.,
    Fred Reichheld and Satmetrix Systems, Inc.

28 Journey map provided by Kerry Bodine & Co. http://kerrybodine.com

29 https://www.forrester.com/report/
Mapping+The+Customer+Journey/-/E-RES55987

30 http://www.concreteproducts.com/news/10076-cemex-adopts-ibm-
platform-for-suite-of-transformational-mobile-apps.html#.WvrRhojRU1s

31 https://www.cleantech.com/how-a-chemicals-as-a-service-model-is-
disrupting-the-traditional-world-of-chemicals/

32 http://www.mckinsey.com/business-functions/marketing-and-sales/
our-insights/the-secret-to-delighting-customers

33 Watermark Consulting graphic used with permission. The Watermark
Consulting Customer Experience ROI Study, available at https://www.
watermarkconsult.net/CX-ROI

34 Image used with permission. All rights reserved. King Fish Media, LLC.
2018. http://kingfishmedia.com/project/nuance

35 https://www.itsma.com/account-based-marketing-hot-topic/

36 http://www.washingtonpost.com/wp-srv/washtech/daily/nov98/
amazon110898.htm

37 https://blog.optimizely.com/2016/03/23/homepage-personalization/

38 https://blog.hubspot.com/marketing/landing-page-navigation-ht#sm.0000
1vb0x0bdbpf4gxskhn7yckwn1

39 https://www.linkedin.com/feed/update/urn:li:activ
ity:6400331247230509056

40 https://blog.hubspot.com/blog/tabid/6307/bid/29274/hubspot-launches-
free-marketing-grader-tool-to-replace-website-grader.aspx

41 https://hbr.org/2015/11/email-is-the-best-way-to-reach-millennials

42 https://www.ftc.gov/tips-advice/business-center/guidance/
can-spam-act-compliance-guide-business

43 https://martechtoday.com/
facing-facebook-google-amazon-brands-pool-data-175424

44 https://blog.mailchimp.com/
insights-from-mailchimps-send-time-optimization-system/

45 https://ga-dev-tools.appspot.com/campaign-url-builder/

46 https://www.bloomberg.com/news/articles/2012-11-29/
the-science-behind-those-obama-campaign-e-mails

47 https://www.marketingprofs.com/charts/2017/31847/
how-special-offers-in-email-subject-lines-impact-performance

48 https://blog.mailchimp.com/
behind-the-scenes-how-we-do-our-own-email-marketing-at-mailchimp/

49 © The Rocket Science Group LLC d/b/a/ MailChimp. Used with permission.
The Rocket Science Group remains the sole owner of the text and images.

50 https://www.thinkwithgoogle.com/marketing-resources/
watchfinder-increases-roi-by-remarketing-with-google-analytics/

51 https://www.linkedin.com/pulse/
sales-enablement-post-funnel-world-thomas-barrieau/

52 http://www.leadresponsemanagement.org/lrm_study

53 Photos of women by Anna Kosali, on Wikimedia Commons, used under
Creative Commons license Attribution-ShareAlike 3.0 Unported (CC
BY-SA 3.0)

54 https://www.forbes.com/sites/kashmirhill/2012/02/16/
how-target-figured-out-a-teen-girl-was-pregnant-before-her-father-did/

55 https://www.marketplace.org/2015/02/27/business/
what-happens-netflix-when-house-cards-goes-live

56 Data provided by Adobe representative at Lattice Engines "AI and Data"
event on September 14, 2017.

57 https://www.nasa.gov/mission_pages/shuttle/flyout/powerdown.html

58 Not everyone thinks that the Keyword Planner is a great tool. This analysis
from Moz discusses problems with the volume figures it gives you. https://
moz.com/blog/unreliable-google-adwords-keyword-volume

59 https://www.hallaminternet.com/
google-adwords-which-ad-position-is-best/

60 Firestone marketing materials used with permission of Bridgestone Retail
Operations, LLC.

61 http://searchengineland.com/7-conversion-rate-truths-will-change-
landing-page-optimization-strategy-191083

62 http://www.mmaglobal.com/case-study-hub/case_studies/view/31739

63 https://searchengineland.com/data-google-monthly-search-volume-
dwarfs-rivals-mobile-advantage-269120

64 http://gs.statcounter.com/search-engine-market-share/desktop/worldwide

65 https://www.semrush.com/
blog/5-reasons-why-marketers-should-pay-attention-to-bing/

66 http://www.idgconnect.com/abstract/16004/
    content-marketing-help-buyers-use-content-help-you

67 Images used with pemission of Maersk Line

68 Email correspondence, April 18, 2018.

69 https://commons.wikimedia.org/wiki/File:Whiskey_Chocolate_Cake.jpg
    Licensed under Creative Commons Attribution-Share Alike 2.0 Generic
    license.

70 http://www.dictionary.com/browse/chocolate. Hat tip to customer creation
    expert Ken Wax who used a similar verbal comparison when training sales
    people how to engage buyer emotions.

71 Photograph ©Herschel Supply Company Ltd. All rights reserved.

72 http://www.mamartino.com/projects/rise_of_partisanship/ Used with
    permission.

73 https://ourworldindata.org/ By Hannah Ritchie and Max Roser. Used under
    Creative Commons CC BY-SA license, https://creativecommons.org/
    licenses/by-sa/2.0/

74 http://neilpatel.com/blog/why-you-need-to-create-evergreen-long-form-
    content-and-how-to-produce-it/

75 revenueassociates.biz/
    hubspot-afford-inbound-marketing-customer-acquisition-cost/

76 Interview with Jamie Scheu in "Modern Sales and Marketing Best Practices"
    ebook, from revenue & associates, pgs 44-45

77 https://www.siriusdecisions.com/blog/2013/jul/
    three-myths-of-the-67-percent-statistic

78 https://ahrefs.com/blog/how-long-does-it-take-to-rank/

79 http://variety.com/2016/digital/news/
    netflix-amazon-prime-video-movies-tv-comparison-1201759030/

80 https://moz.com/blog/the-myth-of-googles-200-ranking-factors

81 https://ahrefs.com/blog/keyword-difficulty/

82 https://moz.com/search-ranking-factors

83 http://www.businessinsider.com/
    amazon-vs-google-online-shopping-product-starting-point-2017-7

84 "Measuring the Long-Term Effects of Television Advertising", Leslie A.
    Wood and David F. Poltrack, Journal of Advertising Research, June, 2015,
    pgs 123-131.

85 https://blog.twitter.com/marketing/en_us/topics/best-practices/2017/how-in-stream-video-ads-on-twitter-help-marketers-tell-their-sto.html

86 http://www.digitalnewsreport.org/survey/2018/podcasts-and-new-audio-strategies/

87 Vidyard 2017 Video in Business Benchmark Report, pg 3.

88 https://digiday.com/media/silent-world-facebook-video/

89 http://variety.com/2017/digital/news/time-warner-snapchat-shows-1202470292/

90 Image used with permission from Variety Media LLC

91 https://marketingland.com/online-vs-tv-72-agencies-say-online-video-ads-effective-effective-tv-survey-118854

92 "The Axe Files" from The University of Chicago Institute of Politics and CNN. Used with permission.

93 http://www.convinceandconvert.com/content-marketing/how-to-produce-a-podcast/

94 http://www.socialmediatoday.com/social-business/asadali/2015-05-24/business-social-media-infographic

95 https://techcrunch.com/2017/06/27/facebook-2-billion-users/

96 https://sproutsocial.com/insights/data/q4-2017/

97 https://econsultancy.com/blog/66901-q-a-how-maersk-line-created-a-brilliant-b2b-social-media-strategy/

98 http://fortune.com/2017/04/24/linkedin-users/

99 Image provided by Clive Roach, Director of Digital Social Media at Sygnify, The Netherlands.

100 http://mashable.com/2017/04/25/tinder-white-rhino-sudan-campaign/#ZxsANpi1BPq5

101 http://www.businessinsider.com/mark-cuban-dont-hire-a-pr-firm-2014-12

102 David Meerman Scott, *Newsjacking: How to Inject your Ideas into a Breaking News Story and Generate Tons of Media Coverage.* Published by Wiley, 2011.

103 https://www.ftc.gov/news-events/press-releases/2016/03/lord-taylor-settles-ftc-charges-it-deceived-consumers-through

104 http://adage.com/article/digital/study-influencer-spenders-finds-big-names-fake-followers/313223/

105 http://www.contentmarketinginstitute.com/wp-content/uploads/2011/12/B2B_Content_Marketing_2012.pdf

106 https://www.forbes.com/pictures/fjle45mkli/ no-5-event-coordinator/#214c53677817

107 http://www.richmediagallery.com/tools/benchmarks

108 Photo Credit: Courtesy of CNN.

109 Cambridge Savings Bank ad used with permission.

110 http://www.adweek.com/digital/u-s-digital-advertising-will-make-83-billion-this-year-says-emarketer/

111 https://www.emarketer.com/Article/ eMarketer-Releases-New-Programmatic-Advertising-Estimates/1015682

112 https://www.crazyegg.com/blog/content-marketing-vs-native-advertising/

113 http://documentmedia.com/article-2555-The-Comeback-of-Direct-Mail.html

114 https://www.iwco.com/blog/2015/04/14/ dma-response-rate-report-and-direct-mail/

115 Lyric Stage mailer Designed by Henry Lussier, Director of Marketing & PR, and Melissa Wagner-O'Malley, Graphic Designer. Photo of Camelot by Mark S. Howard.

116 Image of REI Force of Nature catalog used with permission.

117 https://www.statista.com/statistics/238589/ number-of-magazines-in-the-united-states/

118 Used with permission of Dallas Farmers Market Friends. Creative by agency Firehouse.

119 Used with permission of the American Red Cross. Agency: Red Deluxe Brand Development, Creative Director: Martin Wilford, Copywriter: Justin Dobbs, Art Director: Martin Wilford, Photographer: Allen Mimms.

120 Image courtesy of Creative Agency Animal. Photo: Robin Nilssen, Boon Photography.

121 http://www.feelthereal.org

122 Fearless Girl statue by Kristen Visbal; Charging Bull statue by Arturo di Modica. Photo by Anthony Quintano, used under Creative Commons Attribution 2.0 Generic. CC BY 2.0 https://creativecommons.org/licenses/

123 https://qz.com/1096026/state-street-the-firm-behind-wall-streets-fearless-girl-will-pay-5-million-for-salary-discrimination-against-women/

124 http://fortune.com/2018/04/19/fearless-girl-statue-moved-nyse/

[125] Avinash Kaushik provides an excellent overview of multi-channel attribution modeling, with additional models, at https://www.kaushik.net/avinash/multi-channel-attribution-modeling-good-bad-ugly-models/

[126] https://www.bostonglobe.com/business/2014/01/08/french-firm-keolis-developed-inside-track-bid-for-state-billion-commuter-rail-contract/ZRhC6e4DAhGeJBuRulrWUJ/story.html

[127] https://careers.walmart.com/values

[128] "Revolution at *The Washington Post*", *Columbia Journalism Review*, Fall/Winter 2016, also at https://www.cjr.org/q_and_a/washington_post_bezos_amazon_revolution.php. Used with permission.

[129] https://www.princeton.edu/news/2000/11/28/blind-orchestra-auditions-better-women-study-finds

[130] https://www.inc.com/melanie-curtin/science-companies-with-women-in-top-management-are-significantly-more-profitable.html

[131] http://agilemarketingmanifesto.org/principles/

[132] https://www.flickr.com/photos/robnas/3400482826/in/photolist-6bun5f-a27b5o Creative Commons Attribution License https://creativecommons.org/licenses/by/2.0/legalcode

INDEX

CPSIA information can be obtained
at www.ICGtesting.com
Printed in the USA
LVHW07s0725090818
586478LV00032B/1931/P